Dying for Glory

The Adventurous Lives
of Five Cotswold Brothers

Troopship passing
through the Suez Canal,
early 1890s.

Dying for Glory

The Adventurous Lives
of Five Cotswold Brothers

MICHAEL BOYES

Phillimore

2006

Published by
PHILLIMORE & CO. LTD
Shopwyke Manor Barn, Chichester, West Sussex, England
www.phillimore.co.uk

ISBN 1-86077-394-X
ISBN 13 978-1-86077-394-5

Printed and bound in Great Britain by
CAMBRIDGE UNIVERSITY PRESS

Contents

v

List of Illustrations

Maps

Marginal drawings

Acknowledgements

Many people have helped me during my research for this book. I am especially grateful to Denis Bateman, whose military knowledge and diligent research in the early years of this project were the foundation for much that followed. My particular thanks also to Max Arthur, Lieutenant Colonel (retd) C.D. Darroch (Royal Hampshire Regiment Museum), Scott Flaving at Regimental Headquarters, The Duke of Wellington's Regiment (West Riding), Elizabeth Gallienne (Priaulx Library, Guernsey), Dr Malcolm Llewellyn-Jones (Naval Historical Branch, Ministry of Defence), staff at the Oriental and India Office Collections at the British Library, Alan Readman (West Sussex Record Office), Garry Smith and Jane Davies (Museum of The Queen's Lancashire Regiment), Lesley Smurthwaite (National Army Museum), staff at the Soldiers of Gloucestershire Museum, William Spencer (The National Archives), Tony Sprason (Fusiliers' Museum Lancashire), and Bob Todd (National Maritime Museum) for their valuable assistance.

Over the years that it has taken to complete this book many others have assisted me in various ways. Rosalind Ransford spent many long hours transcribing letters written by the Le Marchant brothers and subsequently offered me much helpful advice, and Tim Graham found time in his busy schedule to read and comment on an early draft of my book; to both I am deeply grateful. My thanks also to David Bishop, John Broadbent, Richard Callaghan, Oliver Crimmen (Natural History Museum), Bill Gallienne (Société Guernesiaise), Norman Good (Abu Klea drawing), Tim Hughes, Gillian Jonas, Mary Lane, Sir Francis Le Marchant, June Lewis-Jones, Judy Mills and Paula Gentil (Corinium Museum), David O'Connor (Charlton Kings Local History Society), Major Edwin Parks, and David Viner for their help and advice.

Finally, a special thank you to my wife, Maggie, and my daughters Emily and Alison for their love, patience and support through the long years it has taken me to bring this project to fruition.

Illustration Acknowledgements

Illustrations are reproduced by kind permission of the following:

John Broadbent, 70; Cotswold District Council/Corinium Museum, 4, 30, 33, 47-9, 107; Duke of Wellington's Regiment (West Riding), Lt Basil Le Marchant (dustjacket), 69, 76-81; Norman Good, 98; *Illustrated London News* Picture Library, 121; Gillian Jonas, 56, 58; Mary Lane, 92; John Montague-Jones, 8, 10, 11, 17, 40, 44-5, 106, 111-12, 115-16, 118, 130-3; Museum of The Queen's Lancashire Regiment, 100, 114, 117, 120, 122-3, 125-6, 134-5; The National Archives (PRO), 59, 60; © National Maritime Museum, 24, 26, 28, 29, 34; Priaulx Library, 1, 25; Regimental Trustees of The Royal Hampshire Regiment Museum, 9, 12, 18-21; West Sussex Record Office, Abu Klea (dustjacket), 97, 101, 105, 109. The maps were supplied by Cartographix, Gloucestershire.

Every reasonable effort has been made to track down copyright and acknowledge it correctly. If you have evidence of different copyright from that acknowledged, please let the author know.

The Burden of Expectation

On the eve of battle Major-General John Gaspard Le Marchant was looking forward to a good night's rest in a comfortable bed – the first for many weeks – when a violent thunderstorm struck. His first thought, as commander of the British heavy dragoons bivouacked on the plain of Salamanca, was that the French were mounting a surprise attack. Pulling on his boots he rushed outside and was informed that a bolt of lightning had caused many of the horses to break free from their stakes and stampede, injuring 18 troopers as they slept on the ground. Lying with his wife in the path of the stampeding horses was second-in-command Lieutenant-Colonel Charles Dalbiac; the pair narrowly escaped serious injury. Most of the horses were later recaptured, but some thirty galloped towards the French lines and were lost. It was to be a long, cold night and torrential rain made sleep impossible. Le Marchant found time to make his peace with God: 'I leave the result in His hands,' he had earlier written, 'with perfect confidence that He will determine what is best for me.'[1]

Eleven months earlier General Le Marchant had been appointed to command the heavy cavalry in the Peninsula. Now, after weeks of manoeuvring, Lord Wellington's Anglo-Portuguese army faced a French army of approximately equal strength a few miles to the south-east of Salamanca. On the morning of 22 July 1812, as the mists cleared after the storms of the night before, the two opposing armies prepared to engage in battle. The turning point came late in the afternoon when Le Marchant, exploiting earlier successes, led his Heavy Brigade of 800 horsemen in a charge at full speed towards the vulnerable French lines, inflicting heavy casualties and destroying some eight battalions of French infantry, virtually the entire left wing of the French Army. Le Marchant himself, sabre in hand, was mortally wounded as he hunted down a small band of fleeing French infantry in the final stages of this brief but decisive cavalry action, which had lasted little more than twenty minutes. Perfectly timed and executed, when the French infantry were already in some disarray, Le Marchant's charge has been described as 'the finest exploit of British cavalry during the entire Peninsular War'.[2]

John Gaspard Le Marchant, the son of a Guernseyman, was born in 1766 at the home of his maternal grandfather, Count Hirzel of Saint Gratien, near

Amiens. Educated at King Edward's School in Bath, he left at the age of 16 to join the York Militia, later transferring to the Royal Regiment of Foot. After several years as a junior ensign in the Royals, and with no immediate prospect of promotion, he purchased a cornetcy in the 6th (Inniskilling) Dragoons, and soon afterwards was given command of the King's escort from Dorchester to Weymouth. The young officer's demeanour, together with his talent for drawing and watercolour painting, so impressed George III that he offered Le Marchant a lieutenancy in the 2nd Dragoon Guards a few months later. With influential friends behind him and his future assured, Le Marchant persuaded his father to allow him to marry, even though he was only 23 years of age. In 1789 Lieutenant Le Marchant married Mary Carey, the oldest daughter of John Carey, one of the 12 Jurats who administered the laws of Guernsey.

Promotion now came rapidly for Le Marchant, and as a captain in command of a cavalry squadron during the Flanders campaign against the French (1793-4) he served with distinction. Concerned about the poor training and equipment of British troopers, he designed a new light cavalry sword and devised a system of sword exercises that was adopted by every cavalry regiment in the Army. The King, impressed by Le Marchant's efforts, appointed him a lieutenant-colonel in the 7th Light Dragoons. Within a year Le Marchant realised that if the professionalism of officers throughout the service were to be raised a uniform system of instruction had to be devised to teach them the principles and practice of warfare, as existed in Prussia and France. With considerable determination and perseverance he overcame entrenched opposition to his ideas, winning the support of the Duke of York for his plans to found the Royal Military College with a department for staff officers, and a junior department for cadets which later evolved to become the Royal Military Academy, Sandhurst. This was his crowning achievement, 'a gift of military education that stands equal with any in the world'.[3] Le Marchant was himself appointed Lieutenant-Governor of the Royal Military College, a post he held until he assumed command of the Heavy Brigade in 1811.

Shortly after arriving in Portugal to take up his new command General Le Marchant received the shattering news that his wife Mary, whom he loved dearly, had died from complications in childbirth. Le Marchant decided to return home to look after his children, but was persuaded to continue in post after learning that the Carey family had made suitable arrangements for their care, and that his five youngest children would go to Guernsey to live with his sister-in-law, Mrs Sophy Mourant, at Candie, a house they knew well. In a letter to his daughter Katherine written a few weeks before his death he expressed concern that she might have succumbed to fever. 'It would break my heart

1. Maj.-Gen. John Gaspard Le Marchant (1766-1812), first Lieutenant-Governor of the Royal Military College. (From a print by C. Hullmantel, designed and drawn by J.W. Harding.)

2. Fort Le Marchant, named in honour of its creator Eleazar Le Marchant, Lieutenant Bailiff, was built on Guernsey's northernmost point in 1796. The bell tents in this photograph (c.1900) may have been used by the Royal Guernsey Militia, in which Basil and Cecil Le Marchant served.

had any sickness deprived me of my dear Kate,' he wrote.[4] Reassuring her that her brother Carey – now his aide-de-camp – was well, the General said how much he valued his son's fluency in French, Italian and Spanish, accomplishments which she might do well to emulate.* 'Let me entreat you to use your utmost exertions towards improving yourself,' he urged her. In all his endeavours Le Marchant set high standards for others to follow.

When Major-General John Gaspard Le Marchant, a courageous leader and 'a born commander of cavalry',[5] was killed at the Battle of Salamanca a grateful Parliament acknowledged his services to the nation by voting the sum of £1,500 for a monument to his memory, together with a pension of £1,200 a year for his nine children.† The General's youngest daughter, Anna Maria, was eight when her father died – old enough to remember him with affection. As she grew up her aunt ensured that his memory was kept alive, and Anna Maria developed a strong sense of pride in her father's many achievements – something that she passed on to her own children some years later.

At the age of 19 Anna Maria Le Marchant married Daniel Tupper at St Martin's Church in Guernsey. Their third child, Eliza Catherine, was born on 21 February 1828. When she was 22 Eliza married the Revd Robert Le Marchant, thus uniting once more two of the island's most distinguished and long-established families. The Le Marchants could trace their ancestry as far back as Peter Le Marchant, Lieutenant-Governor and Bailiff of Guernsey in the time of Edward III. The family had prospered: for hundreds of years they were among the principal landowners, and several buildings in St Peter Port still bear their name. Many of Guernsey's highest offices were once held by Le Marchants, and no fewer than seven members of the family were Bailiffs of Guernsey.

---

* Like his father, Captain Carey Le Marchant quickly earned a reputation for gallantry, distinguishing himself at the storming of San Sebastian. He died in March 1814 from a wound sustained at the Battle of Nive.

† The monument in St Paul's Cathedral features a cameo of Le Marchant and three figures: a Sandhurst cadet looking up at Britannia, and a young woman representing Spain.

Eliza was very proud of her ancestry and the achievements of her close relatives, and she endeavoured to instil this pride into her children at every opportunity. Besides her grandfather, the illustrious Major-General, one of Eliza's uncles, Sir Denis Le Marchant, was Clerk to the House of Commons for more than twenty years and the first Baronet; another uncle, Lieutenant-General Sir John Gaspard Le Marchant, achieved high office as lieutenant-governor of Newfoundland in 1847 and governor of Malta in 1859, ending his career as Commander-in-Chief of the Madras Army. Eliza's brother Gaspard Le Marchant Tupper, an accomplished watercolourist, became Colonel Commandant of the Royal Horse Artillery, reaching the rank of lieutenant-general in 1887. And finally, her great-great-uncle John Tupper (1727-95) was the first Guernseyman to attain the rank of major-general in the British Army, becoming Commandant-in-Chief of the Royal Marines.

Eliza Catherine Tupper and Robert Le Marchant were born into the privileged élite of Guernsey society, but when Robert moved to England as a young curate he and his wife no longer enjoyed such exalted status. Robert qualified as a doctor

3. The Revd Robert Le Marchant with his wife and family at Little Rissington Rectory, 1897. Of their 15 children only Blanche, who had Down's syndrome, is missing.

of medicine from Trinity College, Dublin in 1845, but after only a few years he gave up medicine and entered the ministry of the Church. As a struggling curate he had to rely on private means to support his growing family, but his income was never sufficient comfortably to maintain the family's position in society. In 1862, when he came to the parish of Little Rissington in the Cotswolds as rector, he had been a curate for 13 years and already had nine children to provide for on very little income. Six more children were to follow over the next 10 years.

Eliza now considered herself to be 'poor', a relative term reflecting the family's struggle to keep up with those in society they considered to be their equals. They could not afford to keep a pony and trap, and they employed fewer servants than many of their friends in Cotswold society. Although Robert and Eliza were undoubtedly less well off than many of their relatives, they were nevertheless able to live in reasonable comfort. Robert's annual income from his living was around £300 in the early 1880s, but his expenditure was not less than £1,200 a year. The shortfall was covered by income from investments and occasional windfalls inherited from several of Robert and Eliza's many brothers and sisters. Their nine daughters – none of whom married – were educated at home, and it was only with financial assistance from wealthy relatives that they were able to send their sons to public schools for the last few years of their formal education. One consequence of the relatively short time that each of the sons spent in school was that none of them was able to pass the entrance examination for Sandhurst.

Of their six sons only Gaspard, the oldest, chose not to pursue a military career. Instead he went to Cambridge and obtained a degree in mathematics. Later, after a period as a travelling tutor and a year at the Royal Agricultural

4. After leaving Cambridge in 1875 Gaspard Le Marchant (centre) took groups of students on tours to the Continent and to Egypt.

College, Cirencester, he embarked on what was to be a successful and financially rewarding career in the City. Four sons, brought up to admire the achievements of their famous great-grandfather, gained commissions in the Army and sought adventure in places as far afield as Afghanistan, Egypt, Sudan, the North-West Frontier, South Africa and France; between them Edward, Basil, Cecil and Louis took part in a variety of campaigns, battles and punitive expeditions, large and small, in the service of the Empire. Another son, Evelyn, chose to make his name in the Royal Navy. All of them, however, faced many difficulties in the early years of their military careers.

The extent of the struggle faced by the boys as they embarked on their careers becomes clear from light-hearted entries in the family journal. The sisters, aware of the cost of their brothers' education, chided them for not making the most of their opportunities. 'You [Edward] were somewhat tardily educated,' wrote one of them.

> A smattering of geography and of history you had acquired, and by the age of fifteen you could add up an addition sum with a very good chance of the total being wrong. Having thus progressed under various governesses, it was thought time to send you to school. You went to Shrewsbury, you were put in the lowest form. You gradually progressed to the 3rd form, in which you bobbed about like a cork float, sometimes up and sometimes down until you were sent to a tutor and then into the Militia. Eventually you went up for the line and you failed. You went up again and scraped through.

From an early age the boys were encouraged by their father to appreciate the wonders of nature and the countryside around them. They learned to identify many different flowers, birds and butterflies, and fishing held more of an attraction than the works of Cicero or Shakespeare. 'You [Cecil] were a promising boy,' wrote one of his sisters. 'You were brought to Rissington to run wild … Your education was neglected. Your examinations were unsuccessful.' Basil, too, went to school somewhat late in boyhood. 'You learnt cricket and neglected your studies,' commented his sisters, 'you went up for an examination for the Army and failed, but a generous government gave you a commission.' The youngest of the six sons, Louis, seems to have learnt little from the mistakes of his older brothers and he too struggled academically. 'A liberal-minded and generous uncle, to whom you owe a lasting debt of gratitude, took you in hand and succeeded in having you educated,' lectured his sisters. 'Yet in spite of the very excellent education you received you have not succeeded in your examinations [for Sandhurst].'

It is an irony that, although their great-grandfather founded the Royal Military College, none of the brothers achieved the qualification standard to enter it. Their father could not afford to send them to school at an early age, and once at public school they preferred sports to lessons.

*   *   *

When Eliza realised that none of her daughters would marry a rich suitor of 'blue blood', the focus of all her frustrated ambitions fell upon the shoulders of her sons. That they should succeed in their chosen careers became a matter of increasing concern to her, though at first she was fearful that they might endanger their lives by serving for long periods overseas. Robert, on the other hand, was altogether more laid back. Notwithstanding the fame of their great-grandfather and the pressure to follow in his footsteps, the young boys did not at first show any great enthusiasm for a military career. Perhaps they realised how hard it would be for a gentleman of limited means to keep up with other officers, for regimental life – especially in England – was expensive. But suitable alternative career op-portunities were very limited.

The Le Marchants of Little Rissing-ton owned no country estate to which one of them might aspire and, as the boys had no desire to follow their father into the Church, the Army offered one of the few careers considered suitable for a gentleman. Upper-class customs, manners and values were perpetuated amongst the officers of the British Army and great emphasis was placed on the qualities of character, courage, honour, integrity, loyalty and *esprit de corps*. It was assumed that if an officer was a gentleman, he would possess such qualities by virtue of his upbringing and attendance at a public school. Breeding and education were more important than intellect and academic achievement, and the purchase system – by which an officer could purchase a

5. Evelyn Le Marchant (left), with Basil (centre) and Cecil at home in the Rectory garden, 1890s.

commission and subsequent promotion – enabled wealthy candidates of limited academic ability to pursue a career as an officer. When the purchase system ended many candidates had to have additional tuition after leaving school to enable them to pass the entry examinations for a commission in the Army.

The abolition of purchase in 1871 did not significantly alter the pattern of officer recruitment, for regiments continued to seek officers with the required social attributes and financial independence. It has been estimated that a private income of between £100 and £150 a year was required for an infantry officer and up to £700 for a cavalry officer in those days. Rates of pay for army officers remained more or less unchanged from 1806 until 1914, and many people endorsed the view held by the Duke of Wellington that an officer should be willing to serve the Crown for honour and not material reward.[6]

A newly commissioned subaltern had to purchase his own uniform, consisting of a number of orders of dress, boots, made-to-measure Sam Browne belt, mufti and servant's outfit (particularly in India), together with other items of equipment such as a sword, revolver, compass, cases and furniture. Added to his initial mess contribution, such items could amount to an initial outlay of around £200 for an infantry officer. Thereafter, the young officer would be expected to participate fully in the social life and extravagant hospitality of the regiment, all of which could impose a considerable financial burden on those from less wealthy families. Officers lived well and dined in style in the mess, indulging their taste for champagne and expensive wines and often running up heavy bills in the process. For officers of more limited means, service in India was an alternative option. Not only were most forms of relaxation and sport easily affordable, but there was also more likelihood of seeing active service. And with a chance to fight came an opportunity for distinction.

Perhaps family connections with the Empire influenced the boys in their choice of career. Politics, too, may have played a part. Robert Le Marchant was conservative by nature, and in politics he was an ardent supporter of the Conservative and Unionist Party. Annie, his oldest daughter, joined the Primrose League, and all members were required to sign a declaration pledging themselves to 'the Maintenance of Religion, the Estates of the Realm and the Imperial Ascendancy of the British Empire', objectives with which the Le Marchants could readily agree. Enthusiasm for a comfortable colonial life and a desire for adventure and glory may have persuaded the boys, each very different in character, that the profession of arms was the best option available.

For much of the 19th century Britain extended her influence overseas by means of 'informal empire', involving the negotiation of favourable treaties and the protection of export markets and investments in parts of the world not under direct British rule.* Free trade required safe passage for goods, but there were many areas of instability, corruption, and piracy, where British lives and property were at risk. Informal empire depended on Britain's naval supremacy and the ability to safeguard her interests by persuasion or, if all else failed, the use of force. Sometimes the threat of force alone was enough. In 1879 Evelyn Le Marchant, then a sub-lieutenant, sailed in HMS *Dragon* to the Horn of Africa in an attempt to bring to justice those responsible for acts of piracy and murder on the high seas, and villagers were warned that they would be punished for any further transgressions.

Although anti-imperialist views were expressed in Britain during the 19th century, the prevailing mood was one of support for the concept of empire. Many influential people believed that Britain had a philanthropic duty to bring

---

* Although direct rule may have been pursued with reluctance, Britain nevertheless occupied, annexed or put under protection many territories in a period of some thirty years from 1840, including New Zealand, the Gold Coast, Natal, the Punjab, Hong Kong, the Indian states of Sind and Oudh, Lower Burma, Lagos and parts of Sierra Leone, and Basutoland and Griqualand in South Africa. In addition, new colonies were established in Queensland and British Columbia.

the benefits of a civilised society – sound finance, justice, law and order, security, freedom from oppression, improved communications, public health, schools, and the Christian faith – to what Samuel Wilberforce referred to as inferior nations.* This was to be a recurring theme throughout Queen Victoria's reign. A sense of Christian duty and of moral superiority was frequently expressed; Charles Kingsley spoke of 'the glorious work which God seems to have laid on the English race', and Joseph Chamberlain, who became Colonial Secretary in 1895, believed that the British were 'the greatest governing race the world had ever seen'.[7] Two

6. The six sons of Robert and Eliza Le Marchant, 1897. From the left, standing, Edward, Gaspard, Evelyn; seated, Louis, Basil, Cecil.

---

* Samuel, third son of William Wilberforce, was Bishop of Oxford 1845-69 and of Winchester from 1869 until his death four years later. He initiated the modernisation of the language of the King James Bible.

years later, as an observer at the Diamond Jubilee celebrations, Mark Twain observed that Queen Victoria ruled an empire of some four hundred million subjects across a quarter of the habitable area of the earth.

In his sermons Robert Le Marchant reflected this feeling of self-confidence in the power of the British Empire and its racial and religious superiority. On the first Sunday after Easter in 1859 he preached a thanksgiving sermon for the suppression of the Indian Mutiny. 'The Mohammedan, the Brahmin, the Fire Worshipper – all were restrained by the arts and the power of the Christian,' he declared. For him the Mutiny 'was a contest between truth and falsehood – whether the religion of Christ should still retain its ascendancy in that extensive kingdom'.

The British, with a few notable exceptions, made little attempt to understand or appreciate the indigenous cultures of their subject peoples. In G.A. Henty's novels about imperial wars, read by generations of schoolboys who later took up careers throughout the Empire, the Indian races were generally portrayed as 'inferior to the British in courage and integrity' and as basically dishonest.[8] Henty suggested that British power derived from superior courage, energy and moral uprightness, attributes learned on the playing fields of public schools, a theme echoed by Sir Henry Newbolt and others. A number of eminent politicians, writers and schoolmasters – including the Revd H.W. Moss, headmaster of Shrewsbury where Edward had been a pupil – believed that the destiny of Britain lay in expanding the Empire and founding new colonies. In a lecture to Oxford undergraduates in 1870 Ruskin called on the country's ablest young men to take up the imperial challenge, to make England a beacon of light for all the world; England, he argued, 'must found colonies as fast and as far as she is able'.[9]

In the spirit of the age, the sons of Robert Le Marchant embarked on careers in the Army and Navy in the service of the Empire. But they were not high-minded idealists following a vocation. Indeed, they were tempted to seek more lucrative careers in other fields. What the profession of arms offered them, however, was the prospect of excitement and adventure, and a 'good station in society'. Much was expected of them.

Soldier of the Raj

EDWARD HENRY LE MARCHANT
(1853-1899)

Edward Henry Le Marchant – the second of Robert's six sons – was born in the parish of Somerleyton in Suffolk, where his father was curate. Three years later the family moved to Devon, where the young Edward's education began somewhat tentatively under the first of a succession of governesses. A further five years would pass before Robert, now with nine children to look after, was appointed rector of Little Rissington. Once more Edward's education was disrupted, but when he was about 14 years old he was sent to join his older brother, Gaspard, at Shrewsbury School. The brothers boarded with a Miss Jeffreys in Swan Hill, not far from the school, but attended as dayboys. At Shrewsbury they learnt to play a form of soccer called 'douling', a rough game organised entirely by the boys themselves that was said to be 'a trifle anarchic'. Whilst Gaspard progressed satisfactorily to the 5th form Edward seems to have languished, only reaching the top division of the 3rd form by the time the two boys left school at the end of the Lent term in 1870. Why they were removed from school before the academic year had ended we do not know but Edward, only 16 at the time, was clearly behind in his studies. To catch up he was sent to a private tutor and subsequently to a family in Twistringen, northern Germany, to learn the language.

Edward began his military career in the year that the purchase of commissions was abolished. At the age of 17 he joined the Royal South Gloucestershire Militia, with whom he served as a lieutenant for almost three years. He enjoyed his time with the militia and some years later, by way of thanks, he presented to their Officers' Mess a cup he had won in Burma. In February 1874 Edward was gazetted to the 41st Foot, and the extent of his early struggle is clear from a self-deprecating entry he wrote in the family journal some years later:

> July 1886 – It is some time ago since I embarked for India and having returned to my home, I must endeavour to render some account of myself to my admiring friends. The 1st of January 1871 ushered out the old year of sad memory derived from the classical schools of Shrewsbury, the

instruction of several tutors and crammers and a residence *en famille* in
the house of a German in north Germany where I learnt the language
pure – this was all insufficient to enable me to pass my first essay for the
Army. I was a blockhead, a dunce and an incorrigible idler in the opinion
of my relatives who, with great satisfaction, informed me I would be a
pauper … nevertheless, the 1st January found me medically examined
and measured at Burlington House … about the end of February [1874] I
found myself gazetted to the 41st Regt at Devonport, but an interview with
General Whitmore secured me a transfer to the 67th Regt then serving in
Burma. About the middle of April I joined the depot of my Regt at Fort
Elson near Gosport, having weeks before under the guidance of my very
wealthy relatives secured a first class uniform from a Jew in Tichborne
Street second or third hand – rents were neatly darned and stains were
nicely painted – so at least I thought it was nearly new. My mufti consisted
of three suits which had belonged to my uncles – and had been altered
by the village tailor into a fit that you might get if you sewed arms and
legs to a sack – in this I joined.

It was fortunate that the Le
Marchants had wealthy relatives who
not only contributed towards the cost
of educating Robert's sons but also
helped support them financially in
their military careers. Writing in the
family journal, their sisters commented
that Edward had scraped along in India
partly on his pay and partly on tips
from parents and kind relatives. They
criticised their brothers for draining
the family's resources: 'You [Edward]
have been extravagant and thoughtless.
You have often been wanting in moral
courage to resist the temptations of the
wealthy.' Of all the brothers Edward
made the greatest effort to live on his
pay alone without help from his family,
so such criticism from his sisters was
undeserved. 'You [Evelyn] are now well
off,' wrote one of his sisters after he had
been promoted. 'Did you never think
of putting by for the rainy day – or
spending less to afford your numerous
sisters and parents pleasure.' Louis,
the youngest, received the following

7. Lt Edward Henry Le Marchant, 67th Regiment
(later 2nd Battalion, The Hampshire Regiment).

warning: 'Your experience of some five brothers who have entered life before you should make you avoid their follies and weaknesses. You are still young … you have chosen the Army as your profession and in it you will have your trials like every sub. who does not possess private means … starve yourself before you borrow or ruin will be your end.' A later entry was addressed to Cecil: 'Impecunious, the gods favoured you and you were sent to Cyprus where expenses were small; you could afford a pony and became a member of a London club … you returned to Portsmouth [from Egypt] … and found out that England is not the place for a poor man – you are going to India; never forget some day you may wish to live in England.'

Extensive periods of service overseas were not uncommon in the last quarter of the 19th century. Throughout the 64 years of Queen Victoria's reign there was hardly a year in which the British Army was not involved in an overseas expedition or colonial war somewhere in the world. During that time the Army took part in more than sixty military campaigns involving over 400 separate skirmishes or battles in places as diverse as Abyssinia, Afghanistan, Bengal, Burma, Canada, China, Egypt, New Zealand, Persia, Sudan, Transvaal and West Africa. These colonial wars against the Ashanti, Zulus, Afghan tribesmen, Maoris and Sudanese dervishes were disparagingly called 'gentleman's wars' by Bismarck, but in reality such campaigns were often characterised by considerable brutality on both sides. The British Army became adept at fighting small wars in difficult terrain against numerically superior, though poorly equipped, enemies. However, it lacked the training and organisation to field a large force capable of fighting a major war with modern armaments on the Continent. Compared with the large conscript armies of Europe the volunteer British Army was very small, with about half its battalions stationed overseas at any one time. In 1881 some 91,000 troops were garrisoned in Britain and Ireland, and a little under 96,000 British troops were stationed overseas – of which almost 70,000 were in India.[1]

In addition to the British Army, the Empire could call on the services of the Indian Army. Since the 17th century the East India Company had raised and paid for its own army made up of Indian soldiers, or sepoys, serving under British officers, together with a few European (mainly British) regiments whose recruits normally enlisted for a lifetime of local service. The Company also paid for a number of regiments of the Queen's Army to be stationed in India for tours of duty of up to twenty years. In 1858, following the Mutiny, the administration of India was transferred from the East India Company to the Crown and the local army was reorganised. European regiments were transferred to the British Army and Indian units were reduced in numbers and given inferior weapons. The proportion of British to Indian troops increased significantly, from around one in seven before the Mutiny to one in three thereafter, and every Indian brigade contained a British Army battalion stationed temporarily in India. British officers required for Indian regiments were drawn from the British Army and appointed to a Staff Corps, a separate cadre serving with Indian regiments for the whole of

8. Troopship passing through the Suez Canal, c.1890.

their careers. Both Edward and his younger brother Louis thought seriously about joining the Indian Staff Corps but decided against it, much to the delight of their sisters.

Soon after transferring to the 67th Foot, then serving in Burma, Lieutenant Edward Le Marchant left Portsmouth aboard the troopship *Crocodile* bound for Bombay. An officer heading East did not travel lightly. Edward took with him a portmanteau and several trunks, together with his bath-tub into which he put everything that would not fit elsewhere, including his washstand, jug and basin. In addition to his uniform and several orders of dress, it was also *de rigueur* for an officer to take with him overseas at least one fancy dress outfit. HMS *Crocodile* – one of the famous 'lobster pots', so called after the red coats worn by British soldiers – took five weeks to reach India, and during the long voyage unmarried subalterns often had to endure uncomfortable conditions in an area of the ship below the water-line nicknamed 'the Pandemonium'. Edward, however, was fortunate and shared a pleasant cabin with two army doctors.

When he eventually reached Burma early in 1875 Edward travelled by steamer up the Irrawaddy River to Thayetmyo, the most northerly British station in Lower Burma. From there some of the reinforcements from England had to proceed 140 miles by elephant through rough and little-known country to join part of the regiment stationed at Toungoo, an isolated border outpost on the Sittang River. At Thayetmyo officers and men enjoyed relatively good health, and apart from a bout of dengue fever which laid him up for a couple of weeks, Edward remained remarkably fit and well during his year in Burma. Toungoo, however, was a most unhealthy station and many men unlucky enough to be garrisoned there fell sick. Altogether, 40 officers and men died during the regiment's three years in Burma.[2]

Britain had annexed Lower Burma in 1852 but Upper Burma, with its capital at Mandalay, remained an independent kingdom until 1886, when it was annexed to British India following the Third Anglo-Burmese War. An article in *Our Chronicle*, the journal of the 67th Regiment, explained to its readers why they were serving in Burma:

> One of the most important and ... useful duties the British soldier has to do is to protect our merchants in carrying on their trading business, in remote parts of the world, among semi-civilised people, with whom trading would otherwise be an impossibility ... we are now serving in this country, where there would be little or no security of life or property but for our presence. We are thus in a measure connected with the commerce of our country.

During the mid-1870s relations between British Burma and Burmese Mandalay deteriorated, and any incident which threatened to disrupt trade increased the possibility of conflict. Soon after his arrival Edward commented that everyone in Burma was clamouring for war. He hoped that the Burmese king, whom he disparagingly called 'the King of Umbrellas', would grossly insult the British envoy 'so as to enable him to obtain the drubbing he so richly deserves'. When negotiations resolved matters Edward was disappointed, for he was impatient to see active service. 'I am afraid there is no chance of a war after all, China and Burma have given in and have consented to pay up,' he wrote. He expressed hope that 'we may yet have the chance of whetting our swords against the Burmese king, though it may not be for some years'. Nevertheless, rumours of imminent conflict were rife. 'Tell Mama not to worry even if she hears we are in a war,' he wrote later, 'it will be just a stroll up the river to Mandalay – one good thing, there will be plenty of loot, everyone says.' Evelyn, writing from San Francisco, was envious of his brother's apparent good fortune. 'I see from the papers,' he commented, 'that Edward's regiment is likely to be involved in the Burmese war – what a lucky chap he is.'

9. Thayetmyo on the Irrawaddy River, Burma, 1874.

Constant rumours of war helped to counter the boredom of life in such a remote station. Surrounded by jungle, Thayetmyo lay on the banks of the Irrawaddy, which was more than a mile wide at that point. Wildlife was plentiful. In addition to numerous lizards, toads, butterflies, ants, and birds of every description, 'the place swarms with snakes,' wrote Edward, 'I have killed many in my house.' When a snake charmer visited his garden four snakes, including an enormous python that emerged from the roof of his bungalow, were quickly dispatched or taken away. Scorpions, too, found their way into everything, catching out the unwary. Colonel Jebb, the Commanding Officer, was stung on the hand by one in his sponge, causing him considerable discomfort. Despite such daily hazards the surrounding jungle gave officers an opportunity to get some 'quite fair shooting', and Edward spent many of his evenings improving his shooting skills in pursuit of quail, snipe and jungle fowl. He would have liked to emulate one of his well-off brother officers who had assembled a collection of the skins of more than 500 species of birds, but the cost was too great. 'It is too expensive in powder and shot, and two Burmese employed to skin them,' he explained.

Initially, Edward liked Thayetmyo: 'the place agrees with me,' he wrote. He managed to live within his means, but soon began to suspect that his native servant was stealing small sums of money from him. His suspicions confirmed, Edward marched the man straight to the local jail, hoping that he would be flogged. Instead, he was sentenced by the magistrate to three months' 'rigorous imprisonment'. Edward was determined to live on his pay and so avoid the need to call on his relatives for help, though he was fortunate to receive small sums from them now and again. He was very careful and kept a tight rein on his expenses, for he knew that several other young officers who relied on money lenders had come to grief. In the mess he drank porter rather than spirits, and when he could not afford even porter he simply drank water. He also declined many social invitations. 'I fear I have offended the big wigs here for not going out more, but I do not care twopence to make acquaintance with everybody, it is a nuisance,' he wrote. 'They think one must go out on rides, play badminton, go to balls with the thermometer at 120°, for the sake of the ladies, but I have not. If one dines out that means you must invite the host to mess, and as my bawbees are not so plentiful as a Deputy Commissioner's, I do not go out more than I can help.' He even instructed his family not to ask people to look him up when they came out to the East, as the cost of returning their hospitality was beyond his means. 'I am not a society wallah,' he later confessed, though he did enjoy the company of others on less formal occasions.

Edward, who had never learnt to ride, was the only officer at the station who could not afford to keep a pony. Colonel Jebb, whom Edward regarded as 'first rate', sometimes lent him a pony so that he could participate in events. 'All young subalterns should learn to ride,' Jebb advised Edward, 'as it is part of their profession'. Paper chases, which were very popular, took place once or twice a week when the ground was not too hard, and officers and their wives rode tough little Burmese ponies, no more than four feet high, over ditches and fences that were almost as tall as the ponies. To keep themselves occupied in such a backwater a wide variety of sporting and social events were arranged. Besides the usual badminton tournaments, cricket matches, regimental athletic sports, and penny readings, spectators derived much amusement from native bullock races. These uncooperative beasts kicked and plunged about 'until at length one came in a winner', wrote Edward. Over Christmas and New Year two or three balls were held each week, some of which Edward felt obliged to attend. At other times the men were encouraged to attend regular workshops to learn new trades, whilst officers were required to master Hindustani (Urdu). Edward submerged himself in his studies and spent much of the day learning this difficult language with the help of his *munshi* or native teacher, who smelt disagreeably of beetle nut and bad snuff. Regular musketry competitions also provided a useful diversion and impressed the native population that the soldiers were ready to deal with any raids by gangs of dacoits or robbers, an ever-present threat in the region. Some years later Edward, a crack shot, won a first and several lesser prizes at the annual meeting of the Southern India Rifle Association in Bangalore.

Drawing entitled 'Edward and his Hindustani teacher'.

After a year in Burma Edward accompanied the regiment to Madras, and later to Bangalore. For the ordinary soldier service in Burma or India was 'a life of grinding inactivity dominated by the climate', interspersed with bouts of cholera or malaria.[3] But these were not the only health risks. The incidence of venereal disease was alarmingly high – in 1886, according to one survey, around 45 per cent of troops stationed in Bengal were infected.[4] In an attempt to limit the spread of venereal disease by seeking to control hygiene standards most regiments established licenced brothels, and the tents of 'licensed harlots' were a common sight within or close to every major British cantonment.

Unlike the troops, officers enjoyed a varied social life with plenty of opportunity to play cricket or polo, hunt with hounds, or go pigsticking – the hunting of wild boar on horseback with a lance. Without a horse, which he coveted, Edward was at a considerable disadvantage. He preferred to go snipe shooting, his favourite sport, though wading through paddy fields with mud and water up to his knees was very heavy work. When conditions were favourable he could shoot thirty or forty brace in a few hours. Edward continued to pursue his studies with diligence, setting aside time each day to learn trigonometry, geometry, algebra and logarithms, often writing home to his father for solutions to problems he could not understand. Life in India suited him despite the heat, and for the most part he enjoyed tolerably good health. Several of his teeth, however, were in a very bad state and required extraction, and he anticipated that he would be 'looking out for a cheap second hand set' when he returned to England.

Edward played little part in the hectic social life of Madras and Bangalore, partly from choice but mainly out of necessity. The regimental band, said to be the best in India, proved popular with members of the European community

who turned out in style to listen and
be seen. Men dressed up in frock coats
and tall hats, whilst the ladies appeared
'in the pink of fashion'. Officers were
required to observe the same dress code
as civilians and consequently Edward,
who lacked suitable attire, rarely
attended performances of the band.
Bangalore, 'the Cheltenham of India',
was full of distractions and a subaltern
without means had to be very careful.
'The "Ride" will be crowded in another
week with fair equestrians accompanied
by the Society men,' he wrote, 'and had

10. 'Native conveyance' in Madras, where Edward
was stationed in 1876.

I a horse I would no doubt often show up also.' With so much going on Edward
had to put in an occasional appearance, and at a fancy dress ball he turned up
dressed as a Neapolitan fisherman. 'The dress was entirely of calico and cost me
3 rupees,' Edward informed his mother, 'but it was more admired than many
which cost as many hundreds.' Private theatricals staged in the regimental theatre
were more to his liking, however. 'I don't think I ever saw anything so good
and everyone was delighted,' he commented after one performance.

Eligible young men were in constant demand for the unending round
of tennis and badminton parties, balls and race meetings. At a moonlight
picnic, where he danced and played blind man's buff and hunt the slipper,
Edward met some charming young Armenian ladies, one of whom later
became a great favourite of his. Believing that he might fall for a native
beauty his sisters teased him and warned that his 'olive complexioned loves'
would cause dismay amongst the 'blue blood of the Le Marchants'. Edward

Drawing by Edward
from Bangalore entitled
'Love No.3', March 1876.

did not, however, allow himself to become ensnared, knowing that he would
be in no position to support a wife of any complexion for many years. 'Young
ladies will have most winning manners to catch unwary subs,' he commented, 'I
think I shall cut society and resume my ordinary hermit-like life.' Conditioned by
upbringing to behave with restraint in public, he disapproved of open displays of
affection. 'I see a married couple spooning over there,' he wrote, 'really, I thought
married people gave up that folly after a time, it is perfectly ludicrous.'

The conduit for communication between the Le Marchant brothers was the
Rectory in Little Rissington. Letters home would circulate amongst the nine sisters,
who would take it in turns to summarise and forward news to their brothers
overseas. Sometimes the brothers would write directly to each other, but as they
were often on the move it was easier to write one letter to the 'home party',
and to rely on them to pass on gossip. Edward, the first of Robert and Eliza's
sons to join the Army, was keen that his younger brothers should benefit from
his experience. He wrote to his father at length about the merits of particular

regiments, what equipment should be bought and how to economise. By the age of 25 Edward was already assuming the role of elder statesman within the family, someone to whom others could turn for professional advice. He expressed his opinions freely and was not slow to criticise, especially when he believed that his brother Evelyn was putting an undue strain on the family budget by living beyond his means. But he retained a sense of humour, and his capacity for self-deprecation ensured that he remained on good terms with all his brothers. Edward was a good letter-writer with an eye for amusing detail, and his skills had not gone unnoticed in the regiment. In 1878 he was appointed editor of *Our Chronicle* and soon found that, with few contributions submitted by others, he often had to write most of the paper himself.

It was not only to his brothers that Edward gave advice. A letter to his sister Emma exemplifies his concern for the well-being of his nine unmarried sisters who, he believed, should make much more effort to get out and meet other people. He advised them to follow his example and try something new. 'Have you had any Spelling Bees* at home, or private theatricals,' he asked,

11. Edward may have wished to 'cut society', but entertainment was very much a part of service life and he was expected to play his part. Here guests in formal dress attend a dinner party at the Priory, Simla, 1894.

* Referring to Spelling Bees in a subsequent letter Edward mentioned a cartoon in *Punch* in which an Irish churchwarden asks, 'How do you spell tremenjeous?'

you should begin that sort of fun, plenty of flirtation you know, while you are saying your piece to Mr Simmons, or in the dress rehearsals – capital fun. Penny Readings are also amusing, these harmless recreations would do you all good instead of moping away day by day, looking at a cow or a sheep, or Florence's guinea pigs … of an evening tell stories, sing songs or read aloud and you would find you would all have jolly spirits instead of being so matter of fact. If you see Miss So and So ask her in, laugh and joke, pocket your pride, and have a merry afternoon.

An extract from the family journal – aptly known as Gup, meaning idle gossip in India – purportedly written by an Anglo-Indian friend of the Le Marchants but possibly a satirical piece written by Edward for the amusement of his sisters, gives us an idea of what the social life of an army station in India may have been like at that time:

My father is a colonel in the Indian Staff Corps and my mother, well, she is quite the gay leader of fashion in our station, and I am just out of my teens … Our life is all indolence and easy, like a roving butterfly's, and we live on admiration. I have my horse and pony carriage and I do much as I like. Generally at 6 a.m. and after a cup of tea and a slice of thin bread and butter, my horse comes round to the door at a quarter to seven. Father before this has gone to parade and mother has not yet risen. – I don't quite go for my ride alone on the Mall, there are plenty of gay subalterns willing to come with me. I pick up one, whence we turn off into the country – our conversation will probably be about the station, the latest clique in society or about some awful scandal, for in India we do not get the changes of weather you experience at home to talk about … he comes in for *chota-haziri* or early tea [light breakfast] and before he goes … we have arranged a lawn tennis game for the evening. Father comes in soon afterwards and after a brandy peg he goes back to his dressing room to sleep till 10 or 11 when he gets up for breakfast and I return to my room, and in the lightest of kit lie on my sofa under a pleasant punkah with a breeze through the open window; there I read or doze till breakfast. After breakfast Ma and I prepare to receive visitors, who always call between 12 or two, the hottest time in the day … at 2 p.m. we lunch, afterwards go to ease and indolence in our rooms, perhaps my native dress maker is here in the verandah, in which case I superintend him. At 4 I dress in my lawn tennis get-up, which of course is faultless, and I saunter down to the Gymkhana, a large building around which the lawn tennis courts, cricket ground and polo ground and band stand are distributed. Here we meet nearly every evening and play or sit in our carriages and gossip or walk and flirt in secluded corners, of which there are many – till the shades of night leave us in total darkness. We have lots of fun … if there is a ball coming off, I give most of my dances and fill up my programme with the names of my partners to be.

Although a subaltern without private means might struggle to keep up socially, he could nevertheless live reasonably comfortably in India. Edward rose early each day and by 6 a.m. was ready for a cup of tea with a slice of bread and butter. He made do with the same at 9 a.m., and between midday and 1 p.m. he enjoyed a substantial breakfast of eggs and meat, followed by pineapple, bananas and mangoes. At 7.30 p.m. he settled down to an excellent dinner and 'a good jorum of half and half'* to keep up his strength. Sometimes, on very hot days, he would indulge in one of the decadent pleasures of eastern living – which he termed 'a delicious recreation' – lazing in a cool tub whilst slowly eating mangoes prepared for him by his watchful servant. Edward found life very pleasant in Bangalore, but it was not without its problems. At times mosquitoes and eyeflies nearly drove him crazy, and a severe drought caused terrible famine throughout the Madras Presidency. Despite the existence of relief camps many people died of starvation, cholera or smallpox, and one morning when Edward was out surveying he saw forty or fifty dead bodies being gathered up and taken away for disposal. Though insulated from the consequences of drought, he was moved by the scale of the disaster.[5] He had a good understanding of the local situation, and for six months he was acting interpreter for the regiment in Bangalore.

mango eating

Several years of relative inactivity came to an end in December 1878, when the regiment received orders to proceed north by train to take part in the Second Afghan War. The war had its origins in the Great Game of intrigue played out between Britain and Russia for much of the 19th century. Russian encroachments in central Asia were perceived to be a threat to the security of India, and exponents of a Forward Policy argued that some or all of the Afghan territories bordering India's North-West Frontier should be brought under British influence – part of Britain's indirect empire. Lord Salisbury, previously Secretary for India and now Foreign Secretary, believed that a Russian presence in Afghanistan could encourage a revolt against British rule by the Indian Army and people, and others feared a Russian invasion of India – though that was never likely. Those who opposed a Forward Policy believed that retaining the friendship of the Amir of Kabul, Sher Ali, was the best guarantee of India's security. However, when Lord Lytton became Viceroy he pursued a more aggressive policy and informed the Amir of his intention to send a mission to Kabul. Lord Salisbury hoped that British agents would exert a controlling influence over the Amir by means of moral and intellectual superiority, thereby extending Britain's imperial authority without the need for military force.[6] But Lytton exploited events to further his aim of partitioning Afghanistan. When a Russian officer visited Kabul Lytton sent a British mission to negotiate with the Amir, who refused it permission to enter his country. An ultimatum was then issued which the Amir ignored, and war ensued.

Three British armies invaded Afghanistan in November 1878 and within a month had overcome resistance and opened the way to Kabul. Sher Ali fled, and when he died early in 1879 his son, Yakub Khan, became Amir. The early

---

* Ale and porter.

fighting was already over when the 67th began their 2,700-mile train journey to
the North-West Frontier. For two weeks they travelled by day and spent most
nights in rest camps. Refreshments were not available on the train, and at stations
along the way Edward bought food at his own expense. He also had to purchase
his own tent and warm clothing at a cost of £30, given to him by his uncle James.
On arrival in Jhelum, north of Lahore, the regiment was fitted out with khaki
clothing, first used in India in the mid-1850s when it was made by dyeing white
clothing with coffee, curry powder or mulberry juice. Officers were impatient to
see some action and so qualify for a campaign medal. 'I fear we shall not share
in much of the war,' wrote Edward. Nevertheless, they continued to prepare for
action. 'We all had our swords sharpened today,' he commented, 'and feel very
warlike in consequence.' Kandahar had been taken without a blow but there
were rumours that several officers had been assassinated in the streets. 'If I were
General Stewart,' Edward wrote, 'I would hang up half a dozen of head chaps
and bring them to their senses … a good example is needed to settle it. These
fanatics don't care a bit about what they do.'

From Jhelum – 'a vile place' according to Edward, ankle-deep in dust that blew
everywhere like a thick fog – the 67th proceeded on foot to Rawalpindi, where
they remained for two weeks awaiting additional transport. They then advanced
to the Kurram Valley in stages, marching between ten and fifteen miles a day.
For British forces on campaign in the North-West Frontier the speed of advance
was determined by the mountainous terrain and the need to send out pickets
to guard very long lines of supply – a brigade might have as much as five miles
of transport to protect. Each brigade had to hire many thousands of mules and
camels to carry huge quantities of rations and equipment, from heavy tents and
ammunition to items such as soap, crockery, and officers' personal belongings
– Edward's baggage (excluding his tent) weighed 80 pounds. Considerable
amounts of fodder also had to be transported for the animals themselves. In
addition, teams of elephants were used to pull heavy 40-pounder siege guns. And
depending on available supplies, it would often be necessary to carry additional
quantities of water. The 67th and several other regiments even took with them
their full dress uniforms, though officers had to pay one rupee a day for the
hire of bullock carts. 'It is a great shame making us pay for our baggage on the
march,' complained Edward.

As editor of *Our Chronicle* during the march to Kurram Edward included
a detailed account of each day's journey, from which it is clear that the terrain
posed many difficulties for the transport animals. 'As we approached the Indus,'
wrote the editor,

> the road became more undulating, and after an eight mile march we
> passed through a rocky defile, very narrow and precipitous, to the banks
> of the river, here about 100 yards wide and rock-bound for the most
> part. From autumn to June the crossing is by a bridge of boats … the

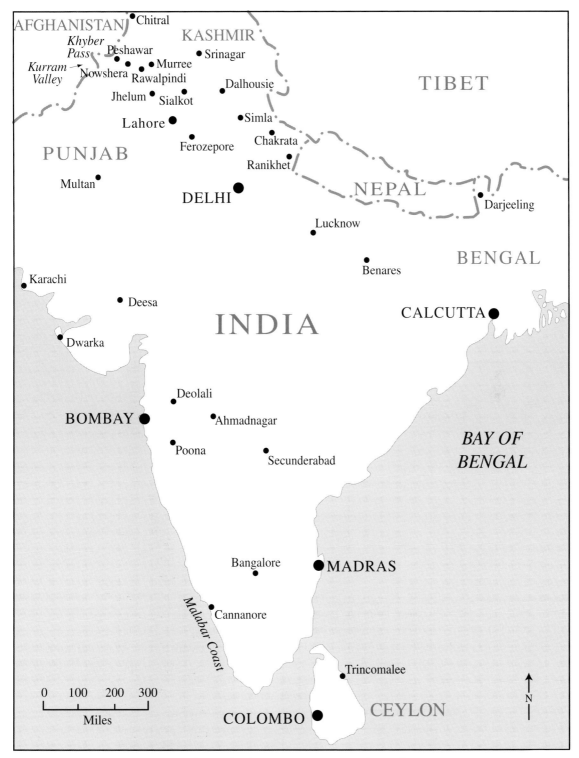

Map 1   India and adjacent countries in the 19th century.

baggage guard had a hard day's work in passing the bullock carts one by one down the steep ghaut [landing area] and over the bridge. At the other side there were a few elephants stationed for the purpose of assisting in hauling the carts up the half mile of steep hill to the camp. Luckily no accident occured, but great care and hard work were required to prevent breakdowns. One camel and one bullock died on the road, and it was surprising we did not lose more, as their drivers never half feed them … At Kooshalgurh some green food for the camels was obtained, not before it was wanted, for the poor brutes cannot do hard work on short rations of bhoosa [straw] alone.[7]

Many of the transport animals suffered from lameness or sore backs, whilst others succumbed to exhaustion and freezing temperatures at night. Losses were enormous, and some 60,000 camels died during the Second Afghan War.[8] Conditions were tough. By day it was very hot but the nights were cold and frosty. 'We have thick ice in our water basins and jugs when we rise in the morning,' wrote Edward, 'lots of bullocks die in the night of cold, and afford a fine feast for the vultures and jackals which abound around us.' And after a heavy thunderstorm which soaked everyone to the skin, the ground rapidly became ankle-deep in mud. 'The beauties of our marches,' commented Edward, 'have often been spoilt by the horrid smell arising from the carcasses of dead camels, horses and bullocks which lie everywhere along the route.' At Kohat, where they halted for five days, the regiment played a cricket match against the garrison and won. When they finally reached the head of the Kurram Valley they had marched more than 300 miles.

For several months the 67th were based near Ali Kheyl, not far from the caves and tunnels at Tora Bora used by Osama Bin Laden's al-Qaeda fighters in 2001. There, at 7,000 feet, they set up camp on a small plateau surrounded by high wooded mountains. 'It is rather pretty, but very cold in the small tents we are now occupying,' wrote Edward on 30 April, 'the hills are all covered with snow and the day before yesterday it snowed nearly all day in camp … Two nights ago we were fired into by some Afghans during the night, and bullets went whising over our heads, but no-one was harmed, it is rather a bore when they do this, as the shots might some night go into our tents and play Old Harry with some of us.' Two weeks later he wrote, 'This Afghan war I fancy is on its last legs … as Yarkoub Khan has arrived in Gundamuck to treat for peace.'

On 26 May Yakub rode into the British camp at Gandamak and signed a treaty, under which the British gained control of the Khyber Pass and various frontier regions. He also agreed to accept a British representative in Kabul who would control Afghan foreign policy. Troops from the 67th accompanied the newly appointed resident, Sir Louis Cavagnari, for part of his journey to Kabul, but once he was safely installed in the Residency with an escort of just 75 men from the Corps of Guides much of the British force returned to India. The 67th were assigned the task of holding the Kurram Valley and the strategic Shutargardan

Pass. Apart from building roads and going out on occasional patrols to search for hostile tribesmen, they had little to do to keep themselves occupied. But the situation remained tense in spite of the peace and Edward anticipated that there would be further trouble in the autumn, as 'the Ghilzais have not come in yet to tender their submission'. By the end of June the Kurram Valley was in a most unsettled state: 'a doctor was sliced up' near Thal, shots were fired at a general, and Waziri tribesmen successfully looted several British mail convoys.

Edward longed to see some real action himself, and he was appalled to read accounts of the conduct of Lieutenant Carey in South Africa, who, when outnumbered and attacked by a force of Zulus, had fled, leaving the Prince Imperial, son of the exiled Napoleon III and a guest of the British Army, to his fate. 'Carey no doubt is much to blame for the Prince Imperial's death,' wrote Edward, 'and I fully believe had he been tried by court martial in Zululand he would have been sentenced to be shot … nothing I can see in the papers justifies his bolting, and the disgrace he has brought on the Army is much too great to allow him to escape.'* Edward complained that the Army was not what it used to

12. The Bala Hissar, an enormous fortress overlooking the Afghan capital of Kabul, was partially destroyed by Lord Roberts in 1879.

---

* Although he was censured, the charge against Carey of 'misbehaviour before the enemy' was not sustained. He later returned to his regiment, but he was shunned by other officers. For a full account of this incident, see *Captain Carey's Blunder: The Death of the Crown Prince Imperial June 1879* by Donald Featherstone (London, 1973), and *With His Face to the Foe: The Life and Death of Louis Napoleon, The Prince Imperial Zululand 1879* by Ian Knight (Spellmount, 2001).

be: some months earlier at Peiwar Kotal, not far from where he was now stationed, a group of young soldiers from the 8th Foot on short-service enlistments had also bolted, leaving their rifles and equipment on the ground.

Months of relative inactivity prompted Edward to return to England in August to attend a two-month course at the School of Musketry in Hythe, Kent. He had been promised the Instructorship of Musketry provided that he obtained the necessary certificate from Hythe, and as the post carried an additional allowance he decided to take this opportunity to return home. After successfully completing the course and spending a couple of weeks on leave in Little Rissington, he sailed for India on the troopship HMS *Malabar* in December. He nearly drowned in Malta when the boat taking him ashore capsized in Valletta harbour. 'It was a very narrow squeak for most of us,' he wrote. 'I never had such a swim in my life, buttoned down to the knee in my great coat.' Utterly exhausted and very cold, he escaped 'with a good ducking'.

By the time he rejoined his regiment in March 1880 much had happened in Afghanistan. Early in September, a few weeks after Edward had left for England, Cavagnari and his entire escort had been massacred by mutinous Afghan soldiers. General Roberts had been ordered to return to Kabul in command of the remaining force in Afghanistan and to strike terror amongst those who resisted, but to avoid a reign of terror. He overcame a strong Afghan force and entered Kabul, quickly establishing martial law. A number of punitive measures were taken, including the burning of villages and demolition of public buildings, stoking up further resentment for the future. The 67th were involved in some fierce fighting and also took part in punitive actions, during which forts were demolished and orchards and vineyards destroyed.[9]

Edward rejoined his regiment in Kabul and for a while he was quartered in relative comfort in the ruined Residency, where Cavagnari had been killed six months earlier. In March, soon after his return, temperatures were beginning to rise, but there was still plenty of snow on the hills. Officers kept themselves warm by adopting a variety of unauthorised forms of dress. Edward had acquired a full-length Afghan sheepskin coat which he wore over a cotton blanket: 'I am as snug as a flea in a rug,' he wrote, 'in my rizai of cotton, and shaggy posteen coat lined with chamois leather and worked in gold inside.' He learned to improvise in any way he could, using old tallow candles to grease his nose as a precaution against sunburn. The approach of summer brought new problems and opportunities. Whilst vegetables were in short supply, fruit was plentiful: peaches, apricots, apples, mulberries, cherries and nectarines could be picked or bought 'for a mere song', and grapes were available by the cart-load. The days grew hotter and there was little do, but Edward never lost his sense of humour. 'The headman of the village here who pays us his respects of a morning has got the largest nose I have ever seen,' he wrote. 'It is quite the largest part of his head. I call him "Noses" which of course he does not understand, but thinks it some English title of rank.'

In June the regiment moved down to Jagdalak, a dry plateau some twenty miles from Gandamak, and once more they had to endure appalling smells emanating from dead camels, bullocks and elephants along the way. Conditions at Jagdalak were extremely uncomfortable. The heat was intense, water was scarce and dust storms compounded their discomfort, the ground was hard and strewn with boulders and pebbles, and there was no shelter from the burning sun – 'not a tree or green scrub to be seen, only bare steep precipitous rocks and deep ravines with stony beds'. But it was the flies that made life a living hell and nearly drove them all mad. 'I have quite come to the conclusion that the plague of flies which greatly troubled one of the Pharohs [*sic*] in Egypt would not have equalled the plague we have lately experienced,' wrote Edward. 'I have scarcely slept a wink for the last twenty days … all was black with them, my bed, blanket, and stones, and chair and all the tent was covered with them, and when I lay down they crawled all over my body.' In another letter full of squashed flies he said, 'I can write no more, am covered with flies, and am in a perfect fever endeavouring to keep them off with a towel.' In these conditions sickness was prevalent amongst the troops, and when the regiment returned to Kabul they were in no fit state to accompany General Roberts on his famous march to relieve Kandahar, where survivors from the disaster at Maiwand were under siege.

Gladstone had returned to power in April and, having denounced British aggression in Afghanistan, he called for British forces to be withdrawn. The war had achieved little and Afghanistan was restored to its former status as a neutral buffer state, under a new Amir, Abdur Rahman. Edward, who had seen very little action during his 10 months of active service in Afghanistan, was unimpressed: 'Abdur Rahman has well fooled the Politicals who are the curse of an army in the field,' he commented. 'No doubt if we retire there will be plenty of scrimmages all the way down … We are wishing to get away from this place, the campaign is a most tedious one, no fighting and very unpopular at home.'

The 67th now faced a gruelling march back to Jhelum under occasional sniper fire. They reached Jalalabad after a series of long marches, one of which involved tramping through deep sand for much of the way in furnace-like heat. Crossing the Indus, swollen by monsoon rains, proved to be another formidable obstacle. 'We all crossed in boats, the planks of which are sewn together with cords,' wrote Edward.

> The current is of course tremendous and directly we were paddled out into the stream the boat, which held forty men, seemed if it would certainly be dashed against the high precipitous black rocks along the bank, but the boatman soon got into the back water and landed us safely amongst the rocks on the other side … It is rather a sight to see a native go down the Indus on an inflated pig skin, at the rate of twenty miles an hour, twisting and turning about, it is a wonder how he sticks to the skin, for he must be drowned did he come off, or if the skin got ripped against a rock, for the current is so strong and very treacherous.

Although the 67th were nearing the end of a long campaign, there were still hazards ahead. At Hasan Abdal, between Peshawar and Rawalpindi, they were delayed for several weeks by an outbreak of cholera which killed 14 soldiers.

Not long after its return to Bangalore the 67th became the 2nd Battalion, The Hampshire Regiment under the linked battalion system initiated by Cardwell, Secretary for War, by which one battalion remained at home whilst the other was on service overseas. Edward regretted the change. 'The Hampshire Regiment does not sound so well as the 67th Regiment,' he commented, for they had earned a fine reputation throughout India as the 'Sixes and Sevens'. Many other ranks on short-service enlistments now returned to England and were replaced by young soldiers trained by the 1st Battalion, but it was to be another five years before Edward returned home. He became disillusioned about his prospects for promotion within the newly formed Hampshire Regiment. 'With all these changes,' he wrote, 'I am sick of the service, and wish I was in the Staff Corps, where the authorities don't play any tricks.' He disliked all the newfangled names and changes of uniform, and felt that the fighting efficiency of the Army was being compromised by the recruitment of too many inexperienced short-service soldiers. Nor did he think much of Sir Garnet Wolseley, then Adjutant General, who was a firm supporter of Cardwell's army reforms. 'Sir Garnet hates the Indian troops,' he wrote, 'and it is so well known in India, that few officers would care to serve under him out here.' In spite of his frustrations, however, Edward decided to bide his time and remain with his regiment, against the advice of his well-meaning uncles whose continual interference he resented. 'Between my relations and I,' he wrote, 'there will be little love lost.'

Early in 1882 the 2nd Battalion were posted to Cannanore on the Malabar coast, a station with good fishing and reasonable shooting but a bad reputation for malaria and prickly heat. Edward found life at Cannanore very dull, though he enjoyed hunting and hoped for a chance to bag his first tiger. 'One shoots

13. Baggage carts, pulled by two or more bullocks depending on the terrain, were widely used by the British Army in India. Drawing by Harriet Gough, 1881.

them on foot, like we do rabbits at home,' he wrote. He was as interested in the natural world as he was in the social life of the station, and in his letters home he tried to excite the imagination of his sisters with descriptions of the dangerous wildlife around Cannanore. Tropical storms fascinated him, and when there was little gossip of interest to pass on he wrote about the awesome power of the south-west monsoon. 'The lightning is such as would astonish you,' he commented, 'we often sit out to watch the electric fluid in the air, really splendid.'

After three years at Cannanore the 2nd Battalion undertook a memorable march to Secunderabad, covering 550 miles across varied terrain in 51 marches. On Christmas day 1884 Robert Le Marchant noted in his diary that 'Evelyn and Louis were at home. Gaspard in Bath. Edward on the march to Secunderabad from Cannanore. Basil at Rawalpindi, and Cecil with the army of occupation in Egypt.' During their long march the officers were able to get some wildfowl shooting and thus to supplement their rations on Christmas day. Supplies of wine, cigars, jams and potted meats carried in the transport carts would also have made life relatively comfortable for the officers, each of whom was accompanied by one or more servants. Much of the route was along good roads, but there were several challenges to be overcome. The Krishna River proved to be a considerable obstacle, and eight men and eight extra bullocks were required to pull each cart across

14. The Rectory, Little Rissington, home to Edward and his brothers when they returned to England after years of service overseas.

the half-mile-wide river bed, which was three and a half feet deep in places. And sunstroke was a constant danger. Major Poole, who had distinguished himself during the Afghan campaign, had to be repatriated. 'He is quite off his head,' wrote Edward, 'must have got a touch of the sun in the early days of our march.'

Not long after reaching Secunderabad the Battalion were held in readiness for active service during the latest Russian scare. The Russians had defeated an Afghan force in disputed territory near the oasis of Penjdeh, north of Herat, renewing British fears of a possible threat to the security of India. 'All India is in ferment over the advance of the Russians,' noted Edward, 'and every preparation is being made to meet any emergency.' However, war was averted and the 2nd Battalion were sent once more to Burma. By now Edward, recently promoted to Captain, was unwell and he returned to England in the troopship *Malabar* in charge of 150 invalids. He reached Little Rissington in December 1885, bringing with him an odoriferous bonnet macaque monkey which he gave to his younger sisters, a troublesome addition to their growing menagerie. He had spent all but four months of the last 11 years overseas, and he was looking forward to seeing Cecil – from whom 'I never get a line', he had complained – to hear all about his experiences during the Nile campaign earlier that year. The two brothers, each of whom had been on active service, would have much to discuss.

It took more than a year and many visits to experts in tropical medicine for Edward to recover his health. He was to spend 12 years in England before returning once more to India. At home on leave he would entertain his family with amusing renditions of songs such as 'The Kerry Recruit' and 'The Long, Long Indian Day'. He tried to teach himself the banjo, and for about a year he edited the family journal. In 1888 he successfully passed a four-day examination to qualify him for his majority, but it was to be another four years before a vacancy occurred enabling him to gain promotion. Robert Le Marchant noted that 'Edward supposes he must have a horse now that he is a major', and indeed, as an officer of field rank, he would probably have had two horses, a government charger and an additional horse owned and paid for by himself.

15. Edward Le Marchant and Miss Mary Christie, 1892.

Besides these extra expenses, the scale and cost of regimental hospitality back in England would have been a considerable burden. It was thus fortunate for Edward that he met and married Miss Mary Christie, daughter of the prosperous William Langham Christie of Glyndebourne. 'I don't know exactly what Mr C is going to give Mary,' he wrote in a letter home announcing his engagement, 'what ought one to live on easily after paying for house and taxes?' A light-hearted comment in the Le Marchant family journal some years earlier observed that Edward had been 'twice nearly married, but the marriage settlements usually broke up the affair'. No such problems arose on this occasion, and to protect his daughter should anything happen to her future husband, Mr Christie gave Mary the very considerable sum of £20,000 as a marriage settlement. He was to leave her a further £10,000 in his will.

The wedding, which took place on 12 October 1892, was celebrated in style; many titled guests were invited to Ringmer Church for the ceremony, which was followed by a wedding breakfast and a selection of music at Glyndebourne. Mary's present to Edward was a silver-mounted travelling bag, and he gave Mary a brooch and a diamond ring. Amongst the more unusual presents they received were a silver grenade, silver-mounted match stands, silver and ivory glove-stretchers, a silver-topped gum bottle, a leather and silver waistband, a silver button hook and an Indian shawl. Edward was 38 when he married, his bride was just 22.* Officers were discouraged from marrying too young, but as a newly promoted major he was complying with an informal army rule which stated that 'subalterns cannot marry, captains may marry, majors should marry, colonels must marry'.[10]

16. Edward and Mary at a seaside photo booth in the early 1890s.

Soon after his marriage Edward was attached to the School of Musketry, South-East District, based at Dover. The couple rented a house at 11 Victoria Park and it was here, early on Sunday 9 September 1894, that their son, Edward Herbert, was born. 'We have a capital nurse,' Edward told his mother, 'the young drummer was not expected until about Wednesday, I believe.' For Edward and Mary their years together in Dover were amongst the happiest of their lives. After three years as Inspector of Musketry Major Le Marchant rejoined his regiment, and it was not long before he was appointed second in command of the 2nd Battalion, then stationed at Birr in the centre of Ireland. This proved to be good hunting country and officers found the opportunities for sport to be better there than in England.

Promotion now came quickly, and a year later Edward was given command of the 1st Battalion The Hampshire Regiment, based at Multan in India. Together with Mary, their baby and a nanny, Lieutenant-Colonel Le Marchant sailed for India on 27 August 1897. Robert Le Marchant had wished them all good-bye and *bon voyage* the previous day, which was to be the last time that he saw Edward. Mary and the baby, however, returned to England the following year. For the men of the regiment conditions at Multan were dreadful. Several died of typhoid and another killed himself by cutting his throat. The overpowering heat 'produces a sort of melancholia' amongst some of the men, wrote Edward, who was fortunate to escape for a while to the *Grand Hotel* in Simla, some 7,000 feet above sea level. To reach the hill station he had to complete an exhausting eight-hour journey from the railhead at Kalka, a distance of 58 miles with an ascent of almost 5,000 feet. 'Simla is built along the crest of a pine covered hill extending some five miles from end to end,' he wrote, 'the hill curves like a crescent … and looks into the valleys north and south some thousand or more

---

* In 1895 Mary's older sister, Agnes Chichester Christie, married Sir Frederick Dixon-Hartland, Baronet; she was 34 and he was 62. It was Sir Frederick's second marriage. Evelyn Le Marchant did not approve: 'no accounting for taste,' he commented. And in a letter to his mother, he wrote: 'What do you think of Agnes Christie's engagement, a widower with 4 children does not sound very exciting, but still he may be very nice and intellectual, and I believe he is a rich man.'

17. At the western end of the Mall in Simla stands Viceregal Lodge (top left and inset) with magnificent views of the surrounding hills, 1895. The lodge was built in 1888.

feet below. It is certainly very pretty.' His thoughts turned to Mary and his son, whom he would never see again.

In October 1898 the 1st Battalion was posted once more to the North-West Frontier. Under the command of Lieutenant-Colonel Le Marchant they marched through the Khyber Pass to Landi Kotal, where they remained for five months on field service without seeing any fighting. When the general in command of the Khyber Brigade returned to Peshawar Edward assumed temporary command, but his promising career was cut short prematurely. On 23 March 1899, two weeks after the Battalion returned to Peshawar, Edward Le Marchant was shot and killed by a ghazi – a Muslim fighter dedicated to killing the enemies of Islam – whilst attending the District Assault at Arms. An eye-witness noted that

> a foul assassin sprang out from behind a tree and shot our poor Colonel, Lt-Col. Le Marchant, in the back with a pistol. The bullet penetrated through the lungs and the poor man died in ten minutes, where he lay, to the inexpressible grief of the whole Regiment. Everyone in the Regiment loses in him a personal friend. Never was there a kinder, more generous,

18. Officers, 1st Battalion The Hampshire Regiment in Landi Kotal, 1899, Lt-Col. E.H. Le Marchant is in the centre, seated. Several officers are wearing Afghan sheepskin coats.

19. Regimental camp at Landi Kotal, Khyber Pass, 1898/99.

more considerate, and thorough English gentleman as a Commanding Officer than the late Lieut.-Colonel E.H. Le Marchant. May he rest in peace.[11]

An officer who was present when Le Marchant was shot wrote:

> The murderer was one of a crowd of thousands looking on, and he was suddenly seen to raise his hand over the shoulder of a shorter man who was with and in front of him, and shoot his victim with an old pistol from three or four yards off … [they] were chased for about 200 yards by Tommies and caught. I am sure their mothers would not have known them when they were rescued from the Tommies' hands. They *did* hammer them.[12]

A private in the Royal Scots Fusiliers who attended the garrison sports that day wrote to a friend and described how the troops had to be restrained:

> It took the officers all their time to keep the men from killing the niggers. There were four altogether in the murder. The one who fired the shot was hanged next morning and the other three men have been imprisoned for life … One of the men of the murdered Colonel's regiment, a colour-sergeant, went forward to bayonet the murderer but was prevented from doing so by an officer … The ladies who were there, that is officers' wives and others, were fainting by the dozen. It was pitiful to see them. Well, before you could say Jack Robinson the sports ground was surrounded by native cavalry [Indian Army]. God knows where they came from.[13]

20. Lt-Col. Edward Le Marchant, Landi Kotal, 1899.

The attack on Colonel Le Marchant – the third ghazi outrage along the Indian frontier within a few weeks – was followed a few days later by the murder of another member of the Hampshire Regiment. The assassin had come to Peshawar from the Afridi stronghold in the Tirah 'with the express purpose of murdering a Christian', and a *Times* correspondent wrote that the relatives of tribesmen killed in the frontier campaigns of 1897 'consider that they have a blood-feud with all white men'. In a letter home at about this time Mrs Anne Wilson, who had spent some years in the region, wrote, 'No Englishman can tell at what moment one of these wild creatures may win a place in paradise by his death. We are prepared as far as possible for off-chances.'[14]

Robert Le Marchant received news of his son's death the next day and recorded simply in his diary: 'Heard this morning from Cecil the sad intelligence of the death of Edward while in command of the 1st Battalion of the Hampshire Regiment at Peshawar.' Although he betrayed little sign of emotion in the words he wrote, the rector was unable to take either of the services in church the following Sunday. It was left to Ethel to express the grief felt by the family in a journal entry of 24 March: 'Terrible day. Telegram to say that dear Cap has been shot. Annie came back from London. Mama very bad in bed, Dr Corser came.' Two days later she wrote, 'Another very sad day', and on Easter Sunday she did not go to church because she was too unhappy. Mary, who had been staying with her mother in Tenby, was informed of her husband's death in a telegram from William Langham Christie at Glyndebourne. Expressing its outrage at the assassination of Colonel Le Marchant, who was known in the town, the *Tenby and County News* commented: 'the tribe to which his murderers belong is extremely blood-thirsty and treacherous, being addicted to rapine, robbery and brutal raids.' In Parliament Mary's brother-in-law, Sir Frederick Dixon-Hartland, MP for Uxbridge, raised questions about Le Marchant's murder and the worsening security situation along the Indian frontier.

In a letter to his mother a couple of months later Evelyn wrote:

21. The grave of Edward Le Marchant, Taikal Cemetery, Peshawar. The stone cross has been broken and the top half now lies beside the grave. The final inscription reads: 'Thou will keep him in perfect peace, until the day break and the shadows flee away.'

> Poor Edward's end was indeed a terrible blow and we have all gone through a very sad time of it and have felt especially for you and Father. It is very gratifying to have had such nice letters from his brother officers in India and to know how much he was liked. The worst is over now and I think Mary would envy his end, it must have been instantaneous. I trust mine will be as quick.

The *Regimental History* described Edward Le Marchant as 'one of the very best regimental officers, who lived for the regiment, never spared himself for it and for his men; helpful and competent, he had set a high standard and left a fine example'.[15] Much loved by his officers and men, Colonel Le Marchant was buried with full military honours in Taikal Cemetery in the presence of the entire Peshawar garrison. To comfort his grieving family a friend, who visited his grave in December that year, wrote:

It is a pretty little cemetery. I think it is a spot where you would quite like those you loved to rest, a little out of Peshawar, lying in the direction of the beautiful hills. It is full of trees and flowers, even now when everything in India is so terribly waterless, and it is all very nicely kept. Over the entrance is a pointed arch, one mass of bougainvillea … The turf on the graves was very nice and short, there was a pretty cross of white roses and a jar of pink ones, and the grave was edged with lovely violets, of which I send some. I don't think anything could be nicer, and he lies in the midst of his comrades. The cemetery is full of lovely roses and poinsettias.

The following year a memorial plaque was erected by members of the Hampshire Regiment in Winchester Cathedral. For the family, news that Edward had not been the assassins' intended target only served to heighten their sense of loss. On 3 June Ethel wrote, 'Heard that those wretches never meant to hurt dear Cap, but the highest in command, General Ellis.'

22. Eliza Le Marchant with her grandchild, Edward Herbert, c.1898.

Mary, left to bring up her only son alone, was to face a second tragedy during the latter stages of the Battle of the Somme. After leaving Harrow, Edward Herbert Charles Drouet Le Marchant followed in his father's footsteps and joined the Hampshire Regiment in April 1914. A year later he was wounded in action at Ypres and invalided home. He applied and was recommended for the Royal Flying Corps but no transfer took place, and in July 1916 he returned to the front in command of a company with the acting rank of captain.[16] On 23 October 1916, whilst leading his company forward during an assault near Guillemont in the face of very heavy machine-gun and rifle fire, Captain Le Marchant was mortally wounded in the chest. Although conscious for long periods, he never realised how ill he was. He died six days later and was buried at St Sever Cemetery, Rouen. Mary, who was then living in Paris, was notified of his death by telegram. After the war she lived for a time in Lucerne, where she died in 1933.

To the Corners of the Globe

EVELYN ROBERT LE MARCHANT
(1858-1949)

During a naval career spanning more than forty years Evelyn Le Marchant witnessed a period of extraordinary change within the Royal Navy, both technological and strategic. When he joined in 1871 many of the Navy's ships were obsolete, and even the most recently completed ironclads were three-masted ships powered by steam but still heavily reliant upon sail. Small squadrons of ships and gunboats were dispersed throughout the Empire to protect Britain's trade routes and imperial interests, though the strategic focus continued to be on the apparent threat posed by France and Russia. By the time Evelyn retired in 1913 the Navy possessed a powerful fleet of 'all-big-gun' modern battleships and battle cruisers, and these were concentrated mainly in the North Sea and the Channel to counter the rapidly expanding German Navy. When he retired for the second time, after the First World War, the Royal Navy had witnessed the complete destruction of her main adversary, the German High Seas Fleet.

Evelyn Robert Le Marchant – the third of Robert and Eliza's sons – began his naval career at the age of 13 as a cadet in the training ship HMS *Britannia*, permanently moored near Dartmouth. There he studied seamanship and navigation, together with mathematics, French and drawing.* He learnt to climb the rigging and received practical instruction in sail-handling aloft. The gun-decks on *Britannia* were used as dormitories and messrooms, and each cadet slept in a hammock above his sea chest. Discipline was tough and the day began with a swim in a cold salt-water bath. Considerable emphasis was placed on hard physical exercise, and after each day's classes and boat-work cadets took part in a variety of sports. Evelyn, whose conduct was 'very good', knuckled down to his studies and participated enthusiastically in all sports. After two years of this insular existence cadets took an examination, before going to sea for the first time as midshipmen.

---

* The future of *Britannia* was under discussion when Evelyn was a cadet. Mathematics was a core skill required by naval officers, and critics believed that cadets as young as 13 were incapable of understanding fully the complex mathematics syllabus. Cramming was necessary to get cadets through their exams, and much of what they were taught in *Britannia* had to be repeated when they attended the Sub-Lieutenants' course at the Royal Naval College some years later.

23. Cadet Training Ship HMS *Britannia* (right) with HMS *Hindostan* at Dartmouth in the 1870s.

Evelyn began life at sea at a time when Britain had enjoyed a period of more than 50 years of unrivalled naval supremacy, despite occasional scares. After the defeat of Napoleon Britain had significantly reduced the size of her enormous Navy, but the Admiralty nevertheless sought to maintain a numerical superiority in ships of the line and cruisers of all types which could provide security against any two other naval powers. This was the age of the *Pax Britannica*. The Royal Navy not only protected Britain's overseas and trade interests but also charted the oceans and took on the duties of world policeman, acting against slave traders and pirates whose actions threatened free trade or stable government. The absence of any serious challenge to Britain's maritime supremacy for many years had induced a growing sense of confidence – or some might say complacency – amongst officers in the Navy. Yet this was a period of innovation and experimentation in warship design, and the Royal Navy led the way in the military application – if not the inception – of major technological advances in ships' armour, weapons and propulsion in the decades before 1914.

The transition from sail to steam was very gradual; early steam engines were extremely unreliable and uneconomical, and coaling stations had not yet been established in all parts of the Empire. During the 1850s and 1860s a number of existing ships of the line were fitted with screw propellers, but most sea-going warships continued to have auxiliary sail power for another thirty or forty years. Captains were required to economise in their use of coal, and most of the ships on which Evelyn served during his first 20 years in the Navy were full-rigged three-masted ships that depended on sail for long stretches on voyages to distant stations.

24. HMS *Lord Warden* in Malta, 1871. *Lord Warden*, a wooden-hulled, ironclad frigate, was the heaviest wooden ship ever built. One of the last broadside ships to be constructed, she fired her guns through ports in the sides, clearly visible in this photograph. Fully rigged, her total sail area was 31,000 sq. ft.

As important as the transition from sail to steam was that from wooden hulls to ironclads, and later to steel-hulled ships. The development of exploding shells by Colonel Paixhans of France – first used in a naval action with devastating effect by the Russians against a Turkish squadron of wooden ships at the Battle of Sinope in 1853 – led to a race between the development of yet more powerful guns and ever thicker protective armour. In 1859 the French launched the first sea-going ironclad warship, *La Gloire*, a wooden-hulled ship clad with a belt of 4½-inch thick wrought-iron armour plates. The following year the Royal Navy responded by launching HMS *Warrior*, usually referred to as the world's first true battleship. Iron-hulled and armoured, she was the largest, fastest and most powerful warship at that time. These two warships made all others obsolete and vulnerable, thus reducing the value of Britain's numerical superiority in warships of all classes.* Yet both *Gloire* and *Warrior* were still full-rig three-masted broadside ships which fired their guns through ports in the sides. *Warrior* could officially do a little over 14 knots under steam and an impressive 13 knots under sail, carrying enough coal to steam about 1,100 miles at full speed or more than 2,000 miles at cruising speed. Formidable though this may seem, one of the Navy's nearest overseas bases outside the Mediterranean – Halifax, Nova Scotia – was more than 3,000 miles from Plymouth. This helps to explain why the Constructor for the Admiralty continued to insist, as late as 1893, that sail power in cruisers was a necessity.

In 1873, at the age of 15, Evelyn sailed to Malta as a newly-qualified midshipman in HMS *Lord Warden*. The construction of *Lord Warden*, a broadside ironclad

---

* Britain, however, possessed the technical knowledge, financial strength and building capacity to outbuild other nations and respond rapidly to advances by rival naval powers.

frigate completed in 1867 which was the heaviest wooden ship ever built, helped to use up remaining stocks of oak timber that had accumulated in the dockyards. The desire to utilise precious stocks of timber is understandable, for it has been estimated that an oak forest of 76 acres was cleared to build one of the last of the so-called 'wooden walls', *Duke of Wellington*, another ship in which Evelyn served for brief spells in Portsmouth harbour. After *Lord Warden*, Evelyn's next ship was HMS *Hercules*, one of the first warships to carry most of her guns in an armoured central battery. Like other battleships of this period she, too, had three masts, not only to conserve fuel on long voyages but also because the Admiralty was not yet willing to rely on steam power alone. And they were right, for on 12 April 1875 Robert Le Marchant noted, 'HMS *Hercules* sailed from Spithead for Malta; had to put into Plymouth, the engines having broken down subsequently'.

By the time he joined *Hercules* Evelyn, now 17, had become frustrated with life in the Navy. There were several reasons for his growing disillusionment. 'The Navy is not the service for a poor man,' he wrote, 'I am quite disgusted with it.' Prospects for promotion and increases in pay were poor, he complained, and leave was inadequate. He wished a war would break out 'just to clear the lists a little', for otherwise it would be another eight years before he reached the rank of lieutenant. Ships in the Mediterranean Fleet called at numerous ports, but at this early stage in his career Evelyn could seldom afford to make lengthy visits ashore with other officers. He was, however, able to make short visits to Athens,

25. Lt-Col. (later Lt-Gen.) Gaspard Le Marchant Tupper, RHA.

Rome and Venice, and from the port of Leghorn he walked to Pisa and back, a total of 26 miles. He got into debt after buying new clothes and deeply resented criticism from his interfering uncle, Frank Tupper. 'I have told Uncle Frank I can live on my pay if I don't get any clothes, or see places but otherwise I can hardly do it,' he wrote to his parents. Nevertheless, he was determined to go ashore and visit places of interest from time to time, even if that meant getting further into debt. Brushing aside criticism from his family, he wrote, 'my debts can wait and the places can't.'

As a midshipman Evelyn could not have survived without an annual allowance of £50 from Frank Tupper, for his expenses, excluding clothes and subscriptions, greatly exceeded his basic pay of £31 a year. But with an allowance came scrutiny of his expenditure, causing continual tension between Evelyn and some of his relatives. He expected his wealthier uncles to help him out with significant items of expense, and when he needed a new naval outfit he approached Gaspard Le Marchant Tupper. 'I am sure your Uncle Gaspard will not assist with your outfit,' wrote Frank Tupper, 'for he considers you don't act as the sons of poor men should, and as we all have done.' Evelyn thought this was 'a very lame excuse for not helping', and he rejected Tupper's suggestion that he should buy a second-hand outfit. 'None of the other midshipmen have to pay for their clothes,' he explained, 'and they are always getting tips from their uncles.' Before matters were resolved Evelyn ran up a bill of around £80, which was eventually settled by his father. When he was able to do so, Evelyn later repaid part of this debt. For Robert Le Marchant, coming on top of the purchase of new uniforms for Basil and Cecil at the start of their army careers, this was 'a very heavy pull on his exchequer'.

Evelyn felt himself to be under considerable pressure to keep up with his fellow officers, a view with which his uncles had little sympathy. Even Edward, then serving with his regiment in India, was critical of his brother's 'extravagance'. 'For myself', wrote Edward to his sister Annie,

> I think it is quite too much of a good thing that Evey should expect to go ashore and visit every place his ship touches at, was I to join in one quarter of the pleasures my brother officers enjoy I don't expect you would see me a month in the Service, I cannot afford to visit, or to drive and see places, or go to evening entertainments, or drink wine, or have three meals a day, and yet Evey can afford to run up a bill of £15 (more than 150 rupees) for clothes and spend £3 or £4 more to see Noah's tomb or the temples of Athens. I am glad to say I owe no man a halfpenny … Evey by this time ought to know what his actual necessary expenses are per month, and money enough to cover them he ought always to have in hand. For six months in Burma I never touched beer at all, only drinking water in order to meet my expenses. At times it was hard work, I allow, but I never felt worse for practising self-denial. Some people think unfortunately it is not right to be in a worse position than that in which they were born, instead of thinking they have to make their way up to that position after they are launched in life. To tell the truth, I think Evey ought to have some self-denial about him, and I am afraid he has none … As far as I am concerned I wouldn't ask for help unless driven into a regular corner, it is much more preferable to be independent on a little than to be dependent on one's relations' largesse. Now I have said enough, but it is only to show you all, the Army is no more *couleur de rose* than the Navy, many fellows in the Service live as I do and I have been in now rather more than two years, and I have never regretted the day I joined.

At 23, Edward was demonstrating a level of maturity and resilience that Evelyn, four years his junior, had yet to acquire.

Evelyn's disillusion with the Navy went well beyond concern over pay and prospects. His sensibilities were offended by the coarseness of many of his fellow officers in *Hercules*, from whom, as a midshipman, he could not escape.

> I live in a mess some 30ft long and 12 wide with some 20 other officers. I won't say gentlemen, as I think it is to only a <u>few</u> exceptions you could apply that term, and I think with the same few exceptions Religion is

pretty well abhored, swearing is the least vice amongst the senior ones, in fact I think you may consider my mess a 'very bad one', <u>not bad though for the Navy</u>, in fact it is considered to be rather a steady quiet mess, I should not like to tell you what it is really like, as it is a great deal too bad to mention … I shall never have a good word for the Navy, as a more utterly hateful profession I don't suppose is to be found. A midshipman certainly learns nothing during the time he does school except navigation, no wonder the naval officers are so ignorant as I have always heard they are … I wish they would invalid me out of the Service …

To survive in this tough environment many officers were indeed somewhat course, intolerant and tyrannical, and a young midshipman could not afford to be oversensitive. Evelyn was having a hard time fitting in. The ethos of a ship depended on the quality of the captain, and *Hercules* was clearly not a happy ship. Evelyn's next ship would be much better.

In a further letter Edward made light of his brother's feelings. 'Is he going into the Church,' asked Edward, 'for we hear he is so religious that he is shocked with his messmates and in fact feels that he was meant to shine elsewhere than in a Middie's Pandemonium.'* Evelyn thought seriously about leaving the Navy for a more lucrative career elsewhere, and the attractions of an expatriate lifestyle led him to enquire about growing oranges in Florida or managing a tea garden in Ceylon, where his cousin Johnny Le Marchant had gone in search of new opportunities. In the end, however, he knuckled down to his chosen profession, worked hard to pass his exams, and waited patiently for promotion. And when promotion came his basic pay improved significantly, from £31 a year as a midshipman to £91 as a sub-lieutenant, and eventually up to £182 as a lieutenant. As a gentleman in the Service needed at least £150 a year to maintain his position, Evelyn would continue to depend on the generosity of his relatives for some years to come.

After an unhappy time in *Hercules* and a brief spell in HMS *Research* Evelyn was glad to transfer to HMS *Monarch*, the Royal Navy's first sea-going turret ship, completed in 1869. The designs for *Monarch* generated some controversy at the time, arising from the need to accommodate heavier and more powerful guns and thicker armour on ships that still carried sail. The ever-increasing weight of guns and armour meant that far fewer guns could be carried, and these were generally protected within a shortened belt of armour amidships. A consequence of this was a reduction in the field of fire. One way to overcome this problem was to place the main guns in centrally-mounted revolving turrets, but the continuing need for masts and rigging prevented end-on fire and thus restricted the usefulness of turrets in ships with sails.

The Navy's Chief Constructor, Edward Reed, believed that warships should carry their heavy guns in a central battery giving broadside fire and that revolving

H·M·S
RESEARCH

* The 'Pandemonium' was a nickname given to an area of a troopship below the water-line where junior officers were quartered on the long, hot voyage out to India.

turrets were unsuited to ships encumbered with masts and spars. Captain Cowper Coles, on the other hand, campaigned vigorously for turrets on sea-going ships that would be designed with a low profile to minimise the risk of being hit by enemy fire. Arising from this debate, *Monarch* was built as an experimental sea-going turret ship to a design approved by the Admiralty. She had two turrets on the upper deck, each carrying a pair of 12-inch muzzle-loading guns weighing 25 tons apiece, the heaviest guns in existence at that time. After further pressure from Coles, approval was reluctantly given to order a second turret ship, HMS *Captain*, in accordance with his designs. The distance between deck and waterline on *Monarch* was 14 feet, but to achieve the low profile advocated by Coles the freeboard on *Captain* was less than seven feet, a fatal design flaw. During a gale in the Bay of Biscay in September 1870 – just six months after her sea trials – *Captain* capsized and sank with the loss of around 470 lives, including that of Captain Coles. Following this disaster *Monarch* was rigorously tested and proved to be entirely seaworthy. Evelyn wrote to his family to assure them that *Monarch* was 'one of the finest ships afloat'.

Still a midshipman, Evelyn joined *Monarch* at a time of tension and conflict in the Balkans when war between Turkey and Russia seemed increasingly likely. Turkish oppression of the Christian races in the Balkans had provoked a series of rebellions, and the brutal massacres which followed, together with Turkey's failure to implement agreed reforms, gave Russia a pretext to attack Turkey and expand southwards towards Constantinople. Disraeli, who believed that Constantinople was the key to India, feared that Russian intervention would pose a threat to the Suez Canal and thus to the security of India. In May 1876 he despatched the Mediterranean Fleet, including *Monarch*, to Besika Bay, near the entrance to the Dardanelles. 'We are anchored about a mile offshore', wrote Evelyn, for there was as yet no British naval base in the Eastern Mediterranean. Lying offshore for much of the next six months proved to be extremely tedious, and occasional trips ashore to play cricket or football did little to alleviate the crushing monotony of the place.

Evelyn followed the developing international situation with interest, and soon after he joined *Monarch* Serbia declared war on Turkey. 'Everyone seems to think that there will be war with Russia soon over Servia [*sic*]. I think it is very hard upon Turkey,' he wrote, 'that they [Gladstone and the Liberals] should bring up all her atrocities when Servia is just as bad, only being Christians [Serbian atrocities] are not brought to light.' Later he commented, 'What a beating the Servians have received from the Turks, and I am very glad of it too.' When Russia declared war on Turkey in April 1877, public opinion in England turned against Russia. Patriotic fervour, or 'jingoism', found expression in the words of a popular music-hall song:

> We don't want to fight, but by jingo if we do,
> We've got the ships, we've got the men, we've got the money too.
> We've fought the Bear before, and while we're Britons true,
> The Russians shall not have Constantinople.[1]

From the comfort of the *Bowring Hotel* in Bangalore where he was attending a Garrison Class Edward, keen for news of his brother, wrote to his sister Annie. 'How is Evey going to provide against torpedo fighting,' he asked, 'we heard today of the Fleet being sent to the Black Sea under sealed orders, it looks rather as if there are black clouds on the horizon* … the Turks through their want of enterprise seem to have lost the advantage of carrying on a war in an enemy country. Russia certainly seems to have the best of it.' Early in 1878, after nine months of war, an armistice was signed. Diplomacy and the threat of British military action had averted a war between Britain and Russia, but rivalry between the two powers continued for some years. In return for agreeing to defend Turkish interests against Russia Britain acquired Cyprus, giving her a much-needed base in the Eastern Mediterranean.

After four years at sea and following his promotion to sub-lieutenant, Evelyn returned to England to attend the Royal Naval College at Greenwich. With promotion came a welcome increase in pay and this, together with the fact that he had no capital with which to invest in overseas business ventures of his own, seems to have persuaded him to make a success of his chosen career. News of the Anglo-Zulu War made him long for an opportunity to see active service, and in a letter to his father in April 1879 Edward advised his brother to consider joining a Naval Brigade. If an opportunity arose to do so he would see action ashore sooner or later. 'I wonder if Evey will get a chance to join the Naval Brigade in Zululand,' wrote Edward, 'there seems to be hard blows falling there,

---

* The first time a torpedo was used in action from a big ship was 1877, when HMS *Shah* fired at the Peruvian turret ship *Huascar* at long range and missed. Edward was clearly aware of developments in naval weaponry and tactics.

but I fancy the Gatling gun will play the deuce with the Zulus, in spite of overwhelming numbers they appear to collect together.'

The chance for a naval officer to go ashore with a detachment of bluejackets and Royal Marines depended on being in the right place at the right time, and Evelyn was nowhere near South Africa. With a renewed sense of commitment to the Navy he sailed in HMS *Dragon* to Aden, from where he would proceed to join his new ship, HMS *Euryalus*. Whilst waiting for *Euryalus* to reach the Indian Ocean Evelyn went for a short cruise in *Dragon* to the Horn of Africa, where they visited several coastal villages to find the 'savages' responsible for committing several murders on the high seas two years previously. The guilty men were never found but the villagers were left in no doubt about the consequences of any further acts of piracy and murder. Back in Aden Evelyn was invited to play tennis with the officers stationed there, most of whom he could beat with ease as he had mastered the overarm service, a new technique they had not yet adopted. He also learned to play polo on a borrowed pony. 'I expect I shall find myself kissing mother earth pretty often at first,' he wrote, 'until I get into it, not being able to ride much.' He was delighted to leave the oppressive heat of Aden after a couple of months and sail to Mauritius to join *Euryalus*, flagship of the East Indies Squadron.

27. Sub-Lt Evelyn Robert Le Marchant, *c*.1878.

During his six months in *Euryalus* Evelyn visited many exotic locations, including Madagascar, the Comoro Islands, Zanzibar, the Seychelles, Trincomalee in Ceylon, and Bombay. *Euryalus* often remained in port for several weeks, during which officers took advantage of the varied social life and generous hospitality of the local expatriate population. In Mauritius Evelyn was too busy to accept invitations to visit the country estates of wealthy sugar plantation owners, but he enjoyed the nightly round of parties and balls, which he considered 'great sport, as one meets some very jolly girls'. Despite his shortcomings on the dance floor Evelyn's presence was much in demand, and he was invited to accompany the Governor and his four daughters on a picnic to the far side of the island, overlooking the harbour at Mahebourg. It was here in 1810 that a French squadron defeated an attack by the Royal Navy, a rare French naval victory over the British during the Napoleonic wars. The victory was shortlived, however, and by the end of that year Britain had captured Mauritius from the French.

Evelyn was now beginning to enjoy life as a young sub-lieutenant. Unlike Edward, who never felt at ease with the social demands of army life, Evelyn seemed to relish the many picnics and parties he attended. 'You are a favourite at home and in society,' commented one of his sisters, 'you have the gift of conversation.' He also indulged his love of sport to the full, making the most of his opportunities. He received numerous invitations to tennis, as much, no doubt, for his handsome good looks as for his prowess on court. In Mauritius he took several wickets against a touring MCC side, and when the chance came to go shooting in Madagascar he borrowed a gun and set off at 4.30 a.m. 'We had capital sport,' he wrote. 'I managed to shoot 5 brace of duck, 2½ brace of widgeon and 1 quail, some of the ponds we shot the duck on were full of crocodiles and so when the duck that were shot fell into the water we were not able to get them, however we brought back a very good bag.'

Still only 21, Evelyn found something new and exciting in each port of call. 'Trincomalee is a very pretty place indeed, so green and hilly,' he wrote. 'The shore all round is thickly wooded, the trees growing right down to the water's edge. Monkeys, snakes, parrots and birds of all sorts literally swarm here, and the plumage of the latter is really quite splendid … I never saw anything like the butterflies.' At Trincomalee, one of the world's finest natural harbours with more than 30 miles of shoreline, officers could relax on Sober Island, which was owned by the Navy. There, in the comfort of the Officers' Club, they could enjoy a cool drink, play billiards, and swim in the warm, clear sea in complete safety. 'We have peacocks here for dinner to say nothing of the venison and other delicacies,' wrote Evelyn, 'but I would give them all up for a little cool weather occasionally.'

HMS *Bacchante* and the Royal Princes, 1880-1882

At this point in his career Evelyn received a very lucky break. He returned to England to study navigation, and soon after gaining his certificate in pilotage he sailed for the South Atlantic in HMS *Forward*. During his time in *Forward* he received excellent reports which, no doubt, were instrumental in securing his next appointment. On arrival in Rio de Janeiro he was astonished to learn from an English newspaper that he was to join HMS *Bacchante* in Montevideo for the greater part of her journey around the world. On board *Bacchante* as midshipmen were Prince George, later King George V, and his older brother, Prince Albert Victor (or 'Eddy'), accompanied by their tutor, the Revd John Neale Dalton. Amongst the other officers were no less than five sons of peers. Evelyn had been chosen to replace an officer who 'did not hit it off with the Prince's governor',

the influential but dull Mr Dalton. 'All the officers in her have been picked out,' wrote Evelyn, 'and no end of officers have applied to be appointed.' The particular qualities for which Evelyn was beginning to develop a solid reputation were competence as a navigator, reliability, tact and judgement – all of which which would be very much in demand during the long voyage in *Bacchante*.

Initially, Evelyn was ambivalent about the opportunity before him. 'The Captain and officers of this ship [*Forward*] say I ought to think it a great compliment and it will no doubt be a great benefit to me by and by in the Service,' he wrote, 'but for all that I am sorry I have got the appointment as it will be a great expense to me, owing to my having to get full dress uniform which I could otherwise have done without, also instead of getting 8/6 per day and being in a ship with little or no expense and every opportunity of saving, I shall only get 7/6 a day and be in to say the least of it an expensive ship, and one that has to entertain a great deal.'

28. Prince Albert Victor and officers on board HMS *Bacchante*. Prince George is standing, 3rd row from the front on the left with his hand resting on the shoulder of a seated officer; Prince Albert Victor is seated, second from the right, and behind him stands the ship's captain, Lord Charles Scott.

Before the arrival of *Bacchante* Evelyn spent two very happy months in Montevideo. There he met many wealthy society ladies and claimed to have fallen in love with at least half a dozen of them. He wrote to his brother Cecil asking him to send a further two dozen photographs of himself without delay, as a young lady had just taken his last one. When *Bacchante*, part of the Detached Squadron, reached Montevideo on 22 December 1880 the British Minister hosted a grand ball, and one of Evelyn's first duties was to introduce her officers to the fashionable ladies attending. Over the next couple of weeks officers from the Squadron were invited to a succession of garden parties, riding parties, picnics, dances, and cricket matches, and everyone seemed quite sorry to leave.

For part of this memorable voyage of more than 40,000 miles Evelyn acted as assistant navigating officer. *Bacchante*'s mission was to sail around the world and show the flag, a task of added significance due to the presence of two of Queen Victoria's grandsons. When Prince George embarked on his naval career the decision was made not to separate him from his brother because it was felt that Prince Eddy, portrayed as listless and backward by Dalton, needed Prince George's company to induce him to study.[2] Whilst Prince George took turns on watch by day, his brother's main task was to continue with his studies. But Dalton was an opinionated, well-meaning but boring teacher, unable to interest or motivate 17-year-old Prince Eddy.* 'The two young Princes are quiet and nice boys,' wrote Evelyn soon after joining *Bacchante*. 'The youngest is much the sharper of the two, the elder being rather more of a fool than most boys of his age I should say, however I daresay he will improve by and by; he has evidently been treated like a child all his life, in the way he has been looked after so that he should not come to any harm.' Evelyn's initial assessment of Prince Eddy may have been influenced by Dalton but later, after living in close proximity with the Princes for many months, he was able to form his own opinion. Though he got to know them well, close friendships with the Princes were discouraged. Courteous, self-assured and easygoing, Evelyn seems to have found favour with Dalton, who later invited him to accompany the Princes on several of their extended visits ashore. At the very outset of the voyage, however, everything could so easily have gone horribly wrong.

On his last night in Montevideo Evelyn dined with the British Minister. At about midnight he left to return to *Bacchante* which was due to sail at 5 a.m. When he reached the landing stage he discovered to his horror that a strong wind had blown up, and he could not find a boatman willing to take him the three miles or more to where the ships lay at anchor. For three tense hours he waited before finally getting away, reaching *Bacchante* with little time to spare before she was due to set sail for the Falkland Islands. In the event, however, departure was delayed for several hours whilst a number of deserters were rounded up and

---

* Dalton's informative two-volume account of the voyage of HMS *Bacchante* is full of tedious facts, figures and lengthy descriptions of places visited, without any spark of humour or imagination whatsoever.

returned to the ship.* The day after reaching the Falklands, Le Marchant and six other officers went out for a day's shooting – three geese and three plover falling to Evelyn's gun. On their way back to the ship they met a party of sailors who had been sent out to search for them, for they were to sail that evening. Instead of rounding the Horn and cruising to the Galapagos Islands, they were to proceed at once to South Africa. The Admiral had received a telegram – which the British Minister had forgotten to give him before leaving Montevideo – ordering the squadron to make all speed to Cape Town to help defeat a Boer rebellion in the Transvaal.

The possibility of seeing some action caused great excitement on board. 'We fully expect to land a Naval Brigade,' wrote Evelyn, 'and I am to go with them.' Preparations were made to land more than 1,000 men, including 200 from *Bacchante*. However, the presence of a naval squadron could do nothing to prevent the Boers inflicting a heavy defeat on a British force at Majuba Hill. Soon after their arrival the Detached Squadron were advised that they would not be required after all, 'to our infinite disgust, rage and disappointment', commented Evelyn, who believed that the Naval Brigade should be landed 'just to show the soldiers how to fight'. And when the peace terms were published the feeling amongst officers was one of astonishment. 'The Boers get all they want,' wrote Evelyn, 'people in Cape Colony are furious and say an Englishman ought to be ashamed to show his face out here.' Evelyn despised Gladstone and accused the Liberal government of weakness for conceding to the Boers' demand for independence without 'retrieving any of our late defeats', a policy which he believed would encourage the 'natives of India … to follow the Boer's example, and try to shake themselves clear of us.'

Once it became clear that the presence of the Detached Squadron was no longer required plans were made to resume their cruise around the world. They remained at Simonstown for six weeks, during which *Bacchante* entertained a good many members of Cape Town society. 'It is most absurd when people come on board the curiosity they exhibit to see the Princes,' wrote Evelyn, 'and the number of questions they ask about them.' During the fleet regatta people had a further chance to see Prince George when he coxed *Bacchante*'s five-oared whaler – in which Evelyn was rowing – to victory in the officers' race. Their win was no fluke, for later in the voyage the same crew repeated their success to win a cup presented by the Hong Kong Club.

From the Cape the Detached Squadron set sail for Australia, a hazardous six-week voyage through heavy seas and frequent storms. During the night of 11 May, as *Bacchante* approached Australia, her rudder was badly damaged in a gale. At daybreak *Bacchante* was missing from the rest of the Squadron, causing considerable anxiety. A search was mounted immediately, but the stricken ship

---

* Desertion was a continuing problem in the Navy at this time. Later in the voyage 70 sailors from the squadron deserted in Melbourne. Desertion was also a problem for merchant ships, particularly in the vicinity of gold fields.

could not be found. Throughout that night the flagship fired signal rockets, but there was no response. For three days *Bacchante* drifted in heavy seas, rudderless. She was not completely helpless, however, for it is possible to control a ship by the skilful use of the sails alone. After five days of searching, with fears for the safety of the Princes growing, the squadron rendezvoused off Cape Otway, south-west of Melbourne. There the Admiral was greatly relieved to receive a signal from land informing him that *Bacchante*, with her damaged rudder temporarily repaired, had managed to limp into port in Albany. For a time she had been in considerable danger.

Bacchante remained in Albany for a month undergoing repairs before rejoining the squadron in Melbourne. Here they were lavishly entertained. The people of Melbourne were generous in their hospitality; officers were invited to stay at country estates, and hardly a night went by without a ball, a banquet or a party. For Evelyn, though, the fun came to an abrupt end when he broke his ankle in a rugby football match, forcing him to lay up in bed for six weeks.* During his enforced idleness he wrote many letters home, including one to his Uncle 'Milly':

> HMS *Bacchante*   Saturday
> Melbourne   9th July 1881
> Australia
>
> My dear Uncle Milly†
>   I was very glad to see by the papers that you have at last been promoted and I congratulate you on obtaining the step which I know you have been longing for, if it was only to get clear of that wretched Ireland … I think any part of England must be infinitely preferable to Ireland as long as the present state of things continue in that country.
>   Many thanks for your last letter, also for your congratulations on my appointment to this ship which as you say ought to benefit me in the service by and by and I trust will; she is a very nice ship and there are a particularly nice lot of officers in her, the only objection I find to her is that she is a trifle expensive owing to the officers all being so well off, however I manage to get on all right and as I hope to get my promotion when the ship returns it will have been a good thing coming here, although I was far better off in the *Forward* as regards pay and expenses.
>   The Princes are quiet and nice chaps and get on very well on board, they live in the Gun Room,‡ as also do I and so of course I see lots of them, they are treated precisely the same as the other midshipmen, except of course when they are on shore in a sort of official capacity. The younger one is <u>much</u> better off for brains than the elder who between

---

* Rugby was a rough game in those days; one of the Melbourne players broke his leg in this match, which was won by the Navy.

† Amelius de Vic Tupper (1836-95) was promoted to Lieutenant-Colonel, Royal Artillery, on 23 April 1881.

‡ A term used to describe the midshipmen's mess.

29. HMS *Bacchante*, an iron screw corvette, 1880. Under sail, with a total canvas area of 38,000 sq. ft, she could manage speeds of up to 11½ knots.

you and me I fancy is rather deficient or else his brains are rather late in developing, however I have no doubt that he will have quite sufficient to fill the billet of King, one thing is his Prime Minister will be able to have it all his own way with him.*

I suppose you have seen in the papers all about our rudder getting broken and about our having to put into Albany W. Australia, in which place we spent a very jolly month getting plenty of shooting, cricket and lawn tennis. The shooting was principally quail and rabbits, the former is capital practice and very good eating, but awfully hard to find without a dog when one does knock them over.

---

* Prince Eddy was clearly a very late developer, as Evelyn observed. A few years later, however, free from the stultifying influence of Dalton, the Prince proved that he could make up his own mind on matters of importance, and he was even considered for the sensitive (though largely symbolic) post of Viceroy of Ireland. In his book *Prince Eddy* (p.81), Andrew Cook surmises that the young Prince's inertia may have been due to a temporary anxiety state, and his apparent blockheadedness can be interpreted as an understandable rebellion against all the restrictions placed on his freedom.

From Albany we came here where we have been thoroughly enjoying ourselves. Melbourne is really a very fine town situated about four miles inland, Sandridge being its seaport off which place we are anchored … Melbourne is quite a little London, it has wide streets with first rate shops, clubs, theatres and an opera house, also Houses of Parliament, Treasury and Law Offices, all of which are very fine buildings. All the people too seem to be a very rich set and I must say are very kind and are certainly entertaining us in a very grand way. There are balls or parties <u>every night</u> and during the day there is either riding, shooting, coursing, pigeon shooting, hunting, football or lawn tennis parties going on. Besides this they are continually giving banquets or dinners in our honour which we like the least attending, as one has to sit and eat and drink for five solid hours, the effects of which it takes at least a good day's violent exercise to work off.

However, altogether we have been having grand sport, but I am sorry to say that I am now quite out of all the fun owing to the effects of a football match that we played last week against Melbourne. When we were about half way through the game my ankle went smash. I was immediately carried off the field and examined by several doctors who happened to be watching the game with some thousands of other people and they pronounced it to be very bad and said it would be some time before I could get about again, so I am now laid up in bed with an iron splint on … the worst part of it is that it is such dreadfully slow work lying in bed when so much fun is going on, and I shall also lose all chance of picking up an heiress of which there seem to be not a few here …

I wonder if Mr Gladstone will pass his Irish Land Bill, I must say the government seem to be quite incapable of managing that country and I hope it will end in their being kicked out, what a pity for England that Old Gladstone did not die the other day instead of Ld. Beaconsfield, however from all accounts I don't imagine the former old gentleman will last very long, he seems to be pretty weak in the head at any rate.*

Last Wednesday we gave an afternoon dance on board to which about 300 people came, and altogether it was a great success … Now with best love to Aunt Milly who I hope is quite well and yourself.

    Good bye   Believe me
                      Your affect. Nephew
                          Evelyn R. Le Marchant

Please excuse the writing as it is rather difficult in bed.

Evelyn was particularly upset to have missed the chance of winning the affection of a wealthy heiress, whether 'young or old'. In his opinion only ladies worth £10,000 a year or more were deemed to be a good catch. 'I wonder Evey did not lose heart there,' commented Edward from Bangalore, 'We shall hear of him emigrating I suspect, and talking of sheep.' Whilst laid up in bed Evelyn

---

* Some years later Evelyn wrote, 'What a state Ireland seems to be in, I believe it would be better to give the Irish home rule,' a view with which his family strongly disagreed.

was not completely isolated, and during afternoon dances on board *Bacchante* young ladies would come to visit him and bring him flowers. No doubt they wished to hear all about the young Princes, who had greatly impressed Australian society; 'the people have made a great fuss over them,' commented Evelyn. When the Detached Squadron sailed on to Sydney with the two Princes aboard the Admiral's ship, HMS *Inconstant*, Evelyn remained behind in Melbourne with *Bacchante* whilst repairs to her rudder were completed.

Early on the morning of 11 July 1881, between Melbourne and Sydney, a lookout on *Inconstant* reported seeing a strange red light approaching. In his private journal Prince George noted the appearance of this light, 'in the midst of which the masts, spars and sails of a brig 200 yards distant stood out in strong relief as she came up on the port bow'.* When the quarterdeck midshipman went forward for a closer look, the phantom ship had disappeared into the pre-dawn light. Altogether, 13 people on board *Inconstant* reported seeing the ghost ship, which was also observed from two other ships in the squadron, *Tourmaline* and *Cleopatra*. According to legend, some 300 years ago a Dutch captain sailed into a terrible storm off the Cape of Good Hope, but refused to turn for shore despite the pleas of his crew. As the storm grew worse the captain challenged God to sink his ship, and for this blasphemy he was condemned to sail the Southern Seas forever with his phantom crew, bringing misfortune to any ship that came within sight of her. By unhappy coincidence, tragedy struck *Inconstant* on the same day that the legendary *Flying Dutchman* was sighted. The lookout who had first seen the apparition later fell to his death from the foretopmast crosstrees. And soon after *Inconstant* reached Sydney the Admiral suffered a stroke, delaying the squadron's departure, though he later recovered.

Prince George and his brother returned to *Bacchante* when she reached Sydney. From there the squadron sailed to Fiji, where they remained for a week. For Dalton, the Fijian Islands were a perfect example of the benefits that flowed from Britain's civilising mission to native peoples around the world. In *The Cruise of HMS Bacchante* he wrote that the government of these islands reflected 'the honour and credit of England in its dealings with native races … The aim has been to infuse British supremacy as a civilising element into the native system … Native customs, unless when they violate morality and humanity, are scrupulously respected.' Later, he described an occasion when many native Fijians came on board *Bacchante*. The chief engineer amused them by passing an electric current through a basin of water, into which they dipped their hands and received a shock. They were not terrified and 'seemed to think it quite natural that we should be possessed of these wonderful powers'.[3]

---

* *The Cruise of HMS Bacchante 1879-1882*, Prince Albert Victor and Prince George of Wales, with additions by John N. Dalton (London, 1886), Vol. I, p. 551. Though claiming to have been compiled from the private journals, letters and notebooks of the two Princes, the book was evidently written by Dalton. 'I fancy old Dalton's book will be very dry reading,' commented Evelyn shortly before it was published. All charts in the book were checked by Lieutenants F.B. Henderson and Evelyn Le Marchant.

Leaving Fiji the squadron sailed north to Japan, a voyage of almost 4,300 miles, mostly under sail. After six weeks at sea they were glad to reach Yokohama, where they were lavishly entertained by the Mikado, Emperor of Japan. The Princes, guests of the Emperor for their two-week stay, greatly appreciated the courtesy and kindness of the Japanese gentlemen who were deputed by the Mikado to look after them. When the Mikado, accompanied by numerous officials in the most gorgeous robes covered with diamonds, came on board *Bacchante*, Evelyn was less complimentary. 'We fired off torpedoes and other things to amuse the Mikado who is certainly one of the ugliest chaps in Japan I have yet seen,' commented Evelyn, who was amazed by many of the new things he saw in foreign lands. At Kobe he was invited out for a day's shooting, much of which was spent travelling, first by train and then for three hours in a rickshaw. This he described as a 'lightly made Bath chair on two wheels and a regular shaft into which a man almost devoid of clothing gets and pulls you about like a pony, they run sometimes as much as 50 miles in the course of the day.' As a young man of 23 Evelyn had already visited more of the world than most Victorian gentlemen could hope to see in a lifetime, and he would see much more before returning to England.

After visits to Hong Kong and China *Bacchante* left the Detached Squadron to begin the long journey homeward. During the return voyage the Princes would meet more foreign dignitaries, including their uncle, King George I of the Hellenes, who visited *Bacchante* several times when she reached Athens some months later. In Singapore the Maharaja of Johor invited officers to stay for a couple of days, but Evelyn chose not to go. There they witnessed ram and cock fights, 'both of which I hear were disgusting sights,' wrote Evelyn, 'the rams simply charging one another until one was killed and the cocks had tremendous, large spurs with which they ripped each other up.' When they reached Ceylon in January 1882 they were invited to witness an elephant kraal, the culmination of a month-long attempt by thousands of beaters to drive two herds of wild elephants into a prepared enclosure. Eventually 12 of the 25 elephants were successfully kraaled, but not without a considerable struggle. The others managed to escape, though one cow had to be shot after charging and wounding several of the beaters.

During his stay in Colombo Evelyn met Walter Waller from Little Rissington, but failed to locate his cousin Johnny Le Marchant, an unsuccessful planter who had to leave Ceylon some years later due to ill health. Many of the planters, who were 'mostly university men and all gentlemen', were facing ruin because blight had destroyed the coffee crop, though some were beginning to plant tea, rubber, or cinchona – from the bark of which comes quinine – instead. Waller had been fortunate: he had been appointed Secretary of the Kandy Club at a salary of £200 a year, considerably more than Evelyn was earning as a sub-lieutenant on 7s. 6d. a day. This seems to have rekindled Evelyn's wish to find a more lucrative profession, and he wrote to his sister Annie asking her to keep an eye out for other opportunities. Later, in Egypt, he met Henry Peveril Le Mesurier, 'a regular Guernseyman' and friend of his parents, who as Director of

Railways earned £3,000 a year, confirming Evelyn's belief that almost every other profession was significantly more rewarding than the Navy. 'If I only had a little money of my own,' he wrote, 'I would go out to Australia and sugar plant.' Yet despite his frustrations he remained in the Navy, earning promotion to the rank of lieutenant before the voyage was over.

Bacchante reached Ismaïlia at the entrance to the Suez Canal early in March. There the royal party – including Dalton, Lord Francis Osbourne and Evelyn Le Marchant – were greeted by Ferdinand de Lesseps and the British Consul-General, Sir Edward Malet, before boarding a special train to Cairo for the start of their three-week visit to Egypt as guests of the Khedive. The visit took place at a sensitive time in Anglo-Egyptian relations, six months after the nationalist, Arabi Pasha, had led a rebellion which challenged the authority of the Khedive's government. Although weak, Khedive Tewfik continued to receive support from Britain and France who believed that he offered the best hope of preventing Egypt from sliding into anarchy, an outcome which would threaten the security of the Suez Canal. Measures taken by these two powers to control the failing Egyptian economy had, however, only served to provoke nationalist unrest and further weaken the Khedive. The royal Princes, ambassadors for their country, were cordially received by the Khedive, but within months of their visit Britain's long occupation of Egypt had begun.

On arrival in Cairo the royal party were driven to one of the Khedive's residences set aside for their use. After changing into full dress uniform they went to pay their respects to the Khedive. 'We were received with a great flourish of trumpets,' wrote Evelyn. 'The Khedive … conducted us to his reception room where we sat round on chairs and then his servants brought us each a pipe about 7 feet long which we had to smoke.' Once the formalities were over the party visited several places of interest in Cairo, before returning to their comfortable residence for a sumptuous dinner. The next day they were driven to the pyramids in the Khedive's carriages. 'We were the lions of the place,' commented

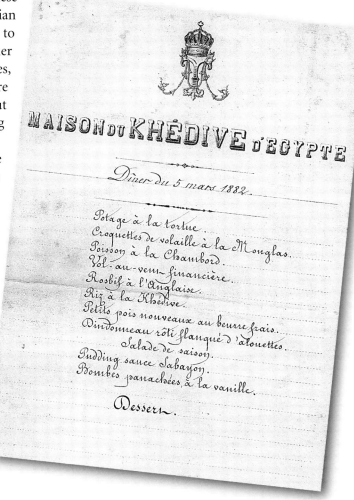

30. Menu for a dinner hosted by the Khedive of Egypt, 5 March 1882, at which Evelyn Le Marchant was present.

Evelyn, 'everybody bowing and scraping as we passed by.' After a hard climb to the top and back, they crawled along a narrow passage inside one of the pyramids, which was unpleasantly hot and stank horribly. The following night the Khedive hosted a dinner in their honour, described by Evelyn as 'a most gorgeous affair'. Among the delicacies on the menu were turtle soup, and roast turkey accompanied by a side dish of larks. During their stay in Cairo they went twice to the opera and saw *Si j'étais roi* by Adam, which Evelyn dismissed as trash, and *La mascotte* by Audran, which he enjoyed very much. The Cairo Opera House, venue for the first production of *Aida* in 1871, had been commissioned by Tewfik's father, Ismail Pasha, to celebrate the opening of the Suez Canal two years previously.

Keen to impress his royal guests, Tewfik arranged for the party to see as many ancient sites as possible. At Saqqara, south of Cairo, they were shown the Serapeum, underground burial galleries where the mummified remains of 28 sacred Apis bulls had been placed in immense granite sarcophagi, the earliest dating from 612 BC. The highlight of their stay was a two-week voyage up the Nile in the comfort of the Khedive's yacht, *Ferouze*. Commencing at Assiut, they sailed as far as the island of Philae, beyond Aswan, a journey of some 300 miles. On the return journey they went aground on a sandbank, and it took more than 18 hours and considerable manpower to pull the boat clear. During the voyage they visited many impressive sites, including the temple at Dendera – 'one of the finest we shall see', wrote Evelyn – and those of Seti I and Rameses II at Abydos, with their exquisite painted relief decoration. At Thebes (modern Luxor) they saw the famous rock-hewn tombs of the Valley of the Kings in which the Pharaohs of the New Kingdom (1550-1069 BC) were buried. The distinguished visitors were accompanied by Émile Brugsch, an eminent German Egyptologist, who told them about his recent discoveries and ensured that they missed nothing of importance. Considerable efforts were made to meet their every need; when Evelyn let it be known that he hoped to see his brother who was somewhere further up the Nile, the Consul-General telegraphed ahead to his officials, who managed to locate Gaspard and give him the message. When the two brothers met they each had many stories to tell.

The royal party rejoined their ship at Alexandria, where a large crowd greeted them on arrival. They were sorry to leave Egypt after such a memorable visit, and could not have foreseen that before *Bacchante* reached England 50 Europeans would be killed in serious rioting in Alexandria. From Egypt *Bacchante* sailed to Jaffa where she remained for two weeks, giving Evelyn and some other officers an opportunity to visit places of interest in the Holy Land. They reached Jerusalem after a day's journey by horse, and the next day, Easter Saturday, they went to the Church of the Holy Sepulchre, which tradition holds to be Christ's burial place. There they witnessed a ceremony known as the Miracle of Holy Fire, said by Orthodox Christians to be the greatest of all miracles. Orthodox Christians believe that on the same day at the same hour every year fire is sent down by

God, striking the sacred tomb and lighting a candle held by the Greek Patriarch of Jerusalem. The miraculous flame is then passed by the Patriarch to followers in the crowded church, leading to a frenzied scramble to be the first to receive it. In 1834 fights broke out and in the ensuing carnage scores of people were trampled to death. As he watched the unfolding drama Evelyn would have been aware that a few ecumenical Anglicans had recently proposed joining up with the Orthodox Churches. Others, however, argued that the ceremony Evelyn was about to see was a trick, evidence of a false religion, heavily dependent on superstition and tolerant of unchristian violence. The Pre-Raphaelite painter William Holman Hunt later satirised the beliefs and practices which accompanied this ceremony in his painting, 'The Miracle of the Holy Fire'.

In a letter home Evelyn described what he saw that day at the Church of the Holy Sepulchre.

> The church was crammed from top to bottom so tight that some people were killed by the squash, a strong body of Turkish soldiers were there to keep order and they lay about them freely with sticks, most of the people (men and women) seemed half drunk and tossed each other up in the air and made an awful noise singing 'Christ is risen. Christ is risen and the Jews are gone to the Devil,' everybody had a bunch of candles ready to catch the Holy fire, which was thrown out at last from the Holy Sepulchre by the Priest inside in the shape of balls of fire, everyone seemed to have a light in a minute with which they singed their faces. The person who gets the first light is supposed to be the most Holy, so you can imagine the fight for it, in fact I never saw such a scene in all my life, a football match is nothing to it.

The events that day made a deep impression on Evelyn, and in another letter he told his uncle that the people were singing 'Our feast is the feast of Christ, the Jew's feast is the feast of the Devil.' Hymns contrasting the Holy Fire ceremony with a Jewish feast are no longer sung, but the Miracle of Holy Fire still attracts faithful crowds of pilgrims today, some of whom claim that their candles have burst into flame spontaneously.* Afterwards they return home, strengthened in faith.

On Easter Sunday Evelyn rode to Bethlehem, where he saw the Church of the Nativity and the manger where Christ was born. Later he bathed in the Dead Sea, before riding on to the River Jordan, 'a filthy muddy stream about twice the size of the brook [the Dickler]'. There he sang the song, 't'other side of Jordan', and dipped himself seven times in the river, but doubted that he was any the

---

* According to author Victoria Clark, Bishop Theophanis of the Greek Orthodox Church in Jerusalem told her during a visit in 2002 that the Patriarch lights his candle from a small oil lamp placed on the tomb before the Holy Fire ceremony begins. That year a scuffle broke out in the inner shrine between the Greek Patriarch and an Armenian priest accompanying him when the latter, in an attempt to hurry proceedings along and perhaps gain some kudos for being the first to pass the Holy Fire out to a waiting priest, used a cigarette lighter to light his own bundle of candles. Victoria Clark, *Holy Fire: The Battle For Christ's Tomb* (Macmillan, 2005), pp. 7 and 18.

cleaner for it. When he reached Jericho he was unimpressed, describing it as 'a miserable dirty place consisting of about a dozen mud huts and the remains of an old castle'. Jericho, he decided, was a place to recommend to anyone you disliked, and he wished that his commanding officer, Lord Charles Scott, would go there and remain for a very long time. The next port of call was Haifa, from where a party of officers set off on another trip, this time to Nazareth and the Sea of Galilee, but Evelyn could not afford to accompany them. Instead, he walked to the top of Mount Carmel and visited the brook of Kishon, where Elijah killed the 450 false prophets of Baal.

Uncomfortably aware that he could not keep up with the extravagant lifestyle of his fellow officers, Evelyn wished he could find 'a good berth on shore. I believe a brewery would be a capital thing if one could only get into one,' he wrote, though he seems to have accepted that he would probably remain in the Navy. In Beirut and Athens he could afford to do very little sightseeing and was now impatient to return home. From Corfu, where *Bacchante* remained for two weeks, he expressed his frustration in a letter home. 'I hope I shall never be in such an expensive ship again, I have not been able to save a sou,' he complained, 'and none of my uncles bar Uncle John have ever sent me a penny and they must know thundering well that a ship of this sort would be more expensive than an ordinary one. I must say I think we are most unlucky in our relations …' When *Bacchante* reached the Solent the Prince and Princess of Wales came on board to welcome their two sons home. Three days later the young Princes were confirmed by Archbishop Tait at Whippingham Church on the Isle of Wight, in the presence of Queen Victoria and many officers from *Bacchante*. Before the ship was paid off the Prince of Wales personally thanked those officers, including Evelyn, who had played a part in the instruction of the Princes during the long voyage and presented them each with a small souvenir of the cruise.

HMS *Wild Swan* and the Pacific Squadron

'You have had wonderful good fortune,' commented one of Evelyn's sisters. 'You have seldom served out of a flag ship. You have made numerous friends and amongst them not the least are the sons of His Royal Highness the Prince of Wales.* You are personally acquainted with the Duke of Edinburgh and won his silver cricket ball in the Mediterranean.' Evelyn, however, who seemed at ease socially amongst this privileged élite, lacked the wealth to feel entirely comfortable. When promotion finally came, which he believed was long overdue, he enjoyed a further substantial increase in pay and could at last support himself without help from his uncles. As a newly promoted lieutenant Evelyn's next appointment was to HMS *Alexandra*, flagship in the Mediterranean, which he joined shortly

---

* When, a decade later, Prince Eddy's engagement was announced Evelyn subscribed to a wedding present from the officers of HMS *Bacchante*. 'Princess May of Teck is a very nice girl from all accounts,' he commented, 'a pity she has not more money as the Royal Family are not well off. To my mind a rich American heiress would have been much more to the purpose.'

after she had taken part in the bombardment of Alexandria. He spent a year in *Alexandra* visiting many places in the Mediterranean, before returning to England for another spell at the Royal Naval College.

In March 1885 Evelyn sailed for Esquimalt, Vancouver Island, as navigating officer in the barque-rigged sloop HMS *Wild Swan*. 'I wish I could have seen him again before he embarked on his long tour in the Pacific,' wrote Edward. 'Though life on the ocean wave to a land lubber like me does not seem to be the most enjoyable one, I really think the Navy is the service now to be proud of, our [the Army's] prestige is gone.' For Evelyn, who would hear of his brother's encouraging comments in due course, it would be another four years before he returned home to England. Such lengthy periods of service overseas were inevitable because of the time it took to reach the most distant foreign stations. The voyage to Esquimalt through the Suez Canal was more than 19,000 miles and lasted almost six months. After 14 years in the Navy long spells at sea were only now ceasing to be a test of endurance for Evelyn. In the Bay of Biscay *Wild Swan* was buffeted by very heavy seas, but Evelyn was relieved to discover that he experienced no seasickness; 'I am beginning to think I have at last got over that terrible feeling,' he wrote.

The outward voyage included a two-day visit to Madeira, before new orders were received to return to the Mediterranean because of the possibility of war with Russia. In Madeira Evelyn accompanied his captain to the top of a hill in Funchal in a bullock carriage, and then came down – as tourists have done for

H.M.S. WILD SWAN.

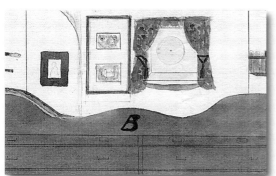

31. Watercolours by Evelyn showing his cabin aboard HMS *Wild Swan*, which he decorated with photographs and pictures from home.

centuries – in a sleigh. 'It took us nearly an hour to get up and we came down in ten minutes,' he wrote. The threat of war provided the stimulus to put in some urgent gunnery practice, and *Wild Swan*'s new breech-loading guns were fired for the first time since she had been rearmed. 'I must say the guns are far superior to the old muzzle-loading ones,' commented Evelyn, 'we made very good shooting.'

Amongst the many ports visited by *Wild Swan* on her outward voyage to Esquimalt were Gibraltar, Malta, Aden, Colombo, Singapore, Hong Kong and Yokohama, places already familiar to the 27-year-old navigating officer. A two-week stay in Hong Kong for repairs to the propeller, which had been damaged as they passed through the Suez Canal, was followed by a pleasant week in Yokohama. There Evelyn visited an amazing 90-foot bronze statue, the inside of which was a temple. 'There is room in his head for several people,' commented Evelyn drily, 'I went inside the chap but found him so hot that I did not get beyond his stomach.' To his great delight a mail steamer arrived just 15 minutes before *Wild Swan* set sail from Yokohama, with many letters from home. These he would read several times to help fill the long hours at sea.

Anything which helped to break the monotony of extended periods at sea was welcome, including a change of diet. The invention of canned meat, dried milk powder and margarine in the mid-19th century enabled ships to stay at sea for longer periods, but gaining access to fresh water was always a concern and the Royal Navy continued to make frequent visits to foreign ports both to take on supplies and to show the flag. Sometimes officers brought animals on board to supplement their rations. In Aden they had purchased two sheep; 'the last was sacrificed today,' commented Evelyn, 'but we could not make much of a meal of him as he was all skin and bone.' And later, in Patagonia, they shot a good many geese which, Evelyn noted, 'were a great addition to our larder'.

Thirty-two days after leaving Yokohama *Wild Swan* finally reached Vancouver Island. Esquimalt, an Indian name meaning a place gradually shoaling, had been developed as a naval base for the Royal Navy's Pacific Squadron during the late 1840s and 1850s. The base was of strategic importance at a sensitive time in Anglo-American relations, enabling the Royal Navy to provide protection for the emerging British colonies of Vancouver Island and British Columbia against foreign encroachments, attacks by native Americans, and the activities of lawless gold miners from the United States. America's belief in her right, or Manifest Destiny, to control the entire North American continent posed a threat to British North America, and when the United States purchased Alaska from Russia in 1867 American Secretary of State William Seward declared that the permanent political separation of British Columbia from Alaska and Washington state was no longer tenable.[4] However, the presence of the Royal Navy acted as a deterrent and Esquimalt, with its sheltered harbour and healthy climate, provided the best available naval base in the eastern Pacific. Plentiful supplies of high-quality timber for masts and spars, together with coal, were readily available on Vancouver Island,

and the value of Esquimalt as a base was further enhanced when a hospital and dry dock were built, increasing the length of time that ships of the Pacific Squadron could remain on station. Esquimalt village itself provided few distractions other than a handful of public houses and brothels, but for a time the goldfields of Pacific America proved to be such a temptation to deserting sailors that shore leave had to be restricted to petty officers and reliable ratings.

Whilst Evelyn was outward bound to Esquimalt the Pacific Squadron took measures to protect the base against a possible hit-and-run attack by Russian cruisers during the war scare of 1885. There had been several such scares since the Crimean War, and the latest crisis over Afghanistan highlighted the lack of adequate protection for the base against enemy bombardment. Accordingly, the Admiralty purchased two torpedo boats from Chile and these were stationed at Esquimalt to guard against a Russian raid. Captain Kelly wrote to Evelyn from Devonport Dockyard to say that if it came to war, a shortage of officers and men would prevent the Admiralty from being able to man all the available warships. 'Everyone seems to think war with Russia is imminent and I hope it is true,' commented Evelyn. 'There may be a chance of some prize money if we can only get inside of Vladivostok.' But if war was averted, he observed, at least 'the scare will have opened people's eyes a bit to the state of the Navy'. A couple of

32. Letter from Evelyn Le Marchant, HMS *Wild Swan*, Panama City, 21 January 1885.

years later, when a war between France and Germany seemed possible, his eagerness for a fight had dimmed. 'I hope we shan't be dragged into it,' he wrote, 'as I have no wish to be shot yet awhile.'

Once the Russian war scare was over the Pacific Squadron resumed its extensive patrol duties in the South Pacific and *Wild Swan* sailed for the tropics. It would be nearly two years before she returned to Esquimalt. The Squadron, under the command of Rear Admiral Sir M. Culme-Seymour, Baronet, called in to take on coal, pick up provisions and show the flag at numerous ports, large and small, along the entire length of the west coast of North and South America, a distance of more than 8,000 miles. Evelyn liked San Francisco very much, with its wide streets, splendid shops, and trams, 'the motive power of which is invisible', he commented. It was here that he was

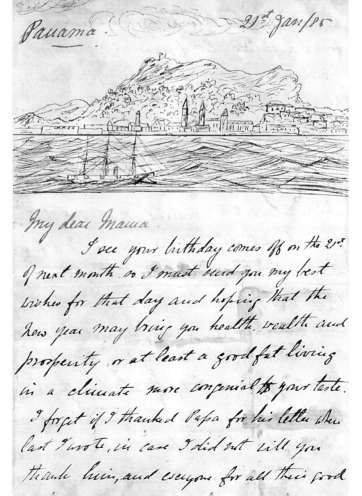

severely bitten on the hand by a large retriever at a lawn tennis party, but within weeks he was back in action. He was unimpressed with Acapulco, 'not much of a place, more like a village of huts than anything else', and he found many of the smaller Central American ports visited by *Wild Swan* on her journey south to be 'dirty, wretched, hot places', entirely without merit. In Panama City, where crime went largely unpunished, a man was stabbed to death close to where Evelyn was playing tennis and nobody showed any apparent concern. Whilst in Panama Evelyn took the opportunity to travel inland to see the canal being constructed and was greatly impressed by the sheer scale of the undertaking.

Whenever he was in port for more than a few days Evelyn played plenty of tennis and cricket, and he quickly immersed himself in the social life of the place. He enjoyed his three-month stay in Lima and thought that the Peruvian girls he met were very pretty. 'They dance awfully well,' he wrote, 'the worst of it is they lose their good looks so soon, at the age of 25 they are quite old, they marry at 15.' Amongst the European society ladies he met was the daughter of the British Minister. The unfortunate young woman, who had a very large, hooked, beak-like nose, was known to everyone as 'the wingless parrot'. It was from Lima that he sent home a parcel containing some very curious eyes – some of which he had dug up himself – that had once belonged to Inca mummies. Imagine, for a moment, what his sisters must have thought when they opened the package. 'They are supposed to be cuttle fish eyes with which the Incas used to fill the eye sockets of the dead,' he wrote. 'You must not mind their smelling a bit when you first open the box, that will pass off and really when mounted they make very handsome pins or earrings.' He resisted the temptation to acquire another Peruvian curio, doubting its provenance. 'In Lima Cathedral,' he wrote, 'old Pizarro is buried, and for a small consideration the priests in charge will give you a piece of his night shirt.'

After a while Evelyn – who by now had grown an impressive moustache and beard – found life on the South Pacific station extremely tedious. Sometimes the work was dirty and unglamorous. 'We are coaling ship today,' he wrote, 'and the coal dust is something quite too awful; being my day on duty I can't get ashore out of it.' Coaling was a thoroughly unpleasant task, a necessary part of naval life which Evelyn detested, but he would not have to undertake this duty again for a while and could now look forward to further spells of leave ashore. During the six weeks that *Wild Swan* remained at Coquimbo, some 200 miles north of Valparaiso, he was able to break the monotony by getting away for long weekends to a ranch owned by the Lamberts, friends he had met five years earlier in Montevideo. There, at *La Compania*, he settled easily into the comfortable expatriate lifestyle of his hosts. On one occasion he rode out with a party to round up and lasso 80 head of cattle, which he found very exciting even though he failed to lasso a single steer. Another time he took part in a hilarious donkey race, riding bare back with no reins; although he fell off six times he still managed to finish fourth.

'The wingless parrot', drawn by Evelyn.

Before returning once more to Esquimalt *Wild Swan* sailed to the Galapagos Islands and on to Honolulu. During the long voyage several blue whales, one nearly 100 feet in length, followed the ship for a time. 'Jonah might have done a 3 years' commission in it without any inconvenience to himself,' wrote Evelyn to his sister Annie. In Honolulu, where he spent a lively week, Evelyn rode out with several friends for a picnic in one of the prettiest valleys on the island. 'Our party consisted of 5 girls and 5 men, no chaperones allowed and it was a great success,' he wrote, 'and we took a photograph machine with us.' Though he sent home lots of photos, many either never reached England or have subsequently been lost.

After a lengthy absence Evelyn was delighted to return to Esquimalt, his base for the next nine months. He lived a comfortable life ashore, and in his garden he kept 19 young chickens from which he obtained a daily supply of fresh eggs. The surrounding woods and mountain rivers provided excellent opportunities for shooting and fishing, and in season Evelyn was able to enjoy the taste of fresh wild salmon almost every day. Life was good, local people were very friendly, and though the winters were cold and wet, summer was a wonderful time on Vancouver Island. 'We are having a first rate time,' wrote Evelyn the following June, 'what with tennis parties, cricket, picnics and fishing.' But social traditions

33. Evelyn aboard HMS *Wild Swan* dressed in a fur skin bought from local traders in Patagonia, 1888.

were slow to adapt to change in a society that was inherently conservative by nature. For some colonial families the idea that women might play cricket with men was too much of a challenge to their sense of propriety. In 1888, when the first such match was played in nearby Victoria, Evelyn commented that 'some of the people were shocked at the idea and would not allow their daughters to play.'

Social life for the officers centred around Victoria, more than five miles away. Several of his fellow officers kept a pony and trap, but at £10 a month the cost was more than Evelyn could afford. Occasionally he hired a carriage, but mostly he depended on others for a lift to Victoria. There they met plenty of pretty girls, though none of them, observed Evelyn, had much money. His initial impression of the womenfolk of Victoria had not been favourable. After one of the best balls of the season he commented, 'I never saw such a collection of old hay bags as the majority of ladies were. There were hardly any unmarried girls, the young married ones were along [*sic*] way the best of the show.' Few families in Victoria were wealthy enough to employ domestic servants and as a consequence, observed Evelyn with regret, if the '<u>old</u> married things who ought to have been in bed instead of flirting away at balls' wanted a night out, their unmarried daughters had to stay at home to look after younger siblings. The best way to meet the prettiest girls in Victoria, he discovered, was to take part in amateur theatricals, and he looked forward to rehearsals with enthusiasm. By the end of his stay Evelyn had made many new friends and was very sorry to leave Esquimalt.

On the return voyage, lasting more than six months, *Wild Swan* was home to an exotic collection of pet animals that had been acquired over the past couple of years. Only the cats and dogs seem to have made it safely back to England, however. A monkey and an armadillo, which had kept the crew amused for some time, jumped overboard and drowned, and an ant-eater – 'a jolly little animal' – ate something poisonous and died. Evelyn brought three Japanese bantams and seven caged birds with him, but several died of cold before they reached the South Atlantic. In Patagonia, where Evelyn successfully charted a course through the Straits of Magellan and the narrow Smith Channel, now rarely used, *Wild Swan* was buffeted by hurricane-force winds and dragged her anchor in port, nearly going aground before putting to sea to ride out the storm. Despite steaming at full power the ship was driven backwards by the power of the gale, but she survived until the winds abated. *Wild Swan* spent each night in port, as the channels were so narrow that navigation was only possible in daylight. The scenery was spectacular, but persistent high winds, snow, hail and rain afforded only fleeting glimpses of the steep mountains nearby. Many of the officers, when they were stranded ashore for two days, bought splendid fur skins from local traders to protect themselves against the extreme weather.

At the end of January 1889 *Wild Swan* reached Plymouth. Evelyn had performed well during the long voyage and returned with his reputation enhanced. He was held in high esteem by his commanding officer who regarded him as a very good navigator and pilot, noting that he was 'most zealous; a very cool and clear-headed officer in case of emergency'.[5] After several more weeks of duty in Plymouth and a detour to Bath to meet his brother Edward, whom he had not seen for almost sixteen years, Evelyn returned to Little Rissington. Robert Le Marchant noted his arrival in his diary entry of 2 March 1889: 'Evelyn came home after his return from the Pacific station in *Wild Swan*. He was absent nearly four years and navigated *Wild Swan* during that period some sixty-five thousand miles. He went quite round the world.'

Cruising the Mediterranean – HMS *Phaeton*

A year later Evelyn joined the cruiser HMS *Phaeton* in the Mediterranean. Although the Royal Navy was undergoing a period of rapid technological change, some of the prevailing attitudes and procedures were still rooted in the past. Discipline was strict and flogging with a cat-o'-nine-tails, though rare, did not finally disappear until 1879. Conditions had improved somewhat for ordinary seamen, but they still faced much discomfort and were expected to eat meals using their fingers or iron spoons as cutlery was considered to be an unwarranted

34. HMS *Phaeton*, a second-class protected cruiser, with her guns carried on the broadside, 1897.

expense. Officers, whose social standing had risen during the reign of Queen Victoria, were often men of private means who numbered among their ranks several princes, dukes, baronets and other titled members of the aristocracy. They lived like gentlemen, and senior officers were supported by an entourage of personal servants.

Extended visits to foreign ports were interspersed with short drills and exercises at sea, for which it was hard to generate any great enthusiasm. 'Next month we go to sea for a day or so to do our firing,' wrote Evelyn, 'it will rather interfere with my trip up country.' The appearance of a ship was all-important, so much so that gunnery exercises were unpopular and guns were fired as little as possible because they made an awful mess and blistered the paintwork. Yet throughout this period the Royal Navy remained the dominant force on the world's oceans, relying not only on its numerical strength and reputation for success but also on its ability to harness and implement technological change. And as technology advanced, so naval tactical thinking evolved. Senior naval officers recognised the importance of tactical training and understood that tactics – systems of attack and defence involving the control of fleets in battle – depended first and foremost on good seamanship, which included skilful ship-handling and co-ordination in close formation. Thus time spent honing such skills was vital, for they 'were the foundations on which victories would be built, not the method that would secure them'.[6] Most naval officers understood these distinctions well enough, but Evelyn nevertheless believed that good admirals and generals were born, not made, and that no amount of tactical training would compensate for a lack of innate ability.

MEDITERRANEAN FLEET REGATTA, 1891.

VICE ADMIRAL, SIR GEORGE TRYON, K.C.B.

COMMANDER-IN-CHIEF.

REAR ADMIRAL LORD WALTER KERR.

Committee.

PRESIDENT:— Captain THE HON. M. A. BOURKE, H.M.S. "VICTORIA".

Lieut.	Barr,	H.M.S. "AGAMEMNON".	Lieut.	Travers,	H.M.S. "NILE".
„	Harbord,	„ "AUSTRALIA".	„	Le Marchant,	„ "PHAETON".
„	Tippinge,	„ "COLLINGWOOD".	„	Carr,	„ "SCOUT".
Comr.	Shakespear,	„ "COLOSSUS".	„	Sandeman,	„ "SURPRISE".
Lieut.	Meldrum,	„ "DREADNOUGHT".	„	Ricardo,	„ "TRAFALGAR".
„	Haworth Booth	„ "EDINBURGH".	„	Growse,	„ "UNDAUNTED".
„	Macnamara,	„ "FEARLESS".	„	Digby,	„ "VICTORIA".

Mr. Franklin, Hon. Secretary, H.M.S. "VICTORIA".

Judges.

Comr. Inglefield, H.M.S. "TRAFALGAR"   Staff Comr. Tully, H.M.S. "VICTORIA",

Starters and Umpires.

Comr.	De Lisle,	H.M.S. "AGAMEMNON".	Lieut. Ommaney,	H.M.S. "EDINBURGH".
„	Dicken.	„ "AUSTRALIA".	Comr. Prothero,	„ "NILE".
„	Tate,	„ "COLOSSUS".	Staff Comr. Bullmore,	„ "TRAFALGAR".
Lieut.	Smythies,	„ "DREADNOUGHT".	Comr. Lowry,	„ "UNDAUNTED".

COURSES.

Rowing.	*Sailing.*
	A triangular course of about 4 miles.
LONG:— about 2½ miles.	LONG:— 3 times round.
SHORT:— 1 mile.	SHORT:— twice round.

DISTINGUISHING FLAGS.

H.M.S. "AGAMEMNON", Dark Blue.   H.M.S. "FEARLESS", Black with Yellow ball.
  „ "AUSTRALIA", Red.   „ "NILE", Red and Yellow.
  „ "COLLINGWOOD", White with a Red C.   „ "PHAETON", Light Blue.
  „ "COLOSSUS", Red and White diagonal   „ "SCOUT", White Black White (vertical)
       with Maltese Cross.   „ "SURPRISE", Red with White Cross.
  „ "DREADNOUGHT", Blue with Crown,   „ "TRAFALGAR", Red flag with White T.
  „ "EDINBURGH", Blue and White,   „ "UNDAUNTED", Letter C.
          H.M.S. "VICTORIA", White with Red Cross.

35. Programme, Mediterranean Fleet Regatta, 1891.
Lieutenant Le Marchant was a member of the
organising committee.

During their many visits to port officers spent much of their time sightseeing, entertaining and playing sport. In August 1890, after a visit to Sorrento, *Phaeton* spent a week at Naples. There Evelyn was able to explore at leisure the excavations at Pompeii and climb Vesuvius at night with several other officers. As they approached the mouth of the crater their guide tried to stop them from proceeding further, warning them that conditions were too dangerous, but they were determined to continue. 'I never saw such a mass of fire, smoke and sparks,' wrote Evelyn, 'and there was a continuous shower of red hot pumice stones and scoria being thrown up to a great height and one had to keep one's weather eye lifting as to where it would fall and dodge about like anything to avoid it, some of the pieces were very large measuring several feet across.' After a hazardous descent, the intrepid officers made it safely back to the ship by 3 a.m. They had been closer to danger than many would ever be during their entire naval careers. In peacetime, deprived of the excitement of war and the chance to prove themselves under fire, officers sought adventure in other ways.

From Naples *Phaeton* returned to Sorrento to pick up Lord Dufferin, ambassador in Rome, for a short cruise to Capri, Amalfi, Salerno and Pesto. Evelyn was particularly impressed with the ancient temples at Paestum, some of the finest Doric temples anywhere. Back in Naples *Phaeton* hosted an afternoon dance to which many prominent members of local society were invited, including a number of dukes, duchesses and princesses. Evelyn, now a good dancer himself, enjoyed these social occasions and wrote to his sisters encouraging them to practise this 'most important accomplishment', as it would greatly improve their marriage prospects. A week later *Phaeton* returned to Sorrento for a few days, where officers were entertained by Lord and Lady Dufferin. Their next destination

36. Rome; watercolour, probably by Evelyn Le Marchant.

was the lovely island of Ischia, where Evelyn walked up Mount Epameo and visited Casamicciola, which had been destroyed by an earthquake several years earlier. In Toulon, where 'it was visiting, eating and drinking all the time', Evelyn observed that the French 'have some very fine ships and they are much more practical and manage things better than we do in our naval ports'. Information gleaned during this and other visits would later be of use to Evelyn when he took charge of Devonport dockyard.

Over the next three years Evelyn explored many of the Mediterranean's most popular islands, including Menorca, Crete, Rhodes, Lemnos, Santorini, Cyprus and Capri. At Maddalena Bay on the north coast of Sardinia, which was 'fast becoming a strongly fortified port and naval arsenal,' they found the Italian fleet in port and had to go through 'much the same kind of entertainment as we did with the French'. Such visits not only fostered good diplomatic relations but also provided the Royal Navy with piecemeal intelligence about the capabilities of navies that might one day be ranged against them. Other notable ports of call included Beirut, Cannes and Salonica. In Spain he enjoyed a splendid run with the Calpe hounds: 'I shall miss the hunting when we leave here,' he wrote from Gibraltar. From Marmaris in Turkey, with its fine natural harbour, Evelyn organised boating picnics in his spare time to secluded spots along the coast. In a sailing race at the Fleet Regatta he was disappointed not to win a handsome silver vase donated by the British ambassador to Constantinople. Whenever *Phaeton* returned to Malta Evelyn enjoyed a busy and varied social life amongst friends and relatives ashore. As well as the usual round of dinner parties, grand fancy dress balls and amateur theatricals, he was a regular guest at the opera and the races. A friend of Evelyn's from Guernsey, Captain De Lancey of the Highland Light Infantry, owned three horses called 'Implicit Confidence', 'Confidence', and 'Misplaced Confidence', on which he won many races.

37. Nancy La Primaudaye, *c.*1890 – one of the young ladies whom Evelyn met during his many visits to Malta. Captain Clement La Primaudaye, RN, was Commissioner of Police in Malta from 1890 to 1903.

It was during manoeuvres carried out by the Mediterranean Fleet in June 1893 – in which Evelyn Le Marchant took part in *Phaeton* – that the Navy suffered another terrible peacetime disaster.* Two columns of ships were steaming towards Tripoli with the Commander-in-Chief, Vice Admiral Sir George Tryon, leading the starboard column on board HMS *Victoria*. At the head of the port column was HMS *Camperdown*. As they approached their anchorage Tryon signalled for the two columns to reverse course by turning inwards, a spectacular manoeuvre when executed successfully. On this occasion, however, Tryon made a fatal error

---

* Previous disasters included the loss of HMS *Captain* in 1870 and the sinking of HMS *Vanguard* in 1875 after she was accidentally rammed by HMS *Iron Duke* in fog in Dublin Bay.

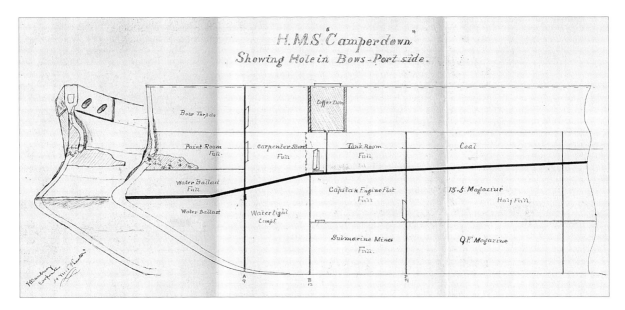

of judgement, for the columns were too close together. The two leading ships turned towards each other, one inside the other's turning circle, and *Camperdown* rammed the starboard bow of *Victoria*, holing Tryon's flagship below the waterline. With no time to close watertight doors or portholes, *Victoria* capsized and sank in less than 15 minutes with the loss of more than 350 of her crew, including the Commander-in-Chief himself. Nothing better illustrates the critical importance of achieving consistently high standards of seamanship before conducting more challenging tactical exercises. A letter from Evelyn to his father describing the sinking of HMS *Victoria* took 12 days to reach Little Rissington, where, no doubt, it would have been the central topic of conversation on many social occasions. That letter has since been lost, but Evelyn later acquired a diagram of the damage to *Camperdown* drawn by a ship's carpenter on *Phaeton*. When accounts of the incident reached India, Louis concluded from newspaper reports that the admiral had made an 'error in his calculations'.

The following year Evelyn was cautioned for a navigating error which caused the battleship *Benbow* to be grounded temporarily on a sandbank in the English Channel. The ship sustained little damage and the incident proved to be no barrier to his subsequent promotion. HMS *Benbow* was one of only three ships in the Royal Navy to be armed with two massive 16.25-inch guns, each weighing 110 tons. These monster guns proved to be unsatisfactory, for they were slow to operate and tended to droop at the muzzle. The period before 1890 was one of experimentation in warship design and armament in which each new development was rapidly made obsolete by the next advance, and no government would permit more than a 'fleet of samples'. Gladstone, reluctant to increase naval expenditure, commented that 'the fashion in ships of war is as fickle as that of ladies' hats'.[7] However, when the report of the Carnarvon Commission

38. A drawing by M. Banbury, a carpenter on board HMS *Phaeton*, of the damage to HMS *Camperdown* after her collision with the flagship *Victoria*.

was published indicating that the Navy's assortment of ships was incapable of defending the sea lanes, Lord Salisbury's government passed the Naval Defence Act of 1889 which authorised the building of 70 new warships to counter the growing threat posed by the expansion of European navies. The Act confirmed that the size of the Navy should be equal to the combined strength of any two other navies, the largest being those of France and Russia at that time.

HMS *Bonaventure* and the East Indies Squadron

H.M.S. BONAVENTURE.

Evelyn's next ship, HMS *Bonaventure*, was one of the 42 cruisers built as a result of the Naval Defence Act. She sailed from Plymouth in 1894 for a three-year tour of duty as flagship of the East Indies Squadron. Entertaining expenses were high on board a flagship and officers received an additional allowance of 3s. a day on station. Added to the 14s. a day he received as a lieutenant of his standing and 4s. for navigation, Evelyn now received 21s. a day which, he reassured his father, 'will do me fairly well'. For several months each year the flagship was based at Trincomalee in Ceylon, and here Rear Admiral Drummond, his family, and all the officers were considered part of the permanent society of the place. For officers life at Trincomalee was very free and easy, with little to worry about and plenty of opportunities for shooting and sport. Cricket matches against the garrison attracted 'all the beauty and fashion' who turned out to hear the band from *Bonaventure* playing at teatime. Evelyn turned in some impressive performances, once taking nine wickets in an innings. As mess caterer life was particularly busy for Evelyn during Trincomalee Week, for there were dances almost every evening and by day the entertainment included cricket, tennis, golf, polo, a regatta, and a gymkhana.

When life was less hectic Evelyn took a spell of local leave and travelled up to the hill station of Nuwara Eliya, where he could easily imagine that he was back home in a traditional English village in the Lake District. 'It is most lovely scenery up here,' he wrote, 'so green and wooded with all kinds of shrubs and flowers that are cultivated at home growing wild. We are about 6,100 feet above sea level.' Writing at about the time of Evelyn's visit, Henry Cave, author of many books on Ceylon, claimed that in Newara Eliya and its surrounding districts could be found 'a combination of the most delightful conditions under which man can desire to live'.[8] Europeans came here to get away from the sultry heat of the lowlands and to recuperate from fever in the cool mountain air. With its comfortable rooms, fine billiard table and well-stocked library, the Hill Club was *the* place to stay, and it was here that Evelyn spent a very relaxing week. He was able to enjoy several rounds of golf at the adjacent 18-hole course, one of the finest and most picturesque in Asia. Caddies, mostly young boys who were often no taller than the clubs they carried, could be hired for just threepence a round.

When he was not playing other sports Evelyn loved to go shooting. He enjoyed his tennis and cricket – in both sports he played for the Fleet and

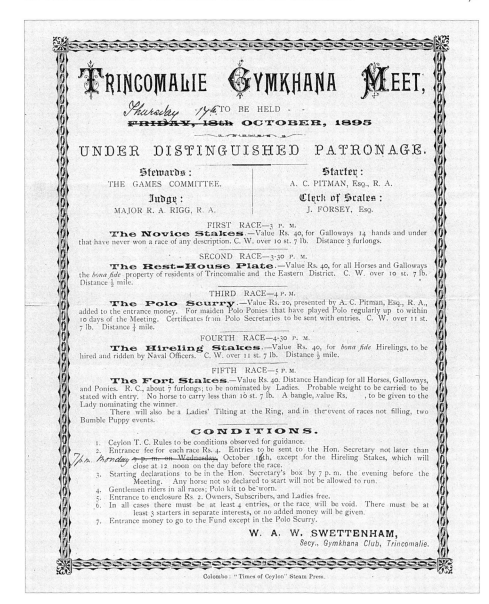

TRINCOMALIE GYMKHANA MEET,

Thursday 17th. TO BE HELD - -
~~FRIDAY, 18th~~ OCTOBER, 1895

UNDER DISTINGUISHED PATRONAGE.

Stewards:	Starter:
THE GAMES COMMITTEE.	A. C. PITMAN, Esq., R. A.
Judge:	**Clerk of Scales:**
MAJOR R. A. RIGG, R. A.	J. FORSEY, Esq.

FIRST RACE—3 P. M.

The Novice Stakes.—Value Rs. 40, for Galloways 14 hands and under that have never won a race of any description. C. W. over 10 st. 7 lb. Distance 3 furlongs.

SECOND RACE—3·30 P. M.

The Rest-House Plate.—Value Rs. 40, for all Horses and Galloways the *bona fide* property of residents of Trincomalie and the Eastern District. C. W. over 10 st. 7 lb. Distance ½ mile.

THIRD RACE—4 P. M.

The Polo Scurry.—Value Rs. 20, presented by A. C. Pitman, Esq., R. A., added to the entrance money. For maiden Polo Ponies that have played Polo regularly up to within 10 days of the Meeting. Certificates from Polo Secretaries to be sent with entries. C. W. over 11 st. 7 lb. Distance ¼ mile.

FOURTH RACE—4·30 P. M.

The Hireling Stakes.—Value Rs. 40, for *bona fide* Hirelings, to be hired and ridden by Naval Officers. C. W. over 11 st. 7 lb. Distance ½ mile.

FIFTH RACE—5 P. M.

The Fort Stakes.—Value Rs. 40. Distance Handicap for all Horses, Galloways, and Ponies. R. C., about 7 furlongs; to be nominated by Ladies. Probable weight to be carried to be stated with entry. No horse to carry less than 10 st. 7 lb. A bangle, value Rs.   , to be given to the Lady nominating the winner.

There will also be a Ladies' Tilting at the Ring, and in the event of races not filling, two Bumble Puppy events.

CONDITIONS.

1. Ceylon T. C. Rules to be conditions observed for guidance.
2. Entrance fee for each race Rs. 4. Entries to be sent to the Hon. Secretary not later than *7 p.m. monday* ~~5 p. m. on Wednesday,~~ October 16th, except for the Hireling Stakes, which will close at 12 noon on the day before the race.
3. Starting declarations to be in the Hon. Secretary's box by 7 p. m. the evening before the Meeting. Any horse not so declared to start will not be allowed to run.
4. Gentlemen riders in all races; Polo kit to be worn.
5. Entrance to enclosure Rs. 2. Owners, Subscribers, and Ladies free.
6. In all cases there must be at least 4 entries, or the race will be void. There must be at least 3 starters in separate interests, or no added money will be given.
7. Entrance money to go to the Fund except in the Polo Scurry.

W. A. W. SWETTENHAM,
Secy., Gymkhana Club, Trincomalie.

Colombo: "Times of Ceylon" Steam Press.

39. Programme, Trincomalie (now Trincomalee) Gymkhana Meet, 17 October 1895.

everywhere his skills were in great demand – but shooting offered a different challenge. Recognising that he needed more practice he wrote, 'I am taking a good lot of cartridges, as not being a very good shot I shall require 3 or 4 for each bird I get.' Whenever *Bonaventure* moved on to a new port Evelyn sought out opportunities to improve his skills in the hope that some day he might bring back a stag's head as a trophy to hang in his cabin. From Karachi he travelled by train and then by camel to find some of the best shooting around, and over the next three days he bagged plenty of snipe, partridge and quail, but on four legs he was able to shoot nothing bigger than a hare. One night when he and several other officers were asleep in a hut in the jungle near Trincomalee, some 'scoundrels of natives' robbed them of everything, including their guns, bags and clothes. Furious, Evelyn sought out the headman of the nearest village and made a tremendous fuss, but to no avail despite an offer of a reward of 100 rupees. Evelyn's rifle, together with a replacement shotgun given to him by friends of the family, were subsequently sent out from England. Later, on a visit to Farquhar Island north of Madagascar, Evelyn and a party of officers shot about 150 guinea fowl 'and found them capital eating.' To keep themselves amused in the evenings they went sea-fishing, and with the help of the islanders' seine-nets they caught a considerable quantity of fish. With a seemingly endless supply of fresh food, they lived very well.

After a month in Mauritius and several weeks in the Seychelles *Bonaventure* returned once more to Ceylon. Earlier, Evelyn had spent a pleasant month in northern India, but much to his annoyance he almost missed the start of his leave. '*Bonaventure* put to sea to do her quarterly practice of gun firing and torpedo work, but as we lost a torpedo we were detained longer than we expected,' he wrote. As soon as the ship reached Bombay Evelyn hurried to the station, travelling first to Ahmadabad and then on to Jaipur, from where he set out to see the deserted city of Amber. 'We drove five miles along rather a pretty road and then one of the Maharajah's elephants met us and took us the other two miles. I have never been on an elephant's back before and am not anxious to do so again, the animal rolled about like a ship in a gale of wind.' After the magnificent palace at Amber Evelyn visited many other places of interest, including sites made famous during the Mutiny of 1857. At Cawnpore, on the River Ganges some 250 miles southeast of Delhi, he made a brief pilgrimage to the Satichaura Ghat where hundreds of European survivors of the siege, including many women and children, had been massacred.

From Cawnpore Evelyn travelled to nearby Lucknow where he stayed for several days with his youngest brother, Louis, a lieutenant in the East Lancashire Regiment (formerly the 30th Foot). 'I was very glad to see Louis again,' he wrote, 'the 30th seems a nice Regiment.' Together they visited the ruins of the Residency, scene of another epic siege, and saw the place where Sir Henry Lawrence had been mortally wounded. 'I wish he could have stayed longer,' Louis informed his mother, 'but we had to go out and bivouac for two days to do night firing. It was most unfortunate.' A month or so later (April 1895) Evelyn received a letter from Louis who relished the prospect of seeing action during the Chitral campaign. 'I expect he will get plenty of it,' Evelyn wrote to his Sister Dora, 'I only trust he will keep a whole skin.'

From Lucknow Evelyn travelled to some of the great sites of India, including the Taj Mahal, 'the finest building in India,' and the holy city of Benares. Each new location elicited more superlatives. Of the many buildings he described as very fine, the Hall of Private Audience in the Palace of Delhi, built entirely of white marble and 'beautifully inlaid with precious stones in designs of flowers', impressed him the most. 'It is a long way the best thing I have seen yet and I

Opposite:

40. The ruins of the Residency, Lucknow, *c.*1890.

41. View towards Kanchenjunga, the third highest mountain in the world, from Darjeeling, early 1900s.

think it quite beautiful,' he wrote, 'over one of the arches is written in Arabic the following lines: "If on earth there be an Eden of Bliss, It is this, it is this, it is this."' Later, in Darjeeling, as Evelyn looked out over hills that fell away steeply towards the world's highest mountains beyond, a scene of unrivalled grandeur and beauty, he must have thought that more than one place in India could justly lay claim to be an earthly paradise.

The distractions of life ashore could not overcome Evelyn's impatience for promotion and his fear that he was being left behind. He wrote to everyone he knew who might have influence, including the Duke of York and John Dalton, and encouraged his relatives to do the same. However, he quickly grew tired of writing solicitous letters to people. 'I don't think it does any good,' he commented, 'if I had been of a rich or strong political family I should have got promotion some time ago.' In June 1895 Rear Admiral Drummond recommended him for promotion, but although he was praised for his tact, judgement, trustworthiness, and skilfulness as a navigator, his name did not appear on the list of officers promoted that year. Having little influence in high places and no war service, Evelyn felt that at least 20 officers had been promoted over his head. In December 1895 Robert Le Marchant wrote directly to the cabinet minister responsible for naval affairs, G.J. Goschen, First Lord of the Admiralty, to press the case for Evelyn's advancement, and a year later he was promoted to the rank of commander. Robert immediately wrote to the Admiralty asking that Evelyn be retained as navigating officer on *Bonaventure* until she returned to England, later noting that they 'assented to my request which they had already anticipated'.

42. Evelyn Le Marchant's programme for the Calcutta Races, January 1897. The prize for the winner of the first race, the Tally-Ho Plate, was 1,600 rupees (about £100).

The newly appointed commander was much in demand in colonial society. When the cruiser made a final visit to the capital of India, Evelyn, a keen race-goer, was once more a guest at the Calcutta Races, one of the highlights of the social season. January was a popular time to visit Calcutta, and *Bonaventure* had spent several weeks there at the same time the previous year. 'We are having a very jolly time of it here, the weather is perfect,' wrote Evelyn. 'The Races are great fun and there is a great show on the Viceroy's Cup day. Like Ascot Cup day at home everybody turns out in their smartest and the Viceroy goes down in State.' After a while, however, Evelyn tired of all this high living, the constant round of balls, dances, and dinners. By the spring of 1897, when *Bonaventure* left Trincomalee for England, Evelyn had had enough of the tropical heat and was delighted that he would soon be home with his family in the pleasant Cotswold countryside.

CALCUTTA RACES
❖ 1896-97 ❖

❯❯ SECOND MEETING ❮❮
FIRST DAY.
SATURDAY, 16th JANUARY 1897.

Stewards:

A. A. APCAR, Esq.
Col. J. L. HUNT.
C. C. McLEOD, Esq.   } Calcutta Turf Club.
Hon. Mr. W. MACPHERSON, c.s.
CHARLES H. MOORE, Esq.
      AND
ALLAN ARTHUR, Esq.   Col. J. L. HUNT.
Judge   ...   ...   Mr. F. BEATY.
Starter   ...   ...   R. BOTELER, Esq.
Handicapper & Clerk of the Scales   Dr. R. SPOONER-HART,
Veterinary Surgeon   ...   M.R.C.V.S., L.E.V.M.A.
                                 W. M. BERESFORD, Esq.
Secretary & Clerk of the Course   ...

43. Calcutta Races; drawing by H. Bird, published by the Calcutta Turf Club in 1891.

44. The racecourse, Calcutta, 1895.

45. The stand, Calcutta Races, where the cream of Bengal society gathered to watch riders compete over 1¾ miles for the Viceroy's Cup.

The Mediterranean, Marriage and Home Waters

46. Evelyn at home on leave, Little Rissington, 1897.

If Evelyn had hoped for an extended period of home duty, he was to be disappointed. After two months' leave on half pay and several months of duty in home waters, he was posted to the newly completed battleship HMS *Caesar* for a tour of duty in the Mediterranean. Initial technical problems delayed her departure, as Robert Le Marchant noted on 30 January 1898: 'The *Caesar* left Portsmouth harbour at 10 a.m. last Thursday for Malta, but the gun trials proved so unsatisfactory that she returned to Spithead.' Once the problems had been overcome *Caesar* sailed for the Mediterranean to take up duty at Chania, on the island of Crete. On this occasion there would be no sightseeing trips inland and no hectic social life. They were here at the behest of the Great Powers to guarantee the status quo on the island and maintain peace between Christian and Muslim Cretans.

Two years earlier Greece had attempted to annex the island following a rebellion by Christian Cretans against repressive Turkish rule. Fearful of the potential consequences of any uprisings against Turkey in the Balkans, the Great Powers intervened and imposed a blockade against Greece. Thwarted, Greece went to war with Turkey in April 1897 and was heavily defeated. Again the Powers interceded, but the future of Crete remained unresolved. As occupying powers,

47. HMS *Caesar*, a first-class battleship with 12-inch guns in circular barbettes fore and aft, in Malta, *c.*1898; from Evelyn Le Marchant's album.

48. The admiral's day cabin under the quarterdeck on HMS *Caesar*, looking aft, with doors leading to the admiral's walk at the stern. Capt. Edward Gamble, seated, commanded *Caesar* between April 1899 and December 1901.

Britain, Russia, France and Italy maintained a military presence on Crete until international agreement could be reached on the island's future, but matters remained tense. 'The island at present is fairly quiet but by no means settled,' wrote Evelyn in May 1898, 'no one can see an end to the present state of affairs …

we have always to go ashore in uniform and can't go very far inland.' At Suda Bay, a few miles from Chania, the British laid out a golf course, tennis courts, and cricket and hockey pitches, and an area was set aside for clay pigeon shooting. Unable to explore the island, Evelyn kept himself occupied playing sports during his spare time. Nearby the Russians built a tennis court for themselves which the British – reflecting Great Power rivalries in the Far East – called 'Port Arthur'. In response, the Russians named the British sportsground 'Wei-hai-wei', after the port of that name recently leased by Britain from China.

Soon after *Caesar* left Crete for duty elsewhere in the Mediterranean Cretan Muslims massacred hundreds

49. Using a lifeboat
from HMS *Caesar*,
with Cdr Evelyn Le
Marchant at the helm,
several officers find a
quiet spot for a picnic.
The caption in Evelyn's
album reads, 'River,
Marmaria'.

50. A firework display
for the visit of Joseph
Chamberlain, Colonial
Secretary, to Malta in
November 1900. The
ships (from left to
right) are: *Canopus*,
Renown (wearing the
flag of Vice-Admiral
J.A. Fisher), *Ocean*, with
Royal Sovereign in the
near line, and *Royal
Oak*, with *Ramillies* in
the near line.

of Christians in Chania. Several British sailors and soldiers were also killed, prompting swift action by the Powers. Turkish troops were ordered to leave the island and the Powers appointed Prince George of Greece to govern as High Commissioner. Two years later *Caesar* returned to Crete with the Mediterranean Fleet on a diplomatic mission for the British government. It was here that Admiral Fisher invested Prince George with the GCB before proceeding to Constantinople to pay his respects to the Sultan, for Crete was still under the nominal suzerainty of the Ottoman Empire.

For the most part life aboard *Caesar* followed a now-familiar pattern. Extended cruises gave officers many opportunities to visit historic sites and places of scenic beauty. Evelyn explored Florence and Pisa, walked to Amalfi from Ravello, and went trout fishing in Sardinia. 'I rather enjoyed our last cruise,' he wrote, 'some of the Levant islands we went to are really lovely, and we did plenty of boating and picnics, it was quite a change after Malta.' Soon afterwards he embarked on a two-month cruise to Sicily, Sardinia, Gibraltar, Morocco, the Italian Riviera and the west coast of Italy. In Malta he dined with Sir John Fisher soon after the latter had taken command of the Mediterranean Fleet. And when Joseph Chamberlain, Colonial Secretary, visited Naples with his wife, the couple spent some time in the company of officers from HMS *Caesar*. When they dined on board, 'we illuminated the ship in their honour and after dinner had a "sing song" for them … which much amused Joe,' wrote Evelyn, 'at the end of the performance … he made an excellent patriotic speech which brought the house down.' Several of the senior officers, including Evelyn, dined with the Chamberlains at their hotel one evening and accompanied them on a visit to Pompeii the following day. Before bidding their illustrious guests farewell, *Caesar* invited them to witness a torpedo practice at sea and afterwards took them on a short cruise to Amalfi. 'They all said how much they had enjoyed the *Caesar*,' Evelyn noted.

On 25 January 1901, his 43rd birthday, Evelyn wrote, 'it is sad to contemplate how old we are all getting and to think that the more vigorous and greater part of one's life is already expended.' He was pleased to have news of his brothers Basil and Louis in South Africa, for 'we do not correspond much with each other', he told his father. He began to think about his return to England later that year and to speculate how long it might be before he would be promoted to the rank of captain. This was the critical step up on the slow escalator of promotion in the Service. If promotion did not come quickly he feared that the Admiralty would consider him to be too old, and he would be passed over. In that event he planned to join the Coast Guard at a salary of £500 a year for five years, after which he could retire on an annual pension of £400.

On his return from the Mediterranean Evelyn was appointed to the Dockyard Reserve at Portsmouth. After spending more than sixteen of the last twenty or so years on extended cruises overseas, this was his first opportunity to spend a couple of years on home soil. In December 1902 he was promoted to the rank of captain but then spent around nine months on half pay of 12s. 6d. a day awaiting his first

51. Beatrice Le Marchant, one of Evelyn's nine sisters, wearing a Royal Navy captain's full dress uniform.

52. Miss Edith Ann
Crocker, of Gawcombe.

53. Capt. Evelyn Le
Marchant.

command. He was not idle during his enforced leave and shortly before taking command of HMS *Brilliant*, at the age of 46, he announced his engagement. 'Heard from Evey that he was engaged to be married to Miss Edith Crocker, the marriage to take place in three years' time on his return from his cruise in the South Atlantic station,' noted Robert. Eliza did not approve of Evelyn's choice, for she had high hopes that her sons and daughters would marry rich spouses of blue blood. Just before he set sail he wrote to his mother to say that when she got to know Baba – as he called Edith – she would come to love her as he did. But he sounded a note of warning: 'don't forget Baba belongs to me,' he wrote. To underline the point he recounted how, at an Admiralty reception in London, the Prince of Wales had sent for him and warmly congratulated him on his recent engagement.

As the newly appointed captain of HMS *Brilliant* Evelyn found himself extremely busy. 'I have got all my servants,' he wrote, 'but they are an ignorant lot and require a lot of looking after.' Evelyn's period in command of *Brilliant* was cut short by the sweeping reforms of the Navy introduced by Admiral Fisher. The South Atlantic station was disbanded, and *Brilliant* returned to Portsmouth at the end of November 1904 and was paid off shortly afterwards. The strategic disposition of the British fleets would in future be concentrated mainly in the North Sea and the Channel to meet the threat posed by the build-up of a modern German navy. Over 150 obsolete ships were scrapped – including many older vessels held in the Dockyard Reserve – but the Royal Navy retained a powerful force of cruisers with which to defend Britain's worldwide trade routes, wherever these might be challenged. Fisher pushed through the introduction of a new type of fast, all-big-gun armoured battleship, HMS *Dreadnought*, which at once rendered all other battleships obsolete. He also commissioned the world's first battle cruiser which, because of its lighter armour-plating, was faster but more vulnerable than the new battleships.

For Evelyn the most welcome consequence of Fisher's reforms was that he no longer had to wait three years to get married. Furthermore, his cruises to overseas stations became much shorter and less frequent. On 17 May 1905 he married Edith Ann Crocker of Gawcombe, near Little Rissington. The ceremony took place in London, followed by a grand reception at *Bailey's Hotel* attended by some two hundred guests. Evelyn gave Edith a diamond ring and she gave him a gold sovereign purse. Amongst the many gifts received by the couple were a silver rose bowl from parishioners and a silver bon-bon dish from the servants at Little Rissington Rectory. As Evelyn was now based at Devonport in command of the battleship HMS *Nile*, the newly married couple were able to spend the next 18 months together in Plymouth. During the spring of 1907, and again the following year, Evelyn captained the cruiser HMS *Hogue** on goodwill visits to the Caribbean before returning once more to Plymouth to take over command of HMS *Sutlej*.

On 28 December 1908 a massive earthquake utterly destroyed the town of Messina in Sicily and caused considerable damage to Reggio di Calabria and surrounding villages. Some 30,000 people were killed in Messina and many more died in Reggio and elsewhere. *Sutlej*, already in the vicinity, was ordered to proceed to Messina to render assistance and was the first British warship to arrive on the scene. Under the command of Captain Le Marchant *Sutlej* made several round trips to Syracuse, carrying more than 550 injured survivors to safety. Men from the ship's crew went ashore to help rescue survivors, returning with harrowing accounts of terrible injuries and of people being shot for looting. Several days later the King of Italy came aboard *Sutlej* to visit the injured and

List of Wedding Presents.

E. A. C.   May 17th, 1905.   **E. R. Le M.**

DONOR.	PRESENT.
Bridegroom to Bride	Diamond Ring.
Bride to Bridegroom	Gold Sovereign Purse.
Father of the Bride	Diamond Pendant.
Mother of the Bride	{ Diamond Watch Bracelet. / { Household Linen.
Father and Mother of the Bridegroom	Silver Coffee Pot.
General and Mrs. Abadie	Pair Silver Bon Bon Dishes.
Lieutenant Maxwell Anderson, R.N.	Silver Napkin Rings.
Mr. Ashburnham	Pair Silver Candlesticks.
Mrs. and Miss Aikman	Fan.
Brothers and Sisters of Bridegroom	Large Silver Salver.
Captain and Mrs. Bacon	Screen.
Captain and Mrs. Bennett	Armenian Table Cloth.
Captain O. de B. Brock, R.N.	Set of Old Silver Salt Cellars.
Captain Blackburn, R.N.	Pair Silver Candlesticks.
Revd. and Mrs. Blake	Set of Carvers.
Mr. and Mrs. Byass	Ivory Paper Knife.
Mrs. Brind	Silver Date Calendar.
Admiral Sir N. Bowden-Smith	Tortoiseshell and Silver Paper Knife
Commander and Mrs. Walter Carey	Pair Silver Flower Vases.
Mrs. Walter Carey	Cushion.
Commander and Mrs.Creagh Osborne	Silver Ink Stand.
Mrs. Carey	Pair Silver Pepper Pots.
Mrs. Carey	Pair Silver Dessert Spoons.
Miss Dora Carey	Glass Punch Bowl.
Mr. and Mrs. Herbert Crocker	Clock.
Mr. and Mrs. Weston Crocker	Gilt Flower Vase.
Mr. and Mrs. Jack Crocker	Complete Coffee Set and Silver Tray
Mr. and Mrs. A. A. Crocker	{ Pair Silver Dessert Dishes and / { Silver Tea Caddy.
Miss Emmeline Crocker	Irish Lace Scarf.
Miss Maude Crocker	{ Silver Fitted Dressing Case. / { Telegram Case.
Mr. Reginald Crocker	Bracelet.
Miss Colvin	Card Table.
Mrs. Cholmley	Set of Coffee Cups.
Miss Cooper	{ Silver Photo Frame and Paper / { Cutting Book.
Mr. and Mrs. Charles Denny	Bridge Box.
Directors of Crocker, Sons & Co., Ltd.	Large Silver Centre Piece.
Bertie and Nellie Dix	Pair Flower Vases.
Miss Esland	Silver Pepper Pot.
Commander Godfrey Faussett, R.N.	Whiskey Decanter.
Captain and Mrs. Floyd	Pair Glass Flower Vases.
Dr. and Mrs. Frossard	Silver Tea Spoons.
Captain and Mrs. Ffinch	Picture.
Mrs. Foster	Flower Box.

54. The first page of three from Evelyn and Edith's list of wedding presents. Adm. Gamble gave a pair of silver candlesticks, the Ward Room officers of HMS *Nile* a silver lamp and shade, and Maj. Ayshford Wise an Irish Terrier pup.

---

* HMS *Hogue* was sunk by a German submarine within weeks of the outbreak of the First World War.

55. At the time of his marriage to Edith Crocker Capt. Le Marchant was in command of HMS *Nile*, a heavily armoured second-class battleship, now consigned to duty in home waters.

56. This picture of HMS *Sutlej* was drawn in Capt. and Mrs Evelyn Le Marchant's visitors' book by Gillian Lee Warner in September 1908.

57. Mrs Edith Le Marchant on board one of Evelyn's ships.

58. Nutfield, Nursling, near Southampton, 1909. 'Our residence number three,' wrote Evelyn, 'Nutfield is a nice compact little house with a large garden.'

personally thank all those involved in the rescue. For his services during this operation Evelyn was awarded the Order of St Maurice and St Lazarus by the King of Italy who, Robert Le Marchant noted, had been 'greatly pleased with Evy's arrangements for the sick and wounded'. A couple of weeks later Evelyn arrived home in Little Rissington. We can only imagine the impact that his eyewitness accounts would have had on his family and local society in the days before television and radio.

In April 1909 Evelyn took over command of the Southern Coastguard District, and he was subsequently appointed Captain of Devonport dockyard, Deputy Superintendent, and King's Harbour Master for the Hamoaze. This was a particularly happy time for Evelyn and Edith, and over the next two years their son, Valentine, and daughter, Valerie, were born. During his service in this triple post Evelyn was promoted to Rear Admiral, but a month later, in January 1913, he decided to retire. He was now comfortably well-off, for as a retired Rear Admiral he received half pay of £650 a year. During his naval career spanning more than 40 years he had seen massive changes; the Navy's most modern dreadnoughts launched during his final years at Devonport dockyard bore little resemblance to the full-rigged three-masted ironclads on which he spent his early years.

The First World War and Retirement

The outbreak of war in 1914 interrupted Evelyn's retirement and he volunteered to serve in a lower rank, taking a commission as Captain in the Royal Naval Reserve. After a few months on patrol duty as Captain of the armed yacht *Vanessa* he was appointed to command the Auxiliary Patrol Base of Kingstown (now Dun Laoghaire), a post he held for several months in 1915. In January 1916 Rear Admiral Le Marchant was posted to Malta to take command of auxiliary patrol vessels operating from there. Towards the end of April a German mine-layer succeeded in laying mines off the Grand Harbour, and within a period of 24 hours three ships, including the minesweeping sloop HMS *Nasturtium*, sank after hitting mines.

At a subsequent court-martial the captain and surviving officers of *Nasturtium* were cleared of any blame. However, the court concluded that the area should have been cleared by trawler-sweepers before any larger vessels were used to search for mines. As to where responsibility might lie, they noted that 'Rear Admiral Le Marchant is still Rear Admiral of Patrols but Vice Admiral Sir A. Limpus [Senior Naval Officer, Malta] is now on half pay'.[9] The Admiralty later wrote to Sir Arthur Limpus in London and sent a copy of this letter to Le Marchant to acquaint him with their conclusions, 'as you were doubtless concerned in the detailed instructions issued on that occasion'.* The Admiralty concluded that Sir Arthur Limpus knew that mines had been found in the area, but destroyers and sloops had nevertheless been ordered to search for mines in dangerous waters despite the fact that their sweeps were not ready for use. 'In the circumstances,' Limpus was informed, 'their Lordships cannot but regard the arrangements as unsatisfactory and ill-considered and they are of the opinion that you showed want of judgement on this occasion.'[10] Le Marchant remained in post in Malta for most of 1916, but a note of the incident was placed on his personal file.

The following year Rear Admiral Le Marchant undertook 'special services' for the Admiralty, and by September he was in charge of convoy escorts across the Atlantic – a recent innovation against submarine attacks. He hoisted his flag in HMS *Knight Templar*, a medium-sized mercantile warship armed with three 6-inch guns.† Officially known as a Commissioned Escort Ship, she was slower and more economical to operate than an armed merchant cruiser. On 4 September *Knight Templar* left Lamlash Bay off the Isle of Arran with a convoy bound for New York, arriving there 16 days later. From New York she sailed to Norfolk, Virginia, departing on 30 September with a return convoy destined for Glasgow. By 14 November Evelyn was once more preparing to leave Lamlash in charge of a convoy, this time bound for Halifax, Nova Scotia.

---

   * Arthur Limpus served as a midshipman in HMS *Bacchante* with Evelyn Le Marchant in 1881. Although junior to Evelyn then, Limpus progressed more rapidly up the ladder of promotion and was subsequently knighted. From 1912-14 he was Naval Adviser to Turkey, and for a time exercised actual command of their fledgling fleet.

   † *Knight Templar* was probably armed with a couple of 11-inch anti-submarine howitzers also. It was not possible during the First World War for a moving ship to detect a dived submarine.

59. HMS *Knight Templar*, a medium-sized mercantile warship assigned to convoy protection duty in the Atlantic, 1918.

Knight Templar docked in Halifax on 27 November, unaware of the catastrophic events that would soon follow. Early on the morning of 6 December the Belgian relief vessel *Imo* set off for New York, and at the same time a French munitions ship, *Mont Blanc*, approached Halifax harbour prior to joining a convoy that was forming up to cross the Atlantic. *Mont Blanc* was laden with 2,925 tons of explosives – TNT and picric acid – together with gun cotton and benzol, a highly explosive and flammable cargo.[11] At the entrance to the Narrows separating Halifax and Dartmouth the two ships collided. Although the damage was not severe and they were able to separate, sparks from the grinding metal ignited vapours from *Mont Blanc*'s cargo of monochlorobenzol stowed in barrels on deck. As the fire began to spread the crew, fearing an immediate explosion, took to their lifeboats and abandoned ship. They reached the Dartmouth shore and, before taking cover, observed *Mont Blanc* burn and drift towards Halifax on the opposite shore. There a crowd began to gather to watch the blazing ship, oblivious of the approaching danger.

For 20 minutes *Mont Blanc* burned, coming to rest against a pier at the northern end of Halifax. Then, at just after 9 a.m., the ship exploded, vaporised. Nothing remained of the hull of a ship weighing more than 3,000 tons, and white-hot debris from the explosion fell onto buildings over a wide area. Entire streets were flattened. The half-ton anchor shaft flew through the air and landed over two miles away, and all glass in a 20-mile radius shattered, causing terrible injuries. The explosion was so powerful that J. Robert Oppenheimer, the 'father of the atom bomb', later studied its effects to predict the devastation likely to be caused by an atomic bomb. In the Halifax explosion and its aftermath more than 1,900 people were killed, and over 6,000 were injured, many of them permanently.

Almost three hundred people were blinded in one or both eyes. Over 1,600 homes were completely destroyed and another 12,000 were damaged.

The staggering force of the blast created a tidal wave 20 feet high which lifted *Imo* up onto the shore and tore large ships from their moorings. The wave carried the British supply ship, *Curuca*, three-quarters of a mile to Tuft's Cove, where she sank with the loss of 45 lives. *Knight Templar*, some distance away, sheered about badly before breaking adrift, pulling posts out of the wharf where she had been tied up.[12] Some time after the dust settled a party from *Knight Templar* landed ashore to render what assistance they could amid scenes of utter devastation. A note on Evelyn's service record expressed appreciation for 'efforts to save life in [the] Halifax explosion'.[13] The sights which Evelyn witnessed ashore must have reminded him of the destruction he had encountered at Messina nine years earlier.

Five days after the explosion *Knight Templar* left Halifax to resume escort duties, arriving in London on 31 December. In January 1918 Evelyn was awarded the DSO for 'services in charge of convoy escorts', and early in April, soon after returning safely with a convoy from New York, he sailed once more for America. On the afternoon of 6 April, in rough seas and with a Force 6 wind blowing, the German submarine *U-53* sighted the convoy and shadowed it until darkness fell. At around midnight, about 120 miles south-west of the Scilly Isles, *U-53* closed in to attack. The first torpedo hit and sank the merchant ship *Fort Campbell*. The second torpedo struck *Knight Templar* in the centre of the ship killing several men in the engine room, but she remained afloat. An approaching destroyer caused *U-53* to dive, but she later resurfaced to resume the attack. Towards daybreak, despite adverse weather conditions, *U-53* struck again. A torpedo hit the tanker

60. A drawing of the damage sustained by HMS *Knight Templar* after a torpedo struck her engine room during the night of 6 April 1918.

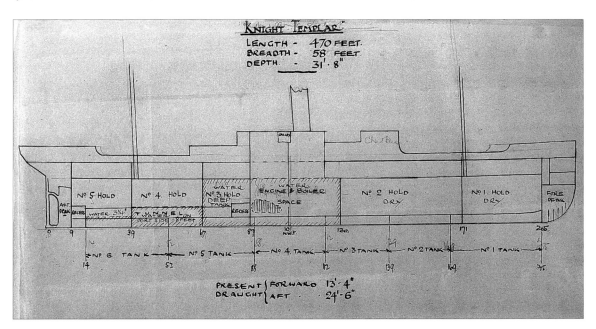

Cadillac, which managed to continue under her own steam and reach port safely. After 37 hours, hampered by continuing bad weather, *U-53* ended her pursuit of the convoy and returned to Wilhelmshaven.[14]

The crew of *Knight Templar* took to their lifeboats and were picked up later by a destroyer. Evelyn and his servant, together with the captain and two other officers, remained on board until 2 p.m. the following day when a destroyer was able to take them off, despite very rough seas.[15] Damage was contained within the engine room and number 3 hold, though some water reached 4 and 5 holds through a tunnel running aft. *Knight Templar* was later towed back to Devonport by the rescue tugs *Epic* and *Revenger* for repairs, which took almost four months.[16] On a visit to see the ship in dock Evelyn's sister Ethel commented, 'She has a frightful hole. A perfect wonder she kept afloat.'

An unusual incident occurred more than a month after *Knight Templar* reached Devonport. On 14 May police removed two badly decomposed bodies from the damaged engine room, later identified as 4th engineer Douglas Leadbetter, aged 23, and greaser Alfred Renshaw, aged 20.[17] Why the bodies had lain there undiscovered for so long is not recorded, though the internal damage to this part of the ship had been extensive. *Knight Templar* was re-commissioned on 30 July, and just over two weeks later Evelyn left Devonport for Halifax. His final months at sea were uneventful, and he had just sailed from Baltimore in *Knight Templar* when the war ended. After the war he returned once more to civilian life. He was promoted to Vice Admiral on the retired list in 1917 and to Admiral in 1921.

Evelyn retired to Woodgreen in Hampshire with his wife and two children, where they lived happily for many years. During the General Strike of 1926 he volunteered without hesitation to serve as a Special Constable, receiving a letter of thanks from Downing Street. Amongst his interests was horse racing, and both Valentine and Valerie inherited their father's passion for horses. Between them they owned and bred several racehorses after the Second World War, the most successful of which was 'The Ghost', a chestnut gelding owned by Lieutenant Colonel Valentine Le Marchant and trained by Vernon Cross. During the early 1970s 'The Ghost' won five steeplechases, including the Kim Muir Handicap Chase at the 1972 Cheltenham Festival.[18] That year he started as favourite for the Whitbread Gold Cup but was unplaced, and the following year Valentine entered the horse for the Grand National. Before his debut at Aintree, however, the Ghost was run down and killed by a car, and Valentine received an insurance payout of around £20,000.

In the years between the wars Evelyn and Edith, affectionately known as 'the Honeybuns', were regular visitors to the family home in Little Rissington. Evelyn

61. Letter of thanks from Downing Street following the collapse of the General Strike, May 1926.

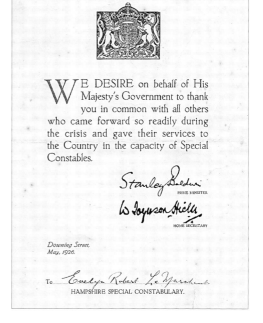

WE DESIRE on behalf of His Majesty's Government to thank you in common with all others who came forward so readily during the crisis and gave their services to the Country in the capacity of Special Constables.

Stanley Baldwin
PRIME MINISTER

W Joynson Hicks
HOME SECRETARY

Downing Street,
May, 1926.

To *Evelyn Robert Le Marchant*
HAMPSHIRE SPECIAL CONSTABULARY.

62. St Peter's Church, Little Rissington, where Adm. and Mrs Evelyn Le Marchant are buried. In the foreground are the graves of men of the Royal Air Force and Royal Canadian Air Force from RAF Little Rissington who died during the Second World War.

was always kind to the domestic staff, who remembered him with affection. During the Second World War he spent much time at his club in London, often staying up at night to watch the Blitz instead of taking refuge in a nearby air-raid shelter. He was slightly hurt during a raid in February 1944, but was able to leave hospital after receiving treatment.

Admiral Le Marchant died in 1949, aged 91, and is buried in the beautiful churchyard in Little Rissington. Luck had played a part in his successful career, but he made the most of his opportunities and lived life to the full. Gregarious, socially confident and dependable in a crisis, he showed concern for others and got on well with most people. He had the strength of character to overcome early setbacks, and it is not surprising that in the end he found fulfilment and success in the Navy. On his tombstone are the following verses from Tennyson's poem, 'Crossing the Bar':

> Twilight and evening bell,
>   And after that the dark!
> And may there be no sadness of farewell,
>   When I embark;
>
> For tho' from out our bourne of Time and Place
>   The flood may bear me far,
> I hope to see my Pilot face to face
>   When I have crost the bar.

4

From Paardeberg to the Khyber

ERNEST BASIL ST JOHN LE MARCHANT
(1859-1956)

63. James Le Marchant, *c.*1880.

Born in Devon in 1859 when his father was curate at Dawlish, Basil Le Marchant grew up to become a sensitive and caring child, very much his mother's favourite. His easygoing and thoughtful disposition would serve him well throughout life, endearing him to everyone he met. He was sent away to school somewhat late in boyhood, attending Somersetshire College in Bath where Alexander Graham Bell had taught a decade earlier. Basil's attendance at this minor public school was made possible by his uncle James, who lived in Bath and knew the city well. With no children of his own, James took the young boy under his wing and paid most of the fees. Yet despite his uncle's generosity Basil was, in the opinion of his sisters, incorrigibly idle, neglecting his studies in favour of cricket. He played for the school in the 'Football Fifteens', a form of rugby, and in a match in which Somersetshire College beat Bristol Grammar School by two goals and 11 touchdowns to a try and a touchdown, Basil was 'conspicuous by his good play'. His favourite sport, however, and the focus of much of his energy and enthusiasm, was cricket. In this he excelled, becoming one of the best bowlers the school had ever produced. Later he developed into an excellent all-rounder, much in demand wherever he went.

During his final year at Somersetshire College Basil still had no idea about a possible career. His older

64. Basil Le Marchant, aged seventeen.

65. Basil as a cadet in the 2nd Regiment, Royal Guernsey Light Infantry, 1879.

brothers tried initially to steer him towards a more lucrative profession than the Army – Edward hoped that a visit to Guy's Hospital might persuade him to 'take up the knife', and Evelyn suggested he become a naval surgeon. 'Basil I hope has decided at length on a profession, for it is full time he should,' wrote Edward, 'perhaps Mr Sawbones would suit him the best, as it is very paying if one can get a start in private practice, and if this is impossible there is always the Army with 10/- per diem or more in England, and R350 per mensem in India to commence on, both very good considering the small expenses attached to a medical man in the Service.' Other options suggested at one time or another were the Church, a clerkship in the Mint, and the Indian Civil Service.

Basil wrote to Edward in Madras for advice, saying that he was considering the Army. Edward, aware that his mother and sisters were against this option, told Basil that the decision was his and he must make up his own mind. 'In the Army it is very hard work to keep straight and one has to pinch and deny oneself a good deal to live on one's pay. I am very fond of the Service and work hard to get on in it, but I cannot do many things I should like to do,' wrote Edward, encouraging his brother to weigh up the pros and cons of service life. 'It is all bosh saying you cannot get into the Army – of course you can if you wish it,' he continued.

> You and I both know that the rest of the family want us to flourish within sight of the tulip tree at home, no going to India or those awful climates where cholera and fevers are continually breaking out, where people die in a couple of hours etc. Now you must put aside all that nonsense, commonly called sentiment, and make up your own mind now and at once, without paying any attention at all to Em or Annie or Mother saying 'five sons, one in India, one on the seas, one in Germany, one going into the Army, and now you too. Oh please don't, go into the Church and have a nice little Rectory, plenty of dibs, no parishioners, and one sermon a Sunday'. All this bosh you must not believe.

And in answer to a subsequent letter from Annie suggesting yet more possibilities, Edward wrote, 'Now if Basil will take my advice he would sit down and work hard for the Army, it is out and out the best thing and the Staff Corps is most excellent; good pay and a first rate station in society.'

With his resolve stiffened Basil decided on a career in the Army, and he joined the 2nd Regiment, Royal Guernsey Light Infantry – soon to become the Royal Guernsey Militia. He subsequently failed the entry examinations for a regular commission and was sent to Mr Goldie at Farmington for private tuition. At 13 guineas a month, excluding drawing which was extra, tuition was not cheap, but the investment paid off and he passed his exams at the second attempt. In February 1881 he was commissioned into the 76th Regiment of Foot – shortly to become the 2nd Battalion The Duke of Wellington's (West Riding Regiment) – and was posted to the Curragh Garrison in Ireland. There he fell in and out of love before returning to England and transferring to the 1st Battalion, previously the 33rd Foot, then stationed in India.

When Basil reached Nowshera early in 1883 the 1st Battalion had just completed a long march from Lucknow to its new quarters in the hills to the east of Peshawar. His six and a half years in India were to be largely uneventful and he settled down to the routine of regimental life in the cantonment, including learning to speak Hindustani. After two years at Nowshera the battalion moved to Rawalpindi, where he was appointed adjutant after recovering from a bout of malaria. There were plenty of opportunities for sport and Basil encouraged all young officers to

take part, irrespective of their level of skill. An accomplished fisherman and shot, Basil led by example, taking up *shikar* (hunting) with enthusiasm. He quickly established a reputation as a fine cricketer and sportsman, and it was during his period as adjutant that the battalion won success on the polo field. He often met up with his brothers Cecil and Louis, both of whom were serving in the Punjab at this time. Of his social life we know little, though a letter from his brother Evelyn enquired how he was getting on with the prettiest girl in India. 'I trust he won't go and marry for love without plenty of dollars to back it up,' commented Evelyn. And Edward informed his father that 'Master Basil evidently contemplates marriage in early life, for he writes, "I think, if I go home, I shall look out for a wife."' In 1888, at the age of 29, Basil was promoted to Captain, shortly before the battalion undertook another long march, this time from Rawalpindi to Mian Mir cantonment outside Lahore, a distance of nearly 200 miles. They had been at Mian Mir for less than a year when the battalion was posted to Aden, where

66. Sergeants, 33rd Regiment – now 1st Battalion The Duke of Wellington's (West Riding Regiment) – Rawalpindi, 1885. Lt Le Marchant, adjutant, is seated in the centre.

67. 33rd Regiment – Basil continued to use the former title – at Camp Topa, Murree Hills, 1885.

68. Capt. Basil Le Marchant, 1895. As Inspector of Musketry for the Southern District, he is wearing the frock coat and cocked hat of an officer on the Staff rather than the uniform of his parent regiment.

Basil spent several months before returning to England and home to Little Rissington in 1889.

During his long leave of almost six months Basil indulged his love of sport to the full, playing cricket for Bourton Vale against MCC and other prestigious touring teams and accompanying his sisters to all the fashionable tennis parties in the area.* He was soon on good terms with the new occupant of Little Rissington Manor, Major Walter Wynter, who had moved to the village with his family two years previously. The two men had much in common.

Walter Wynter had spent 15 years in the 33rd Foot, resigning in 1881 after taking part in the Second Afghan War. Earlier he had served as an ensign with his regiment in the Abyssinian campaign of 1868 and was the only officer to march to Magdala and back on foot, a distance of some 800 miles. During the final assault on King Theodore's capital at Magdala the Regimental Colour was carried by Wynter. Looting followed the British victory, but in his account of the action some years later Wynter noted that orders about loot were very strict. Anything not taken at the point of a bayonet had to be handed over to the prize master, in this

---

* Amongst his cricketing achievements were the following: eight wickets in an innings for the Curragh Garrison in a match won by County Kildare Club (1881); 87 runs for Bourton Vale CC against Charlbury (1890); five wickets for 11 runs for Heythrop Hunt CC against Croome (1891); and several times playing for the '33rd Duke of Wellington's Regt' he took five, six or seven wickets in an innings (Strensall Camp, 1890; Dover, late 1890s).

case a Colonel Fraser of the 11th Hussars. Wynter had to hand in the silver head of a processional cross, but he managed to acquire a large rhinoceros-hide shield, heavily plated with silver. This he purchased for five dollars from a sergeant in the 33rd, who had gained it 'at the point of the bayonet'.[1] Wynter also brought back a couple of illuminated parchment scrolls, and these trophies would, no doubt, have been prominently displayed in Little Rissington Manor for many years. Wynter saw action again in West Africa during the Ashanti War of 1874 but was invalided home after contracting malaria, from which he continued to suffer intermittently for many years. Not long after moving to the village he joined the 5th (Militia) Battalion of The Royal Fusiliers, which he later commanded for some years before retiring as a full colonel.

Basil, who was to spend the next 10 years in England, often dined with Colonel Wynter when he returned to Little Rissington, and the two men liked to go off for the day to shoot or play golf. One evening in May 1889 two other former officers of the 33rd Foot joined Walter Wynter and Basil Le Marchant for dinner at the Manor. Colonel Basil Fanshawe, who commanded the regiment from 1873 until he retired five years later, had served with Wynter throughout

the Abyssinian campaign. During his military career Fanshawe also saw action in the Crimea and again in 1859 at the siege and occupation of Dwarka, a coastal town some 400 miles north-west of Bombay. A small expeditionary force, including the 28th Foot (later the 1st Battalion The Gloucestershire Regiment), sailed from Bombay to secure the surrender or capture of a notorious band of Rajput pirates, or Waghurs. Their fort on Beyt Island was attacked and taken, but many of the rebels escaped inland. Soldiers looted gold and jewellery from sacred Hindu temples, but orders were later given that the booty be returned. Meanwhile

69. Major (later Colonel) Walter Wynter, 33rd Regiment.

70. Devubha Jivanbha Kara, whose great-grandfather fought for the Waghurs at Beyt in 1859.

a smaller force, with Captain Fanshawe second in command, set out from Deesa to reinforce the troops already at Dwarka. Covering 500 miles in 30 days Fanshawe and the men of the 33rd Regiment endured many hardships, frequently wading through flash floods caused by heavy monsoon rains.* They arrived just in time to take part in the bombardment of Dwarka, which lasted for 11 days. After the town

---

* Describing conditions during the march Corporal (later Colour Sergeant) John McGrath of the 33rd Rgt wrote, 'Scarcely a day past [sic] without our wading through water 3 or 4 times … [you] can imagine what an unpleasant thing it is to walk or march in wet socks and boots'; later McGrath commented that he and his company went '8 days without taking our boots off'.

71. Little Rissington Manor, home to the Wynter family for 14 years, 1890s.

had been taken sporadic fighting continued for some time in the surrounding jungle, ending with the capture of several hundred Waghur prisoners. Fanshawe and his men remained at Dwarka for three months before marching at a more leisurely pace back to Deesa, their boots in tatters.[2] Much to their consternation those who had taken part in this long-forgotten campaign received no batta,* no medal and no share of the prize money available for distribution to other regiments on active service elsewhere in Central India.

The other dinner guest that evening was Colonel Robert Waller. Waller was no stranger at the Manor, for it was here 13 years earlier that he had attended a wedding breakfast to celebrate the marriage of Miss Mary Waller to William Snooke Stenson of Bourton-on-the-Water. Shortly before the wedding the bride's brother, Captain J.H. Waller, a veteran of the Indian Mutiny, had leased Little Rissington Manor from the Bennett family for three years. The Wallers had enough money to enable Robert to purchase a commission in 1861, and four years later he purchased his promotion to the rank of lieutenant. Basil Fanshawe had also purchased his commission, something that Wynter's family had not been able to do for their son. Instead Walter Wynter had gained his commission through Sandhurst, of which he gave a depressing account. Robert Waller spent much of his career in the 53rd Regiment, and it was not until 1882 that he transferred to

_____

* An additional allowance paid to officers and men on campaign in India, perceived by most to be an entitlement.

72. United Services Cricket XI, Portsmouth, c.1895. Basil Le Marchant is seated, far right.

the 33rd (now the 1st West Ridings*), then stationed in India. There he served for several years with Basil Le Marchant, and over a drink at the club the two men would talk together about home and the people they both knew. Reunited on that evening in May, the four officers of the old 33rd had much to reminisce about.

In 1895 Basil Le Marchant was appointed Inspector of Musketry for the Southern District based in Portsmouth, a post he held for three years before returning to his regiment in Dover. He was promoted to Major in March 1899, a couple of months before the battalion took part in extended exercises on Salisbury Plain. Soon afterwards the battalion received orders to embark for South Africa following the outbreak of the Boer War.† Before leaving, officers took their ceremonial swords to the armourer to be sharpened, but on arrival in Cape Town these were put in store. So that they could not be easily identified by Boer marksmen, officers were required to carry rifles and wear the same equipment as the men.

After the failure of Dr Jameson's raid into the gold-rich Boer republic of the Transvaal in 1896 – ostensibly to support an expected uprising by foreign (mainly British) immigrants or *Uitlanders* who were denied any political rights – Britain's new high commissioner in the Cape Colony, Sir Alfred Milner, sought a pretext for war which would lead to the annexation of the Transvaal. The Orange Free State agreed to support the Transvaal in the event of war, and both Boer republics imported large quantities of modern weapons in preparation

---

* The full name for the 1st West Ridings at that time was the 1st Battalion The Duke of Wellington's (West Riding Regiment), but for ease of reference I will use the shortened title.

† Also known as the Anglo-Boer War or the Second South African War.

73. 1st Battalion The Duke of Wellington's (West Riding Regiment) in Dover, late 1890s.

74. Lt-Col. G.E. Lloyd (left, killed at Rhenoster Kop), Lt F.J. Siordet (centre, killed at Paardeberg), Basil Le Marchant (right) and 2nd Lt H.J.L. Oakes (wounded at Rhenoster Kop) take time off from exercises on Salisbury Plain to visit Stonehenge, early summer, 1899.

75. The 33rd Regiment's gong, Salisbury Plain, 1899. On the gong are inscribed the names of the garrisons, mostly in India, where the Regiment – now 1st Battalion The Duke of Wellington's (West Riding Regiment) or 1st West Ridings for short – had been stationed. The soldiers are wearing the dark blue Home Pattern helmet common to all line infantry regiments at that time, the design for which was probably based on the German pickelhaube.

for a war that appeared increasingly likely. The British government still hoped to achieve its ultimate aim – the maintenance of overall British supremacy in South Africa – by peaceful means and believed that if President Kruger was put under enough pressure he would accede to British demands. But although Kruger was prepared to compromise on voting rights for the *Uitlanders*, he refused to accept that Britain enjoyed any suzerainty over the Boer republic. Above all, he was determined to maintain the Transvaal's independence. The collapse of negotiations between Milner and Kruger in June 1899 was followed in September by the movement of British troops to vulnerable border towns in Natal and the Cape and a call-up of reservists in Britain. Kruger demanded that British troops be withdrawn and on 11 October, when his ultimatum expired, Boer commandos invaded Natal and the Cape Colony. They hoped to defeat the 22,000 or so British troops in South Africa before further reinforcements could be shipped out from England and the Empire.

The British Army was about to face its longest and most expensive war since the defeat of Napoleon. The 1st Army Corps of 47,000 men was rapidly mobilised and sent to South Africa under the command of General Sir Redvers Buller, and the British public confidently expected victory by Christmas. There was widespread complacency, and most British officers regarded the Boers as back-country yokels. Captain J.E. Gough endorsed this view when he wrote, 'how on earth men who call themselves Englishmen could allow themselves to be turned off a hill [Spion Kop] by a pack of Dutch peasants, I am damned if I know.'[3] Many years earlier Lord Salisbury (now Prime Minister) had written home from Cape Town saying that the Boers were 'as degraded a set of savages as any white men in the world: many of them can't read – few of them can write'.[4] The British were in for a shock or, as Kipling put it, 'no end of a lesson'.

The war which the British were confident would be over in a few months lasted two years and eight months and involved some 450,000 British and Empire troops. The Boers, who never fielded more than 40,000 or so irregulars at any one time, proved to be a formidable enemy. Possessing no infantry they were highly mobile, and by living off the land they minimised the supplies they carried with them. They knew the terrain intimately, were expert shots and made good use of cover to conceal their positions. The British, on the other hand, advanced at the pace of their infantry and supply columns in unfamiliar territory and depended on tactics which had served them well in numerous small colonial

Map 2   South Africa, 1899.

wars but which had not kept up with advances in technology. Furthermore, small colonial campaigns had given them no experience of coordinating large bodies of troops successfully, and this was to be a factor in the defeats suffered by the British during 'Black Week' in December 1899. 'What bad news from South Africa, all three of our Generals being defeated,' commented Evelyn, then serving in the Mediterranean, 'I am surprised at Buller, the truth is Generals and Admirals are born not made.' And from India a friend of the Le Marchants wrote, 'How much sadness there must be in England this Xmas. Last week one felt absolutely ill after three such sickening blows … Twenty in the house [in Lahore], and much gaiety, for which one doesn't feel in tune, but it would not do for the ruling race to seem disturbed out here!'

After the defeats at Stormberg, Magersfontein and Colenso Major-General Lyttelton reflected on the differences between the battles of Omdurman – won so decisively just 15 months earlier – and Colenso. At Omdurman, he observed, '50,000 fanatics streamed across the open regardless of cover to certain death, while at Colenso I never saw a Boer all day till the battle was over and it was our men who were the victims.'[5] Acknowledging the difficulties posed by the terrain around Ladysmith and Colenso, the Commander-in-Chief in Whitehall, Lord Wolseley, wrote of the area:

> It is above all others that I know of, the best suited for Boer tactics and the worst possible country for a Regular army to operate in. It was said long ago that in Spain a large army would be starved and a small one destroyed by the enemy. Of the country forming the triangle I have drawn [between the Draconsberg, and the Buffalo and Tugela rivers], the same may indeed be well said also.[6]

The towns of Kimberley, Mafeking and Ladysmith had been under siege for several months when Major Le Marchant reached Cape Town on 20 January 1900 with the 1st West Ridings. They proceeded north by train to join the 6th Division, part of a larger force now commanded by Lord Roberts, whose immediate objectives were to relieve Kimberley and then take Bloemfontein, capital of the Orange Free State. Leaving the railway the 6th Division marched for days through drenching rainstorms and exceptionally hot weather to reach the Modder River south of Kimberley, not far from where General Cronje was dug in with some 4,000 Boers. The marches were arduous, up to twenty miles a day with little to drink, and even when they did find water it was sometimes 'as thick as pea-soup', wrote Basil. With the arrival of the 6th Division, Lieutenant-General John French's Cavalry Division was able to sweep round in a wide arc and outflank the Boers, entering Kimberley on 15 February.

Cronje, fearing that he might be cut off, decided to leave his entrenched position and move east towards Bloemfontein. His route brought him into contact with the advancing British troops, but he could have escaped had he abandoned his cumbersome wagon train. These wagons, however, were the property of his

Boer farmers and represented a significant part of their capital. On 16 February Basil Le Marchant and the West Ridings were involved in fierce fighting to clear Boer positions on a ridge overlooking the Modder River, part of a larger action by the 6th Division that day to maintain pressure on Cronje. The West Ridings were ordered to make a frontal attack at Drieput Drift and were under fire all day. 'A man was shot through the shoulder close to me,' wrote Basil. 'However, we got along the river bank and at last captured their first position and some waggons containing food, the Boers retiring to some hills further back.' The battalion continued their advance and soon came under heavy fire. For much of the day, wrote Basil, 'we were left lying on the veldt with no cover'. Eventually, after the Oxfords and Gloucesters had worked their way around the flanks, the battalion succeeded in driving the enemy from the higher ground. 'This [action] was brilliantly carried out, the two kopjes [hills] on the left being carried, thus taking the big kopje in front … and causing the enemy to retire.'[7] The battalion's losses that day were 29 wounded and one killed.

During the night Cronje moved away but, unable to make good his escape, he decided to laager his wagons and dig in on the banks of the Modder River at Paardeberg, where he was soon surrounded by a vastly superior force. The West Ridings, together with the Gloucesters and other infantry battalions of the 6th Division, marched all the following day with very little rest and caught up with Cronje early the next morning (18 February). 'Soon after 3 a.m. we were up and off again without water in our bottles,' wrote Basil. To make matters worse the battalion had been on half rations of dried biscuits for several days, following the capture of their food convoy by General De Wet.

76. Officers' Mess, 1st West Ridings, Modder River, February 1900, with Lt-Col. Lloyd seated, far right.

Despite their hunger and exhaustion the men were not allowed to rest. Lord Kitchener – now in temporary command in South Africa whilst Roberts was indisposed – ordered an immediate and costly frontal attack on the entrenched Boer positions. The West Ridings, with Major Le Marchant commanding a company of 120 men, advanced in extended lines through broken cover and then across open ground into a 'well-aimed and terrible fire' from an unseen enemy well dug in on the river banks. 'We eventually reached the river, the first to get there I believe, closely followed by the Highlanders,' commented Basil. 'The carnage going down this frontal attack was awful … most ghastly to witness,' wrote Major Townsend of the West Ridings. Together with the Oxfordshire Light Infantry they succeeded in driving the Boers out of their forward trenches on the south bank of the Modder River, forcing them to retire to their stronghold on the northern bank. But as some of the men, desperate with thirst, stopped to fill their water bottles, they were hit by enemy sniper fire. During the confusion that followed men of the West Ridings in forward positions were also fired on by the second line of their own regiment. It was only after Colonel Lloyd – with complete disregard for his own safety – stood up to signal their position in semaphore that the firing from behind ceased.

By the end of the day repeated and wasteful attacks involving the 6th and 9th Divisions had failed to break into Cronje's fortified laager, though many of his oxen and horses had been killed by artillery bombardment. The British suffered more casualties – 1,270 – on this day than on any other single day of the entire war. The losses suffered by the West Ridings were particularly heavy, with 22 men killed and 106 wounded. 'I really don't know how any of us escaped,' wrote Basil, 'as the ground was simply ripped up with bullets – at night time all the firing ceased and we could drink – the thirst was awful and lying out in the hot sun and no water was bad.' That night after other battalions had withdrawn the West Ridings held the river bank alone, attending to all the wounded they could find. Next morning they too were ordered to retire. 'I left with the rear guard and buried many poor fellows on my return to camp,' wrote Basil. From his own company alone 26 were killed or wounded; 'it was a desperate fight and no mistake,' he commented, 'and the Boers still hold the river but we have completely surrounded them.'

For the next few days Basil and his men were on outpost duty, often under fire, but they were soon ordered to return to the front line. They waded across the river and advanced towards heavily defended Boer positions. Finding the Hampshire Regiment dug in about 1,200 yards from the Boers, the West Ridings took over the forward positions and began to dig trenches so that they could edge closer to the enemy. 'We sap at night,' wrote Basil.

> I was in charge of 250 men on 25 Feb. when the Boers opened a terrific fire on my working party. We lay low in the trench we had been constructing and no one was hit but they kept up the fire for some ten minutes. I did

not return a shot for fear of disclosing our position. As soon as the firing ceased we continued our work and this is now the most advanced trench of all. We lie along the river bank and have cut holes to sleep in. We are under fire all day long and there are a few men hit every day. The banks are steep and high and the willow trees are splendid. – 27 Feb. Majuba day, Hurrah.* Cronje has surrendered, his trenches only 800 yards from us and we can see them all trailing out.

77. 1st West Ridings crossing the Modder River after Cronje's surrender; watercolour by Lt M.V. Le Poer Trench.

The Battle of Paardeberg on 18 February 1900 – with its uncoordinated and unnecessary frontal attacks – had been a costly prelude to victory. With 100 guns surrounding his position Cronje had been bombarded and starved into submission, and nine days after the battle he had surrendered with 4,000 men.

The British had won their first major victory and now prepared to take the war into Boer territory. As Roberts advanced towards Bloemfontein the West Ridings were involved in further action at Poplar Grove and some hard fighting at Driefontein, but the Boers retreated to avoid capture. Conditions for Basil Le Marchant and the men of the 6th Division were tough; since landing at the Cape

* The humiliating defeat of a British force on this day in 1881 at Majuba Hill marked the end of the First Boer War. Soon afterwards the British concluded a peace agreement which restored full internal self-government to the Boers in the Transvaal, whilst Britain retained ill-defined rights over the Transvaal's foreign affairs. Evelyn Le Marchant had sailed for Cape Town aboard HMS *Bacchante* in 1881, arriving just too late to render assistance to British forces then in South Africa.

they had been without tents or campbeds and had slept on the ground in the open in all weathers. 'I must say the men have marched and fought splendidly, and have always followed wherever led and under very heavy fire,' wrote Basil. 'They have had very long trying marches in a burning sun, often soaked to the skin with the rain, for many days on half rations and worst of all they suffered a good deal from thirst, often from 12 to 16 hours under arms. Of course General French [cavalry] has done excellently well, but except for our troops to support him he would have achieved nothing.' Describing the conditions faced by infantrymen in action in blazing hot sunshine many miles away in Natal, Captain H.P. Gough, 16th Lancers, wrote, 'It must have been awful for the infantry, burdened with rifle, ammunition, water and food, climbing the steep slopes and under a hot fire … it is they who suffer the greatest hardships and who give up their lives three times as much as any arm'.[8]

The West Ridings had indeed faced many hardships, so it must have been a great relief when they entered the Free State capital, Bloemfontein, on 13 March. 'We certainly have had the brunt of it all and we were selected to march through the town,' wrote Basil, 'though why the Guards did also I do not know as I do not think they have fired a shot since entering the Free State.'* Any sense of relief, however, was shortlived. Roberts rested his force in Bloemfontein for seven weeks, but a severe epidemic of typhoid broke out, and in conditions of appalling squalor and overcrowding more British soldiers died of fever than were killed in action during the whole war. Men rationed to half a water bottle a day drank from any source they could find, including the waters of the Modder River beside Cronje's camp at Paardeberg, polluted by the rotting carcasses of dozens of animals killed during the battle. In their desperation, noted Basil later, the men also drank greedily from dirty puddles along the roadside. When Colonel Lloyd went down with fever in Bloemfontein and Colonel Carnac, second in command, suffered a severe bout of dysentery, Basil assumed temporary command of the regiment.

Conditions began to improve after the town's waterworks reopened, but army hospitals remained hopelessly understaffed and overcrowded. Roberts resumed his advance early in May and reached Pretoria on 5 June, but the West Ridings remained behind as part of the garrison. To keep himself occupied in his spare time Basil acquired a pony and often went out riding or shooting, once bringing back several guinea fowl and an ox-eyed plover to supplement his rations. He was delighted to receive from home several much-needed parcels containing woollen underwear, a long Shetland scarf, socks, khaki handkerchiefs, pencils, cigarettes and tobacco.

On 15 May Basil wrote to his family about life in the town:

> We are all very tired of Bloemfontein and shall be very glad to get out of the place. It is pretty and there are some fine trees and houses but owing to the vast army that has been encamped here and the numbers of carts and

---

* The Guards Brigade had been in action at Belmont and Graspan, just outside the Free State.

78. Officers, 1st West Ridings, Bloemfontein, 1900. From the left, standing: 2nd Lt M.V. Le P. Trench, Lt R.E. Maffett, Maj. H.D. Thorold, Lt H.J.L. Oakes, Lt A.M. Whitaker, Lt E.V. Jenkins, Lt F.S. Exham, Surg. Capt. E.W. Siberry (RAMC), Lt E.N. Townsend; seated: Capt. L.R Acworth, Capt. F.D. Behrend, Lt & Adjt W.E.M. Tyndall, Lt-Col. G.E. Lloyd, Maj. B. St J. Le Marchant (holding a slouch hat), Capt. O. Harris, Capt. E.R. Houghton; front row: 2nd Lt W.E. Maples, Lt P.B. Strafford.

horses etc that have passed backwards and forwards through the place the dust is awful. It is scraped off the roads like snow and put in great heaps and then carted away but it seems to collect again almost immediately … Lady Roberts is still here and goes a good deal to the hospitals. She is living in the ex-President's house which is quite the finest in the place … We have at last got our things up from Cape Town, so now we have our camp bedsteads and sleep off the ground for the first time since we landed 10th Jan. last … We had a tremendous storm of locusts over the camp yesterday. They came in millions and made a noise like the wind as they came over us. I met Conan Doyle yesterday. He is here in charge of the Langham [volunteer] hospital and has asked me to tea. I am going to see him in a day or two … 18 May – Good news today … [Roberts] moving forward quickly now and the Boers in full flight. Perhaps they will surrender soon. They must either do so or fight. Emma can move the flags a long way up the map, <u>never</u> to be moved down again.

Such optimism was, of course, misplaced. Barely two months later Basil conceded that 'De Wet seems too clever for our Generals and it is rather humiliating considering the number of troops we have and the few he has got'.

In June the battalion proceeded by train to Winburg, where Colonel Lloyd was appointed Commandant. Basil took command of the half-battalion responsible for defending the north of the town and immediately began preparing trenches. 'Outpost work here is very harassing,' he wrote,

> as the Authorities seem to be always expecting an attack, consequently we are always standing to arms from two hours before daybreak and it is bitterly cold. I have only one subaltern and he is going into hospital today with fever … It is a pouring wet day and has been raining since early morning. We are all right in tents but my poor men in outposts must be drenched to the skin. At last we hear that Lord Roberts is sending a force down to clear out the Boers in this part of the country.

A friendly rivalry existed between the two Le Marchant brothers fighting in South Africa, who had last met in Bloemfontein early in March. 'Louis I have heard nothing of but presume he is in Johannesburg,' wrote Basil four months later. 'He was lucky to get in the general advance and I think it was hard lines the 6th Division [including the West Ridings] being left behind.' Basil, acknowledging that Louis 'must have been in a warm corner when fired at from three sides' at Zand River, nevertheless believed that his younger brother had got off lightly so far. 'We all think the 7th Division [including the 1st East Lancs, Louis' regiment] has had a comparatively easy time of it,' commented Basil in a letter to his father. Basil was keen to know if the family in Little Rissington had heard from his brothers recently. 'Any news of Evey? I have not heard from him for ages.' And when his father wrote back Basil commented, 'Evey seems to be in the height of high society and I expect is enjoying himself muchly.' If Basil envied the life enjoyed by his brother in Malta whilst he endured long months of discomfort and danger on the veldt, he did not show it. And he was pleased that Cecil, who had returned to India the previous year, was apparently enjoying life. 'I heard from Cecil last mail,' wrote Basil, 'he seems very well and in capital spirits.'

In an effort to keep up morale Florence Le Marchant sent her brother an unexpected parcel. 'Tell Flo the boar turned up all right and caused a good deal of amusement amongst the Subs,' wrote Basil in a letter to his mother. He also recounted what had happened to the unfortunate Captain Macleod of his regiment who, whilst acting as signalling officer to the Highland Brigade, had been wounded at Magersfontein and invalided home. When he had recovered he rejoined the Battalion in Bloemfontein, before proceeding to Winburg. 'He came here to act as galloper to General Colvile,' Basil continued.

> On arriving he found General Colvile gone. He followed him to Lindley with a company of Yeomanry, and on nearing Lindley they found it occupied by the Boers who attacked them. They held out for five days and then surrendered, so he was taken prisoner. They took him to Reitz where he got enteric fever, so they released him and he is now invalided home again. He says the Boers were very kind to him and treated him exceedingly well.

In August the West Ridings were posted to Pretoria, from where they took part in operations north and east of the capital. Basil was given command of the half-battalion, which included the 1st Volunteer Service Company, and he led them in action when they came under fire for the first time. Some volunteer units, such as Paget's Horse, were raised by wealthy individuals on their own initiative, a practice adopted to boost recruitment in times of need. When a strong force had been sent to Bechuanaland in 1885 to establish British control over the region, Colonel Methuen raised an irregular force of mounted rifles for the expedition. One of those to join Methuen's Horse as a volunteer was Dr Moore's son Arthur from Bourton-on-the-Water. Previously he had been a bank clerk in Cheltenham on £40 a year, but as a lieutenant in the South African Irregular Force his rate of pay increased significantly to 11s. a day. These 'volunteers of a respectable class' were engaged for a minimum period of six months, and were divided into three groups: 'the A troop composed of the class of gentlemen; the B troop of old soldiers, and the third of the rustic class, including labourers and sons of small farmers'.[9]

The West Ridings, part of a mobile column under General Paget, spent long weeks pursuing elusive Boer commandos, searching their farmsteads and punishing those who aided them. Basil, now Intelligence Officer and acting Staff Officer for the Battalion, disliked this phase of the war. 'We returned to Waterval [140 miles east of Pretoria] on 18 October. Since leaving Waterval we captured some 120 prisoners, thousands of sheep and cattle, burnt a lot of farms and laid waste the country through which we marched,' he wrote. 'It is sad to see the waste but I suppose it is an absolute necessity to stop the guerilla fighting.' One morning Basil accompanied Colonel Lloyd and two companies of infantry, together with the Queensland Imperial Bushmen – 'splendid men' – on a raid to capture some Boers about fifteen miles from Waterval. 'We surprised them so much that they left their coffee undrunk but galloped off before we could get to them,' wrote Basil. 'We burnt their farms and destroyed their crops … I don't know when the war will cease – it is getting awfully hot and I am sick of it.' When they returned three days later they had captured 18 prisoners with their rifles and ammunition, 1,550 cattle and 1,300 sheep, 23 horses, seven wagons and two carts.

Soon afterwards Paget insisted that Basil, an officer on whom he could rely, take charge of another vital supply convoy. 'The rest of the Regt are having a quiet time at Waterval and I thought that I should have been allowed to rest there also,' wrote Basil. 'I have been kept in command of a huge convoy which stretches between 3 and 4 miles … I have an escort of half a battalion, two guns Royal Artillery and some cavalry.' The route passed through thick bush, and during a terrific thunderstorm one night they were forced to stop, tie up the oxen and wait for daybreak. Soon after dawn they reached a river, and it took four and a half hours to get all the wagons across. Later that day they reached their destination, Jericho, without losing a single wagon. 'They tell me that General Paget is very pleased,' Basil told his sister Beatrice. His thoughts turned to home and Sarah Cheetham, whom he would eventually marry. 'Remember me to Miss Cheetham when you see her,' he added, 'and tell her I am going to write to her when I come off this march.'

On 29 November, the day that Kitchener took over command from Roberts, Major Le Marchant and the West Ridings fought a fierce engagement against a Boer commando unit under Commandant Viljoen at Rhenoster Kop, east of Pretoria. As they advanced up a hill they were 'met by an overwhelming fire', and during the day-long battle the West Riding's brave Commanding Officer, Colonel Lloyd, was killed. Five other men from the regiment were also killed that day, and a further 27 wounded. That night Viljoen made good his escape before reinforcements could arrive. Basil remained at Rhenoster Kop for several weeks during which more men went down with dysentery and fever, further depleting the strength of the Battalion. 'The weather is pretty bad now, we get drenching rain most days and then burning sun,' he wrote, 'the men are a bit run down after all their hard work and are more liable to disease than if they were fit … We work every day at the defences and I generally ride morning and evening. Some play hockey, cricket and football but I have not the energy in this heat for any of these games.' In early January 1901 Colonel Carnac arrived to take over command of the battalion, 'or rather what there is left of it,' commented Basil.

The war was now entering its long and bitter final phase in which Kitchener sought to counter Boer guerrilla tactics aimed at cutting his extended and vulnerable lines of communication. He continued Roberts' scorched earth policy, destroying crops and livestock in an attempt to break Afrikaner resistance. Boer women and children, no longer able to feed themselves, were 'concentrated' into camps where it is estimated that some 25,000 died as a result of overcrowding, poor sanitation and disease.* In a further effort to restrict the mobility of those Boers who continued to fight to the bitter end, Kitchener constructed a network of some 8,000 blockhouses across the veldt linked by miles of barbed wire.

For the remainder of the war the West Ridings took part in 'wearisome marches, tantalising pursuits of the enemy and sudden calls to distant stations to check raids of marauding parties of elusive Boers'.[10] They also spent lengthy periods on tedious garrison duty in blockhouses guarding a section of railway line between Pretoria and Pietersburg in the northern Transvaal. Blockhouses – in places just 1,000 yards apart – were usually manned by a corporal and six men, with a subaltern in charge of three blockhouses and a captain responsible for ten or twelve. Life inside these small fortified outposts was much more comfortable than bivouacking on the veldt, though they were often intensely hot by day and

---

* These camps caused a heavy loss of life through administrative inefficiency, poor planning, an inadequate diet and lack of proper medical provision. More could and should have been done to prevent disease, and later conditions did improve as a result of pressure from campaigners such as Emily Hobhouse. Very many Africans also died in their own segregated concentration camps; Denis Judd & Keith Surridge, *The Boer War* (John Murray, 2002), p.196. It should not be forgotten that many thousands of British soldiers succumbed to fever during the Boer War – poor sanitation and disease were indiscriminate killers.

79. A blockhouse under construction, part of a line of blockhouses manned by the 1st West Ridings between Pretoria and Nylstroom, 1901.

below freezing at night. But it was a stultifying existence; no one could venture far from a blockhouse without the risk of being captured. Despite the dangers Basil took the opportunity to do a little fishing or shooting, sometimes bringing back several guinea fowl to supplement his larder. 'There are many beautiful birds here but one has no time to get and cure their skins,' he wrote, 'the Bush is so thick that it is not safe to go far beyond the outposts or brother Boer might have a pot shot at you.'

Basil later recalled how, when he was stationed at Pienaar's River 40 miles north of Pretoria in August 1901, the battalion took possession of President Kruger's saddle and rifle:

> I was at the outposts one morning when I saw a man on a pony with a white flag coming towards the post. When he came up to me he said he wished to surrender and that he was President Kruger's servant. I took his rifle and escorted him to the Orderly Room to Colonel Carnac … On his pony was a saddle with the Transvaal Coat of Arms on it. He said the saddle and rifle belonged to President Kruger. I asked Colonel Carnac for the rifle and he gave it to me. The saddle he gave to the Officers' Mess of the Battalion.[11]

At the end of the war the saddle was brought home to England and placed in the officers' mess, but in 1939 it was returned to South Africa and put on display in the Kruger Museum in Pretoria. Basil also agreed to return the rifle to the Union of South Africa at this time.

With monotonous inevitability the war dragged on through 1901, but not without incident and danger. On 31 August a train, with an escort of 45 men

80. A section of barbed-wire fence between blockhouses manned by the 1st West Ridings, north of Pretoria.

of the West Ridings, was derailed by the Boers near Hammanskraal, north of Pretoria. Also on board, in charge of battalion pay and stores, was Major Le Marchant. Some 200 Boers lay in wait, and as the train entered a deep cutting they detonated a mine under the armoured truck in which the soldiers were riding. As the troops scrambled out without their rifles they came under heavy fire from the Boers and suffered many casualties. The officers, who were travelling with some women and children in the passenger coaches, made their way under fire to the armoured guard's van at the rear. Meanwhile, the Boers swarmed onto the train and took money, clothing and food from the passengers and a number of rifles from the escort, before setting fire to the wreckage and riding off with their loot – including the battalion's pay. They had blown up the track some distance away to prevent help from coming quickly. This attack provoked Conan Doyle – who had by now published his influential history of the Boer War* – to write to *The Times* to propose a controversial solution:

> Would it not be perfectly feasible to put a truck full of Boer irreconcilables behind every engine which passes through a dangerous part of the country? Two of these dastardly affairs in the last few weeks have cost us 40 men killed and wounded, while the sum total of men who have been maimed in this fashion during the war amounts to many hundreds … The Germans in 1870 continually carried French hostages in the trains.[12]

A total of 11 men were killed and 20 wounded at Hammanskraal, mostly from the 1st West Ridings. Basil himself was wounded above one eye and repatriated.

---

* In a letter to his sister Emma, Evelyn asked 'Have you read *The Great Boer War* by Conan Doyle? I think it very good.'

81. An armoured train, South Africa, similar to one in which Basil Le Marchant was travelling when it was blown up by the Boers.

Robert Le Marchant received conflicting reports about the seriousness of the wound: 'Received a letter from Capt. Acworth [also wounded] dictated by Basil who seems to have received a severe injury to his eye and was unable to write – Pretoria General Hospital, 6 Sept. 1901.' Two weeks later a letter from the War Office said that Basil had a slight wound in the eyebrow and another in the back. He had been mentioned in despatches three times during 1901, and he returned home to a hero's welcome, as Robert noted on 26 October 1901: 'Basil arrived at Little Rissington this afternoon, giving only an hour's notice by telegram. When he arrived at the Lodge, the horse was taken out of the shafts and the villagers dragged him up [the steep hill] to the Rectory in an incredibly short time. He came from S. Africa.'

When he had fully recovered Basil was given command of the 8th Provisional Battalion in Belfast. 'I am glad Basil likes his job in Ireland,' wrote Louis to his father, 'please thank him for his letter which I am very glad to have.' In South Africa the war finally came to an end on 31 May 1902. Almost 6,000 British and Empire troops had been killed in action – including Gaspard de Coligny Le Marchant, Basil's second cousin – and a further 16,000 died of wounds or disease. As many as 7,000 Boers were killed in action, and it has been estimated that more than 12,000 Africans also died.[13] The war revealed significant shortcomings in the armaments and organisation of the British Army, and pressure for reform grew. There was a widespread but exaggerated concern about the professional competence of the officer corps, whom some critics viewed as an organisation that existed merely to provide 'an elegant employment for the leisure hours of the wealthy classes'.[14] For middle-ranking career officers like Basil Le Marchant, who did not come from a wealthy background and who had so recently risked their lives for their country, such criticisms must have seemed unworthy and disheartening. The 'fun or glory in soldiering', evident in the many small colonial wars hitherto, was ceasing to be a part of an officer's experience of modern warfare.[15]

In February 1904 Basil was appointed second in command of the 1st Battalion The Royal Munster Fusiliers, then in India. After purchasing various items of tropical kit, he proceeded to Southampton to take charge of some 500 troops bound for Bombay on board the P & O steamer *Assaye*. On the afternoon of 19 March *Assaye* left port but remained in the Solent off Hurst Castle all night because of thick fog. Conditions had not improved much the following morning, causing further delay. Sometime before 1 p.m. an American passenger liner, *New York*, entered Southampton Water and was unable to avert a collision as *Assaye* emerged from the mist. *New York*'s bows ripped a tremendous hole from deck to waterline in the starboard bow of *Assaye* and, noted Robert, 'it was at one time feared that it would be necessary to beach her … All on board behaved beautifully, there was no panic but much excitement. No lives were lost'. The troops mustered on deck and boats were lowered into the water as a precaution, but *Assaye* was able to return to Southampton for repairs. 'The ship was cut right down to the keel,' wrote Basil later, 'so we had a more narrow shave than we thought.' He received a very complimentary telegram from Hugh Arnold-Forster, Secretary of State for War, 'on the discipline of the troops under his command during the trying circumstances of the collision'. A month later he left Southampton for India aboard *Assaye*, now fully repaired.

Basil joined the 1st Battalion in Multan, notorious for its intense heat. Even amongst Punjabis the place had a fearsome reputation, best expressed in the words of a local saying:

> Dust, heat, beggars and tombs
> Are the four specialities of Multan.

In March the following year Basil was promoted to Lieutenant-Colonel, and soon afterwards he escaped from the heat for five months, returning to England to get married. His bride, Helen Carlton Harris – the widow of his closest friend from the 1st West Riding Regiment who had died from a wound received during the Boer War* – was described by Annie Le Marchant as 'a charming lady who will make a very good wife for Basil'. They had a quiet wedding in London,

82. Capt. Gaspard de Coligny Le Marchant, 1st Lancashire Fusiliers, killed in action at Boschbult, Kleinhardts River, 31 March 1902, aged 22. He was a great-grandson of Maj.-Gen. John Gaspard Le Marchant (killed at Salamanca).

---

* Major Owen Harris, whilst in command of the 8th Mounted Infantry Battalion, was wounded as he led an attack against a well-defended Boer laager. He was apparently shot after the Boers had raised a white flag. Though his wound did not appear serious at the time, he never fully recovered and died not long after being repatriated.

85. Capt. Owen Harris
(left), Maj. Basil Le
Marchant, and Lt
K.A. Macleod (right),
Salisbury Plain, 1899.

83. Basil Le Marchant
with his bride, Helen
Carlton Harris, 1905.

84. Gharial barracks,
Murree Hills, north-east
of Rawalpindi.

with just two of his nine sisters and Gaspard present from his immediate family. Basil gave his bride an ivory-bound prayer book and an amethyst, peridot and pearl necklace, and she gave him a gold watch, chain and cuff-links. From Robert and Eliza Le Marchant they received a handsome silver coffee pot, and amongst the other gifts was a silver bowl generously given by the parishioners of Little Rissington. The couple returned to Multan early in November, and a few weeks later the battalion, now under the command of Lieutenant-Colonel Le Marchant, moved to Rawalpindi.

When the battalion moved up to Gharial barracks in the Murree Hills the following April Basil and Carlie hoped to find themselves a house in Murree – a lovely hill-station 7,500 feet above sea level with magnificent views of snowcapped peaks – but none was available. Instead, they settled into a pleasant bungalow in Gharial, where they spent several blissfully happy months together. Carlie was now some five months pregnant, and in a letter home to Eliza she described their journey up from Rawalpindi. 'We came up here on Thursday in a sort of antiquated landau,' she wrote.

> They are more comfortable than the tongas … we left our bungalow at 10 a.m. and arrived here [Murree] just about 5. They change horses about every four or five miles so one comes along at a good pace – 41 miles. I was tired of course, but none the worse. Basil stayed 2 nights and yesterday went back to Pindi to bring the Regt up. They expect to arrive at Gharial on Wed. morning. I have been out there today, the furniture has arrived and I had to see about getting it put in. I hope to get it all straight by the time Basil arrives – it takes about an hour to go out there from here in a dandy, which is a thing something like a boat and 4 men carry it, two at each end, it is rather a horrid feeling as it feels as if it might upset but they say they hardly ever do and I expect one soon gets used to them. We like our bungalow very much, there are 6 rooms and it is on a little mound with steep drops all round and pine trees everywhere … There is still a little snow left in patches along the sides of the roads though it is quite warm in the day – but gets cold at night and one likes a fire – it is lovely up here and the views are beautiful.

86. An officer's house, Murree, *c.*1875, from a watercolour by Harriet Gough. A 'dandy' carried by four people can be seen in the foreground.

87. The Anglican Church, Mall and bazaar at Murree.

To assist her when the baby arrived Carlie engaged a nurse from Bombay, as she was unable to find one locally.

Two months later Carlie wrote again to Eliza, signing herself as 'Your affectionate daughter'. 'Basil has just started collecting some butterflies, but as he only started 4 days ago there are not many yet,' she wrote.

> The native servants are all much interested and excited and leap about with butterfly nets. We have had to stop them today as they were getting more than Basil had room to set, and also they go in for quantity more than quality … I am now busy trimming the cot … with white muslin which has got a spot and a line in it, and lining the sides etc. with white sateen … Mrs Grimston told me she did not even line her cot, just had the netting for fear of animals but I thought it looked rather bare …

When they were not planning ahead for the arrival of their baby, deciding on possible names and writing to prospective godparents, they worked in their garden and took great delight in growing their own vegetables. They had so much to look forward to together.

In July they moved to Murree and two weeks later, on 5 August 1906, their son, Gaspard St John, was born. It was an anxious time for Basil, but after a few days Carlie seemed to be doing fine. However, she never fully regained her strength and two months later, aged just 34, she died. Basil was utterly distraught, and in a letter to his father he expressed his grief:

> Brock Hurst
> Murree
> 9 Oct 06
>
> My dear Father
>
> Since Carlie's confinement she never picked up her strength properly and never seemed to decrease in size. This I believe was due to over feeding by the nurse but of course we thought it was all right at the time. About a fortnight ago she got most awfully out of breath when walking, and it got worse and worse till she had to stop walking altogether. On Saturday she complained of a pain in her chest over the heart but the doctor said it was muscular, that night the pain was very acute and when the doctor came on Sunday morning he said she was very ill, this was about 9 a.m. or 10 a.m. Another doctor came and they had a consultation and agreed that she was suffering from Pericarditis, and if she could get through the next 24 hours all would be well. She went on well all day, and the doctors came several times and were quite pleased with her progress. At 10 p.m. the doctor was again quite hopeful and told me to go and get some sleep, as it was a great thing in her favour not to let her know she was so ill. At 2 a.m. I came down stairs and the nurse said there was a change for the worse. I rushed off for the doctor and then came back to my dear Carlie, and she died a few minutes afterwards and before the doctor came. My loss is a terrible one and almost too hard to bear, it is a cruel cruel blow.

88. Murree Post
Office, from where
Basil telegraphed the
sad news of Carlie's
untimely death.

She and I were just all the world to each other, and now I have lost my
dear beautiful good brave wife. She was so plucky through her illness and
always had a smile for me so as to not let me think she was suffering.
She suffered a lot I fear but she would never say or admit it. I cannot
help thinking the doctors should have found out long before what was
wrong, but they said her heart and lungs were perfectly sound and they
put down the breathlessness to excessive fat by over feeding. She hated all
the food she had to take but did it as she thought for the baby's sake. Oh
how I wish I had brought her home for her confinement, but she wished
so not to and wanted to stay out here. Every minute since we married has
been one of perfect happiness and now my darling Carlie has gone from
me for ever. Everybody loved her and she had such a sweet smile on her
dear face after death and looked so perfectly peaceful. If ever there was a
pure woman she was one.

We buried her yesterday evening. All the officers of the Regiment
came. [General] Sir B[indon] Blood and a lot of others, 20 Colour
Sergeants and Staff Sergeants of the Munsters appeared and carried the
coffin to the bier and wheeled the bier all the way to the cemetery some 2
miles from this house, and then they carried her to the grave and lowered
the coffin themselves. It was very nice of them and I am sure she would
have wished this. She was so fond and proud of the Regiment. I cannot
write more about it now, long before you get this I expect you will get a
wire to say that I am coming home. I must get someone to look after the
baby whilst I come out here again. My poor darling Carlie, to think she
is gone. I always prayed that if either of us had to go that it might be me

so that she would have her boy to see grow up and be a great pleasure and comfort to her. She was so fond of him. It is a terrible blank to look forward to now and life can never be anything again.

Your kind wire of sympathy just received 7.30 a.m. for which my heartfelt thanks. With best love to yourself, Mother and all.

      Yr affectionate son
        Basil

On Carlie's tombstone Basil had the following verse inscribed:

> And they shall be mine saith the Lord of Hosts
> in that day when I make up my jewels
>   Malachi, iii, 17

89. Carlie, in happier times.

Soon afterwards Basil came home to England with his baby son, leaving him in the care of Mrs Paul, Carlie's sister, in London. Basil spent much of the next five months with his family in Little Rissington, though he visited his son often. At the end of March he returned to duty in India.

By February 1908, some nine months after Basil had resumed command of the battalion at Rawalpindi, unrest had once again broken out in what was now the North-West Frontier Province. Between the territory administered by the government of India and the presumptive border of Afghanistan lay a semi-independent area over which the British – through the government of India – assumed responsibility for the good behaviour of the local tribesmen, without exercising direct administrative control. Some of these tribes were paid allowances by the British in return for promises of good behaviour, and when such undertakings were broken fines were normally imposed. This semi-independent area included the Khyber Pass, to the south of which lay the Bazar Valley, home to the Zakha Khels, who had recently been carrying out raids into British territory.

The Bazar Valley Field Force, including Colonel Le Marchant and the 1st Royal Munster Fusiliers, was mobilised to undertake a punitive expedition against the offending tribesmen. Within weeks the Zakha Khels had submitted and the field force withdrew. The 1st Battalion had been held in reserve close to the action but had not been required to take part, and now they marched back to Rawalpindi. However, the Mohmands from north of the Khyber Pass had been persuaded by local mullahs to rally in support of their neighbours and they undertook a series of raids, attacking border posts and coming within 20 miles of Peshawar. *The Times*, reflecting how these matters were perceived, reported that prominent tribal leaders were preaching a holy war: 'the Mohmand mullahs have sent messengers … to the leading men in the Swat district, including the mad fakir who headed the fanatical rising of 1897.'[16] To the British, all fanatics and religious extremists were deemed to be mad. Once more a field force was assembled and the leading brigades were involved in some sharp encounters. The

90. Fortified tribal towers guarding walled villages, Khyber Pass, North-West Frontier Province.

1st Battalion, part of the 3rd Brigade, was initially held in reserve and followed later, reaching Jamrud on 2 May. There they camped, but during the night they were fired on by snipers and two NCOs were wounded. Next day the battalion, under the command of Colonel Le Marchant, marched almost twenty-two miles in intense heat through the Khyber Pass and reached the fort at Landi Kotal in 12 hours. That night snipers were again active, and the following day the battalion advanced under very heavy fire and took a fortified village, causing the enemy to retire towards the Afghan border. After a couple of days the 2nd and 3rd Brigades withdrew, but elsewhere the campaign continued and various punitive measures were taken, including the destruction of fortified enemy towers and villages and the collection of fines.

During a hot and dusty march back to Peshawar the battalion was given strict orders not to drink any water along the roadside because several cases of cholera had occurred in other regiments. From Peshawar they marched north to Shabkadar, but there the battalion was struck down by cholera and was thus unable to take any further part in operations against the Mohmands. They were confined to a perimeter camp where the temperature reached 116°F in the shade and where they were exposed to intermittent enemy sniper fire. Over the next two weeks there were 43 cases of cholera in the battalion, and 35 deaths.

The sheer monotony of camp life was unremitting, but one incident provided some light relief. Late one afternoon, when it seemed that an attack on the camp was imminent, the alarm was sounded, tents were lowered, and the troops stood to arms. No attack materialised and after a while the men were dismissed, but during the disturbance half a barrel of beer had gone missing. Every corner of the camp and every soldier and camp follower was searched, but 'there was not a sign

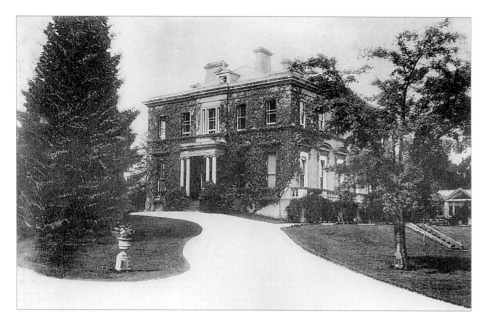

91. Eyford Park, the home of Sarah Crompton Cheetham, Basil's second wife.

either of beer or of its effects'. Some years later it emerged that an enterprising Private Murphy and 12 others, not satisfied with the ration of a pint per man a day, had taken advantage of the confusion to raid the canteen tent. They had each filled a camp kettle full of beer from the barrel and then hidden the kettles in a trench which they covered with earth. There the kettles lay undiscovered during the search and later that night 'thirteen thirsty fusiliers crept quietly out and in a businesslike manner disposed of the fourteen gallons of beer'.

When no fresh cases of cholera had been reported for 10 days the battalion marched 23 miles back to Peshawar, but the march was not without incident. During the night, as they crossed one of the numerous boat bridges over the Kabul River, several officers and men were thrown into the river when a mule stampeded, though all managed to reach the shore safely. Perhaps it is no wonder that after the ordeal of the last few weeks Colonel Le Marchant remarked, 'By gad, I command the finest regiment in the service.'[17] At the end of the Mohmand operations Basil was mentioned in a letter to the Chief of Staff: 'Colonel B. St J. Le Marchant is reported by General Ramsay to have commanded the Regiment to his entire satisfaction.'

Five months later Basil returned to England, and in March 1909, at the age of 50, he retired. Though not wealthy, he received a pension of £300 a year (half pay) and was now comfortably well off. He was offered command of a territorial brigade but turned it down. The following year he married Sarah Cheetham from Eyford Park, known fondly to the family as Sissy, and the couple enjoyed an extended honeymoon on the Continent before returning to their new home near Daymer Bay in Cornwall. Many years later they moved back to Winchcombe in the Cotswolds. Basil used to drive over to Little Rissington as often as he could to

92. Mary Creed (later
Mrs Donald Lane)
worked as a house and
parlour maid for the
Le Marchants in Little
Rissington during the
Second World War.

make sure that his sisters were all right. On arrival he would slip the servants a parcel of food, telling them to keep it for themselves and say nothing to the ageing Miss Le Marchants. 'Hide it,' he would say, 'don't tell them what I have brought.' Mary Lane, who worked for the Le Marchants during the Second World War, remembers him with affection. 'He was a real gentleman,' she said.

Basil, who outlived Sarah by some five years, died, aged 97, at a nursing home in Cheltenham in 1956. He was buried beside Sarah at St Peter's Church, Upper Slaughter. From his obituary in the regimental journal, *The Iron Duke*, one characteristic stands out above all others: those who knew him were struck by his kindliness, especially to junior officers. He was not only a true sportsman and an excellent adjutant, but also a kind and fair adjudicator and a loyal regimental soldier. Sensitive to the needs of others, always courteous and considerate, he was well liked by all those who knew him.

93. A view of St Peter's Church, Upper Slaughter, from the peaceful spot where Basil Le Marchant and his wife, Sarah, are buried.

Egypt, Abu Klea and the North-West Frontier

OSMUND CECIL LE MARCHANT
(1860-1943)

Cecil Le Marchant was not quite two years old when his father was appointed rector of Little Rissington. The family moved to the Cotswolds, and Cecil, according to his sisters, 'ran wild and grew fond of field sports and the natural objects of the country'. As a young boy his formal education was neglected, but eventually he was sent to school near London, where relatives were close at hand in case of need. His time as a boarder at Streatham School was not a success, however. 'I am sorry to hear about Cecil and his school,' wrote his brother Evelyn, 'it seems to me that it is such a bad one, it is a great pity he is not removed to a better one where he will learn something.'

94 & 95. Cecil (left) and Basil, aged three. It was customary to dress boys in frocks until they were three or four.

On leaving Streatham School Cecil was sent abroad to learn French, and when he returned home he had little idea about what he wanted to do. Edward urged his brother – 'a regular *monsieur* and a dapper little fellow' – to make up his mind and join the Army as soon as possible. Further delay would mean that younger men would be ahead of him on the long ladder of promotion, for every 'step' towards the rank of captain depended on length of service. Whenever an officer with longer service resigned or transferred to another unit, those officers below would move a step closer to being in command of a company. Edward suggested that Annie give her brother daily lessons in English history and other subjects to help prepare Cecil for the entrance exams he would later be required to sit. 'I am afraid Cecil does not see the need for exertion,' observed Edward, who knew what struggles lay ahead.

After a long period of indecision Cecil resolved to follow his brothers Edward and Basil and obtain a commission in the Army through what some commentators disparagingly called the 'back door' of the Militia. He began his military career in the Royal Guernsey Militia, with whom Basil was already serving. The bond between the two brothers – only 19 months apart in age – was very strong, and together they received their basic training on the island where their parents had been born. Subsequently, after passing the entry examinations for a regular commission on his second attempt, Cecil joined the 35th Regiment, soon to become the 1st Battalion, The Royal Sussex Regiment. Shortly before joining the 1st Battalion in Cyprus he went to London with Basil – recently gazetted to the 76th Regiment – to buy his outfit and other essential equipment. For Robert Le Marchant the initial outlay for both sons would have amounted to over £300 – as much as he earned in one year from his living – but for a generous contribution from Aunt De Lancey who paid for their uniforms. Amongst the items purchased were the following:

	£	s	d
two waterproof coats	1	14	6
three airtight tin cases	3	13	-
one buffalo trunk	2	14	-
tailoring for Cecil	24	10	6
tailoring for Basil	13	10	6
flannel shirts, trousers & drawers	3	11	3
two Bibles	1	5	-
two prismatic compasses	3	-	-
pocket handkerchiefs, ties, braces, gloves	2	16	2
boots & shoes	5	9	11
forks & spoons; studs	3	17	6
towards Cecil's gun	2	-	-
Cecil for saddle, bridle, bath, tin case *etc*	8	10	6
Hawkes' account [military tailor/supplier] 102	19	6	
Nathan's account + Deane's account	61	10	3
Gaspard's camp bed given to Cecil	3	-	-
revolvers, pouch *etc* given by James	8	19	-

Robert Le Marchant had followed the advice of his son Edward, who by now had been with the 67th Regiment for seven years and knew how difficult it was for an officer without private means to survive on his pay alone. 'I hope the boys [Cecil and Basil] will be able to get good outfits, it looks bad for a fellow to join a regiment in part worn and shabby kit, besides putting him to expense early in his service to get new clothes,' he wrote, hoping they would avoid some of the early hardships he had endured. His second- and third-hand kit had proved to be a false economy. 'My trousers went in the seats, my coats in the elbows, and a year and a half after entering the Service I could not appear in the uniform,' he added. To save money Edward suggested they need not buy full dress trousers, but instead could sew a strip of lace onto the legs of their mufti evening dress when they went to a dance. Furthermore, their old Guernsey Militia kit would be adequate on board ship and for rough work in India. 'White shirts are an important item in a sub's kit, as he has to appear in a clean one every night; also collars and pocket handkerchiefs,' wrote Edward. 'A small solid leather dressing case is very useful, one foot by six inches or so, containing hair brush, looking glass, toothbrush, nailbrush, scissors, two razors, shaving brush, etc. – cost about 30s. – as everything can be packed together, and all ready at hand when wanted,' he advised, drawing on his campaign experience in Afghanistan. They would also need a bath sponge and face sponge in a waterproof bag, he suggested.

96. Cecil as a cadet in the Royal Guernsey Militia.

The choice of a suitable regiment was also a matter on which Edward held strong views. Expensive regiments were to be avoided. 'I do not advise your putting them in either the Rifle Brigade or the 60th [King's Royal Rifle Corps] both of which are monied regiments. The 28th Regt [1st Bn Gloucestershire Regiment] is a very good one, and a County Regiment too,' he wrote to his father. The Rifle Brigade would be far too expensive, said Edward, requiring a private income of at least £200 a year. In that regiment, he wrote, 'all the battalions at different times go in for drags to races, or in keeping a pack of hounds (beagles), or something of that kind, and unless a fellow can stick up for what is called in the Army "the credit of the Corps", he had better keep out of it, and I don't think a man without money for this reason would do for the Rifle Brigade.' If, on the other hand, Cecil were to join the Corps of Guides in India he would enjoy good pay, comfortable quarters, and have a better chance of seeing active service. The Corps of Guides, he wrote, is in 'every way superior to the Line for a poor man, who can just subsist on his pay without enjoying much amusement of any kind'.

Edward also favoured the Indian Staff Corps, though he believed it would be better to join a line regiment first, where Cecil could learn how to treat soldiers

properly and master the elements of drill thoroughly. Once he had passed the
Higher Standard in Hindustani Cecil could transfer to the Staff Corps and thus
be well placed to get an adjutancy at an early date. Aware that his family were not
in favour of a career in the Indian Army, Edward urged his father to consider the
benefits. 'It is a great mistake to suppose the Staff Corps is at all a bad profession,
or that it is altogether life in India, every five years one can go home for a year
on £250 which is too good for a poor man to despise. I earnestly recommend it
to Cecil, as being better than the Line,' he wrote. 'In the Staff Corps where one
can keep horses, shoot and hunt, pigstick, it really is very pleasant … you can
little guess how hard it is to make both ends meet at the end of each month as
one is obliged to do in the Service.' After much thought, however, Cecil obtained
a commission in the The Royal Sussex Regiment. He would later apply for a
transfer, not to the Indian Staff Corps but to the Egyptian Army.

Cecil sailed to join his regiment in Cyprus in May 1881. His voyage aboard SS
Sesostris was not without incident, and soon after leaving Liverpool the boatswain
fell overboard and drowned; Cecil threw a life buoy after him but saw him go
under before a rescue boat could reach him. The following night one of the
passengers caused quite a disturbance in the saloon, breaking everything in sight.
'He has got DT and has been quite mad ever since,' wrote Cecil, 'he was put
in irons for a day and now he is shut up in a small cabin and we look at him
through a window. He fancies himself in London and puts on his top hat and
says he is going to make some calls in the afternoon.' The poor man provided
a welcome distraction from the boredom of the voyage. 'There is very little to
do except play rope quoits which we do nearly all day,' commented Cecil, 'but
it is not much of a game.'

During the short time Cecil was to spend in Cyprus he made the most of
the sporting opportunities available. Because expenses were relatively low he
could afford to keep a pony and learn to ride. Cricket was not his game, but
he was selected to play for the battalion against HMS *Superb*, a match in which
the naval side managed to score just 13 runs in the first innings and 61 in the
second; the battalion won by more than an innings and Cecil, coming in at
number 10, had no chance to shine. He fared rather better in the island's tennis
championships, which were held near the summit of Mount Olympus, the site
of the garrison's summer camp in the Troodos Mountains. With his partner,
Lieutenant Todd-Thornton of The Royal Sussex Regiment, he won the doubles,
each player receiving a handsome trophy carved in polished Troodos stone. Cecil
had been in Cyprus for less than eighteen months when nationalist unrest in
Egypt cut short the battalion's tour of duty on the island.

Since the completion of the Suez Canal in 1869 Egypt – nominally part of
the Ottoman Empire – had been sliding into insolvency, and there was growing
concern that the Khedive of Egypt would be unable to pay the interest on his
foreign debts. In 1875 Disraeli purchased Khedive Ismail's Suez Canal Company
shares, and the following year an international commission was appointed to

supervise the Egyptian budget and economy. The European Powers secured the replacement of Ismail by his weak son Tewfik, who was persuaded to accept Anglo-French control of his treasury. Anti-European feeling grew, and the authority of the Khedive was undermined. In 1881 an Egyptian army colonel, Arabi Pasha, and a group of unpaid army officers rebelled, and Arabi subsequently appointed himself Minister of War with control of the army. Britain and France continued to express support for Khedive Tewfik and a naval force was sent to Alexandria, but these measures only served to increase resentment of foreign intervention. In Britain there were fears, largely unfounded, that the growing nationalist movement posed an immediate threat to the Suez Canal, described by Bismarck as the Empire's spinal cord. When a riot in Alexandria led to the murder of some fifty Europeans in June 1882 there were demands in Parliament for action. Gladstone was opposed to unnecessary foreign entanglements, but his Cabinet were divided on the issue.

An opportunity for action occurred when Admiral Seymour advised the Cabinet that his ships were being threatened by new gun batteries installed by Arabi to strengthen the port of Alexandria's defences. When Arabi ignored an ultimatum to remove the batteries the Royal Navy bombarded the fortifications in Alexandria. Two days later parties of sailors and marines went ashore to restore law and order in the town. Gladstone defended these actions on the grounds that Egypt was 'in a state of military violence, without any law whatsoever',[1] and that 'we are discharging single-handed an European duty', applying the 'resources of civilisation' to restore order in Egypt.[2] An expeditionary force under the command of Sir Garnet Wolseley, including troops of the Indian Army, was sent to Egypt and defeated Arabi at Tel-el-Kabir.

Cecil Le Marchant and units of the 1st Royal Sussex landed at Ismaïlia in September 1882 and took part in operations to restore order in Cairo and protect the city. Soon afterwards the battalion moved a few miles upriver to the barracks at Abbassiyya, where the British army of occupation was garrisoned. Life quickly settled into a predictable routine, and the following year Cecil was selected to play as a forward in a 'football' match for the garrison against the Highland Brigade. The game, which took place on the polo ground, was the first to be played in Cairo under rugby rules. Although the Abbassiyya forwards were considerably heavier than the Highlanders, their advantage up front was neutralised by the superior speed of their opponents behind the pack and the Highlanders won by two goals and two tries to nil. 'Both sides played up well,' commented an observer. But garrison life was not much fun in the desert heat, and during a severe outbreak of cholera, in which 34 soldiers from the battalion died, seven companies were moved back to Ismaïlia for several months. Cecil returned to England to recover from illness, but was soon back in Egypt with his regiment.

Successive British governments declared that the occupation of Egypt would be temporary, but the need to protect British interests and prevent any other power from annexing Egypt led Britain to retain a substantial military presence in Egypt until the 1950s. One consequence of Britain's *de facto* protectorate in Egypt was that she was reluctantly drawn into developments in the Sudan, which had been conquered by Egypt in 1822. Sudanese resentment of Egyptian misrule, unjust taxes and attempts to suppress the slave trade had been growing and Muhammad Ahmad, who proclaimed himself to be *al-Mahdi*, or the 'divinely guided one', was able to channel this discontent into a religious uprising. The Mahdi revealed that God had appointed him to purify Islam and drive out all those who defiled it, including corrupt Egyptians who were betraying the true faith. He proclaimed a *jihad* or holy war, and by the end of 1883 Mahdist warriors (or Ansar – known to the British as dervishes)* had defeated three Egyptian armies sent against them, including one commanded by an experienced British officer, Colonel William Hicks.

The British government now decided that the Egyptians should be pressed into withdrawing from their empire in the Sudan and appointed a special representative, General Charles Gordon, to organise the evacuation of all Egyptian garrisons and personnel. Initially Gordon believed that he could achieve a peaceful evacuation and establish friendly relations with the Mahdi, but when the latter rejected his overtures Gordon realised that such an approach was futile. Once he had reached Khartoum Gordon, a devout Christian, decided to ignore his orders to evacuate the Sudan and instead proposed that the Mahdi must be defeated, at the same time appealing for British military intervention to help save the Sudan from what he believed to be the forces of evil. This represented a complete reversal of government policy, and for many months Gladstone resisted mounting pressure to send an expedition to rescue Gordon, now besieged in Khartoum and surrounded by Mahdist forces. At the beginning of August 1884, as Gordon's position became more precarious and public concern grew for the fate of a national hero, Gladstone reluctantly agreed to send a relief force under the command of General Wolseley.

Wolseley, 'The Very Model of a Modern Major-General', assembled a force of more than 10,000 men and prepared to transport his entire column up the Nile as far as Wadi Halfa in steamers provided by the travel company Thomas Cook. Thereafter smaller boats were required, some eight hundred of which were shipped out from England. Three hundred boatmen were recruited from Canada to help guide the flotilla up the dangerous rapids, or cataracts, between Aswan and Khartoum, but the logistics all took time to organise and implement. At Aswan Cecil saved the life of Lieutenant Stuart Graham in the River Nile, for which he was later awarded the medal of the Royal Humane Society. The 1st Royal Sussex reached Wadi Halfa – 'Bloody Halfway' to the troops – in late August ahead of the main force and led the way as far as Dongola, using local

---

* The word 'dervishes' is an Anglicisation of the Sudanese word *daraweesh*, meaning 'holy men', as the followers of the Mahdi were known. Dervishes were Muslim (mainly Sufi) religious ascetics who had taken vows of poverty and whose order included dancing – hence British references to 'whirling dervishes'.

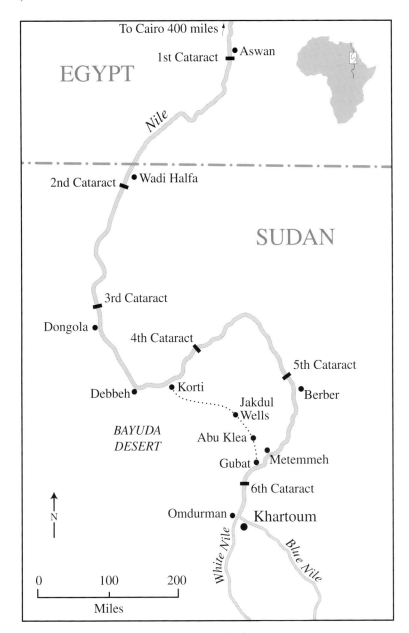

Map 3   Northern Sudan, 1884-5.

sailing craft, called nuggars, which could carry up to forty men with stores and ammunition. Shaped like the bowl of a spoon, these shallow-draughted boats were well suited to the river, but progress was painfully slow as they had to be hauled up the cataracts with ropes and towed by the men when there was no wind.[3] The effort required was enormous, with over 100 miles of broken water to be negotiated. Several nuggars were wrecked in the cataracts and two men from the battalion were drowned.

The Royal Sussex remained at Dongola for many weeks – enduring terrible sandstorms and plagues of white ants that rapidly devoured anything left on the ground – whilst the camel regiments rode up slowly from Aswan. When Wolseley reached Dongola he failed to convey any pressing sense of urgency. Indeed, as one officer had earlier observed, 'The expedition is planted and taking root here … there is nothing but confusion.'[4] The need to stockpile vast quantities of food, ammunition and supplies, including more than 1½ million tins of beef and almost as many pounds of ships biscuits, all took time.* Cecil was fully occupied on temporary secondment to the commissariat department, with responsibility for all the camels and transport in Dongola, a duty he was glad to relinquish at the earliest opportunity.

Learning to ride the camels unaided was no easy matter. 'I was no sooner on than I was off, and that was the case with most of us,' recalled Private Etherington of the 1st Royal Sussex, who complained that nearly all the camels were 'diseased and swarming with maggots'.[5] Camels are well adapted to carrying heavy loads in desert conditions, but the British did not know how to handle these cantankerous beasts. Great care was needed when approaching a camel that was annoyed, for it could spit foul-smelling vomit forwards or spray droppings at anyone to its rear. If caught unawares from behind a camel could kick out and break a man's leg, and males could inflict a nasty wound with their sharp teeth. Even when mounted a rider was not safe, for a camel could bend its head back and bite its rider's leg.[6]

Like everyone else Cecil learnt to ride a camel by trial and error – there were no army instruction manuals – and, no doubt, he fell off several times along the way. Camel and pony races were organised to amuse the troops and familiarise them with their mounts, and first prize in the pony race was a spear given by the Mudir of Dongola, which he had captured in his last fight near Debbeh, about 100 miles to the south. 'I was nowhere near the winner,' wrote Cecil, 'but Trafford came in second.' When some of the Guards Camel Corps passed through Dongola, 'the Mudir and some of the natives of the place were much impressed with their red coats,' commented Cecil, 'and seemed to think they would be quite sufficient to frighten the rebels away from Khartoum.' Indeed Gordon himself believed, as he wrote in his journal on 13 December, that 'one hundred men are all that we require, just to show themselves.'[7]

Early in December a bizarre rumour that the Mahdi was dead reached General Wolseley's headquarters at Dongola. 'I suppose like all other reports it is utterly untrue,' surmised Cecil correctly. Wolseley himself earnestly hoped it was true, noting in his diary, 'What an amount of anxiety his death would take off my shoulders! and how furious all these ambitious young officers would be if the

Opposite:
97. Officers, 1st Battalion Royal Sussex Regiment, Luxor, 1884. From the left, back row: QM McKiernan, Maj. Prevost, Maj. Sunderland, Lt O.C. Le Marchant (sitting, with white Foreign Service helmet above his knee), Maj. Kelly (profile, hands outstretched); middle row, Maj. Dowdall, Lt O.G. Ievers (sitting, wearing a Sola Topee helmet), Lt H.B. Scaife, Dr Headley, Lt P.E.P. Crawfurd; front row, seated: Surgeon Maconachie, Lt S.B. Graham, Lt E.H. Montrésor, Capt. Powell, Lt-Col. W. Tolson; foreground: Lt R.W. Jones.

---

* Troops were given one 2lb tin of beef for two days or three tins per week. Between August 1884 and June 1885 a total of 4,373,704 issues of provisions were made to troops on the Nile Expedition and, according to Wolseley's final report, the total weight of stores used was 17,929 tons (TNA(PRO) WO 147/39).

bubble was to burst without fighting!'[8] Back in England the general public were keenly aware that the expedition was in a race against time, yet by Christmas day – almost four months after leaving Wadi Halfa – most of the Royal Sussex had only reached Korti. From here, as part of the Desert Column, they would strike out across the Bayuda Desert in a desperate attempt to reach Khartoum by the shortest route, whilst the main force continued its slow progress upriver.

The Desert Column, including the recently formed Camel Corps and several hundred men from the 1st Royal Sussex, faced a tough challenge. Gordon had sent a message to say that Khartoum, besieged on three sides, would soon run out of food and could not hold out much longer. The need for speed, together with limited supplies of water, meant that the column was restricted to 1,800 men and some three hundred camel drivers and guides. Mindful of the fate of a considerably larger force under Colonel Hicks little more than a year earlier, they would have been keenly aware of the risks involved. The dervishes proved to be a formidable enemy, and as Kipling observed – using the term 'Fuzzy-Wuzzy' to refer to the Hadendowa, one of the Beja tribes from Eastern Sudan who greased their long, matted hair with mutton fat – these 'first-class fighting men' won the grudging respect of British soldiers. Private William Burge of the Guards Camel Regiment admired the courage of dervishes, who showed no fear and believed that through death they 'could make sure of Paradise and everlasting joy'.[9] And writing in his journal Captain Lionel Trafford, 1st Royal Sussex, commented that 'the bravery of the Arabs was beyond praise'.

Under the command of Brigadier-General Sir Herbert Stewart advance units of the Desert Column set off on 30 December, proceeding without incident as far as the first significant wells at Jakdul, approximately one hundred miles south-east of Korti. With the wells secured and supplies offloaded the camels returned to Korti, and the main body of the Desert Column rode out during the night of 9 January. Their objective was to cover more than 200 miles to Khartoum without delay, where they hoped to reinforce the town until the arrival of Wolseley's larger force. Following a line of wells the column, with some 2,900 camels and 160 horses, made steady progress, but finding the first wells dry carried on to those at El Howeiyat, still some distance from Jakdul. Here the limited supplies of water were 'as thick as pea soup and had a slimy flavour'.[10] With midday temperatures of over 100°F there was a serious risk of dehydration, and it took time to replenish supplies from the muddy wells. The daily water allowance was just two pints per man but the skin water bottles were porous and much water was lost, causing a desperate scramble for the foul water on arrival at the wells. Even the camels suffered: the British, largely through ignorance, overestimated the extent to which camels could go without food and water, and all too often the beasts were loaded incorrectly, causing open sores from chafing. Trafford later noted that 'the mortality amongst the baggage camels was very great'.

When the main column reached Jakdul a detachment from the Royal Sussex Regiment remained behind to guard the wells, whilst the Desert Column, including

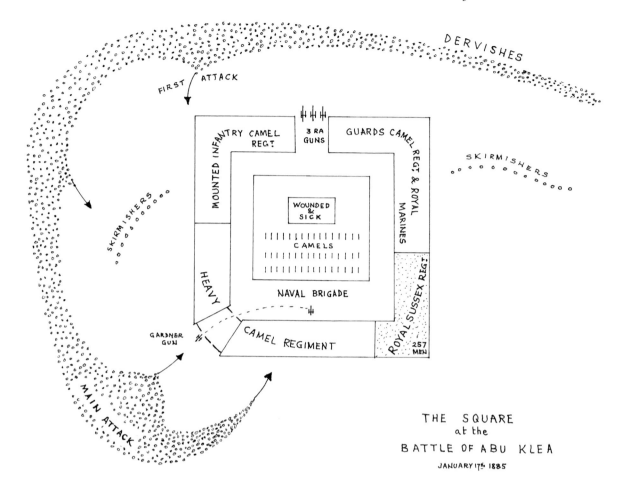

THE SQUARE
at the
BATTLE OF ABU KLEA
JANUARY 17th 1885

Cecil Le Marchant and some 250 men of the Royal Sussex, continued towards the wells at Abu Klea. They were now deep in enemy territory and a force of some 10,000 or more dervishes was waiting for them. As they approached Abu Klea scouts reported that the wells were held by a large enemy force. Stewart's men spent a sleepless night inside a hastily-prepared zareba consisting of thorn bushes, stones, camel saddles and baggage. They were harassed all night by sniper fire and the continuous sound of beating drums. Next morning, 17 January, Stewart decided to attack the Mahdist force. Leaving behind all non-essential stores, most of the camels and sufficient men to guard the zareba, he formed his men into a square with the baggage camels in the centre. Each camel could transport enough food and water for eight men for up to thirteen days, but they proved to be difficult to control in square formation. During the advance a number of men and some of the camels were hit by sniper fire, and recovery of the wounded on stretchers, which had to be tied to camels, continually disrupted the rear face of the square.

98. The Battle of Abu Klea, 1885.

Stewart advanced some two miles towards the wells and had at his disposal fewer than 1,500 men, three screw guns and a Gardner machine-gun. As the square moved slowly forward on foot towards a line of enemy banners a group of some 5,000 dervishes broke cover and charged towards the front left corner of the square, led by disciplined Ansar cavalrymen moving at considerable speed. The screw guns opened fire and the dervishes reacted by changing the direction of their attack, sweeping round towards the left rear corner of the square, where the presence of a group of Stewart's skirmishers temporarily prevented men on the left face from firing at the rapidly advancing enemy. The left rear corner of the square, already in some disarray, opened to allow the retiring skirmishers to enter and a naval party to run out the Gardner machine-gun, but it jammed after a few rounds and was quickly overrun.* Many of the single-shot Martini-Henry rifles also jammed due to sand in the mechanism, but volley-firing nevertheless inflicted heavy casualties on the enemy. However, rifle fire alone was insufficient to prevent many of the advancing spearmen from reaching the vulnerable left rear corner of the square, which was pressed back by sheer weight of numbers.

In the ensuing confusion a number of dervishes succeeded in breaking into the square but could not advance beyond the barrier formed by tethered camels. There followed a critical period of hand-to-hand fighting with bayonets, many of which were substandard and bent on impact. One eyewitness reported that 'the Sussex Regiment, though taken in the rear, rallied and fought desperately'.[11] Some of the troops in the rear rank of the front face, standing on slightly higher ground, turned about and fired on the enemy inside the square. None of those who had succeeded in breaking into the square survived. In the last action of this hard-fought battle the dervishes directed a cavalry charge against the right rear corner of the square but this was repulsed by sustained fire from the Heavy Camel Regiment and the Royal Sussex. With 1,100 of their comrades dead and as many wounded, the dervishes now gave up and walked away to regroup and fight another day. During this short but intense battle nine British officers and 65 other ranks were killed, and nine officers and 85 other ranks were wounded. Although the Royal Sussex Regiment's losses were relatively light – five killed and 26 wounded – those present were shaken by the ferocity of the dervish attack, which had threatened to overwhelm the British square.

Rapid communications and the presence of numerous war correspondents and artists generated intense interest in the race to save Gordon, ensuring that the Battle of Abu Klea caught the public imagination. Kipling commented that 'it was above all things necessary that England at breakfast should be amused and thrilled and interested, whether Gordon lived or died, or half the British Army went to pieces in the sand.'[12] Count Helmuth von Moltke called the Desert Column a band of heroes, and in his poem 'Vitaï Lampada' Sir Henry Newbolt glorified the action with these famous words:[13]

---

* Sir Henry Newbolt, in his well-known poem, refers to the Gardner gun as a 'Gatling'.

> The sand of the desert is sodden red, –
> Red with the wreck of a square that broke; –
> The Gatling's jammed and the Colonel dead,
> And the regiment blind with dust and smoke.
> The river of death has brimmed his banks,
> And England's far, and Honour a name,
> But the voice of a schoolboy rallies the ranks;
> 'Play up! play up! And play the game!'

With the battle over, Stewart moved forward to the wells at Abu Klea. There the men spent an uncomfortable and very cold night bivouacking in the open without blankets or greatcoats, as the baggage had not yet come up from the zareba. Bennet Burleigh, correspondent for the *Daily Telegraph*, described how the troops lay in square formation with their arms ready for instant use in case of attack. Each man had been issued with a pint of water, half his day's supply, and few slept that night. The next day, before the main column set out for Metemmeh and the Nile some 25 miles away, a stone fort was built for the wounded. One hundred men of the Royal Sussex, including Lieutenant Le Marchant, were given responsibility for guarding the wells and looking after the wounded, a daunting task in view of the thousands of dervishes still in the vicinity.

The Desert Column fought and won another battle in square formation before reaching the Nile on 21 January, though Stewart himself was mortally wounded by sniper fire. Sir Charles Wilson assumed command, and after a critical delay of several days at Gubat, embarked with 20 men of the Royal Sussex and some two hundred Sudanese soldiers in two armoured steamers sent by Gordon. In an effort to overawe the enemy, as Gordon had advised, the men of the Royal Sussex wore scarlet tunics borrowed from the Guards, but to no avail. As they approached Khartoum on 28 January it became clear that they were too late. Khartoum had fallen two days earlier and Gordon, who held out for 317 days, had been killed. When news of the death of Gordon – whom Wolseley called 'God's friend' – reached England there was considerable shock and public anger. People blamed Gladstone for his delay in authorising a relief expedition, and Queen Victoria openly expressed her displeasure. Gordon had said that failure to send military help would amount to an 'indelible disgrace' and now Gladstone, the Grand Old Man (GOM), was denounced as the MOG – Murderer of Gordon. This whole episode further increased the antipathy felt by the Le Marchant family towards the Liberals. It would be another 13 years before Kitchener avenged Gordon's death and defeated the Khalifa's army at Omdurman.

Unable to achieve its objective, the Desert Column was ordered to withdraw. British troops left Gubat for Abu Klea, where Cecil and his men had remained for almost a month. The shortage of transport camels was now so severe that most of the men had to march back across the stony desert all the way to Korti. When the column reached Abu Klea Major Herbert Kitchener learned that a large body of dervishes was approaching the wells, and to prevent the enemy from following and attacking the column as it withdrew across the desert he gave instructions for all the wells to be filled in. The troops reached Korti safely, but their boots and clothes were in a wretched state and many men walked into camp with bare feet. Trafford noted that the men of the Royal Sussex had slept in the open without tents from the time they left Korti early in January until their return two months later. Though 'the dust in this place is very bad', wrote Cecil, 'we are all delighted to see the hills and to have as much water as we care for'.

Their hardships were not yet over, however, and for the next nine weeks the Royal Sussex, including Cecil Le Marchant, were quartered at Abu Gus on the banks of the Nile, two days downstream from Korti by whaler. Rumours that they would return to Khartoum in the autumn to avenge Gordon's death swept the camp, and indeed such plans were discussed in government but never implemented.* On 1 June the battalion embarked once more in whalers for the journey back to Wadi Halfa, but descending the cataracts proved to be very hazardous and 'in one rough piece of water alone', wrote Trafford, 'one company [of Royal Sussex] lost all its boats'. No one was drowned in this incident, and the remainder of the journey from Wadi Halfa to Cairo by steamer was uneventful. During their three years in Egypt the battalion lost one officer and 118 men, eight of whom were killed in action or died of wounds. Most deaths, some ninety-five in all, occurred as a result of cholera and other diseases, though nine men drowned and six died from accidents, suicide, or 'sunstroke' – probably dehydration, a condition not properly understood in those days.

99. Cecil at home in the Rectory garden, Little Rissington, 1893.

Cecil returned to England in September 1885, and after an absence of more than four years arrived home at the Rectory with many stories to tell. His sisters were in awe of his various military exploits, as an extract in the family journal the following year suggests:

> You awoke one morning to find yourself famous … you were restored to health and returned to the land of the Pharaohs to receive your baptism of fire … you were one of the lucky companies of your famous regiment. You fought two pitched battles and many skirmishes. You made your name known – you wear medals and two clasps of your hard fought fields [in Egypt and the Sudan] – you have the medal for saving life.

The 'lucky companies' of the 1st Royal Sussex were those present at the Battle of Abu Klea, and Cecil considered

* When Russian troops invaded the Afghan village of Pendjeh in March 1885, it seemed for a time that the resulting dispute would lead to war between Britain and Russia. Such a possibility provided Gladstone with the excuse he needed to justify withdrawing British forces from the Sudan.

himself fortunate to have seen action and been under fire during the campaign. He had been given the opportunity to demonstrate that he possessed qualities which the Victorians esteemed in an officer – courage, *esprit de corps*, stoicism in the face of extreme discomfort, self-sacrifice, and steadfastness under fire. Officers like Captain Donisthorpe Donne, who had remained behind, felt bitter that they had been deprived of the chance to prove themselves in battle.[14] But although Cecil was 'present at the action at Abu Klea' and received the clasp awarded to all those involved in the action on 17 January, he had remained in the zareba with two companies of Royal Sussex guarding the stores and many of the camels. 'We had none of our subalterns in the square,' he wrote, 'in fact only three of us left the Gakdul wells and I was lucky enough to be one of them, but I was unfortunate being left behind to garrison the Abu Klea wells instead of going on to Metemmeh.'

Garrison life in England did not suit Cecil, and within a year he had secured a transfer to the 2nd Royal Sussex, then serving in India. The 2nd Battalion had once been the 107th Bengal Infantry, part of the Honourable East India Company's army and proud of its 'John Company' origins.* Required to learn Hindustani, Cecil struggled to reach the necessary standard. 'I am sorry to hear Cecil has failed again,' wrote Louis from Ferozepore, 'I cannot make it out as he has the very best *munshi* in the country and has been working now for some time. I am rather afraid I shall not have much chance as I have rather a poor class of *munshi*.'

100. A mountain stream near Dalhousie, 1887. The forests around Dalhousie, where wildlife was abundant, offered plenty of opportunities for 'good sport'.

During the summer of 1887 Cecil spent several months in Dalhousie, a hill-station in the Himalayan foothills close to Kashmir. Louis was also stationed there for the summer, and when they were not on duty or studying for military exams the brothers played plenty of tennis together. 'Cecil is looking very well but he is still a little deaf, though not so bad as he used to be,' wrote Louis. 'He has been so busy sketching lately that he has had little time to himself, his examination sketch takes place tomorrow.' Whenever he could Cecil liked to explore. Once, while out walking, he was startled to see lots of small rocks rolling down the steep hillside towards him. He looked up and saw that he was being bombarded by a troop of monkeys, so he hurriedly retreated. Wildlife was abundant in the mountain forests around Dalhousie, and during his stay a couple of officers from the 2nd Wiltshires 'had pretty good sport, they got eight bears, a lot of smaller skins and some very fine horns'. Cecil loved the area around Dalhousie, with its pleasant climate and spectacular scenery, and he often returned to neighbouring Kashmir during his periods of leave in India.

---

* An Indian nickname for the East India Company.

101. The subalterns' camp at Gharial, Murree Hills, May-September 1888, with Cecil Le Marchant on the extreme left. Note the assortment of chairs that the regiment brought with them to camp.

It was not long before Cecil was once more on active service, this time with the Hazara Field Force on one of the many North-West Frontier campaigns of this period. The remote and mountainous frontier region contained a number of strategic passes into India and was home to many local tribes – Afridis, Waziris, Mohmands and others – collectively known to the British as Pathans. The British attitude to the region was clearly expressed by General Sir George White, who said that 'the Indian government could not tolerate on its borders 200,000 of the most turbulent and finest fighting material in the world, unrestrained by civilised government and fired by fanaticism'.[15] When two British officers were killed in an attack on a remote outpost by tribesmen from the Black Mountain region on the north-western edge of the Hazara district, an expedition set out to punish the enemy and impose fines on their leaders in an effort to deter further incursions.

A total of 14,000 British and Indian troops, organised into four columns, made up the Hazara Field Force which took part in the Black Mountain Expedition of 1888. The 2nd Royal Sussex, part of the third column, burnt hostile villages and destroyed fortified towers as they advanced through the mountainous terrain, suffering only light casualties during the month-long campaign. By day, if they were not engaged in pursuing or punishing the enemy, they occupied their time making roads, and during the intensely cold nights men struggled to keep warm with just two blankets and a greatcoat each. Because of the terrain the battalion travelled lightly by contemporary standards, leaving their tents behind after the initial advance. Transport was kept to a minimum, with one mule carrying the kit of 10 men. Officers, whose baggage allowance on campaign was a generous 80 pounds, were allocated one mule between three.* The fiercest fighting involved the fourth column, which repulsed a suicidal charge by more than 180 'fanatical

102. Pathan tribesmen from the North-West Frontier region (now Pakistan).

ghazis' intent on driving out the enemies of Islam. After more fighting and destruction of villages the tribal leaders agreed to pay the fines imposed on them, and the field force withdrew. However, the region remained troublesome, requiring the dispatch of a second expedition two years later. These frontier campaigns – and there were more than 20 between 1863 and 1908 – were glamourised by writers such as Kipling and Henty, who wrote of daring deeds carried out with dash and bravado in pursuit of what they saw as Britain's mission to extend the boundaries of civilisation. Cecil Le Marchant earned further kudos and a campaign medal for his part in the Black Mountain Expedition, and General McQueen, the commanding officer, complimented the 2nd Battalion by saying that he had 'never seen a regiment with more dash and go'.

The battalion now returned to peacetime duty at Ferozepore, south of Lahore, taking over from the 1st East Lancs, his brother Louis' regiment. 'I don't think Cecil cares very much about this country,' wrote Louis to his mother. Because of his partial deafness Cecil must have found the social side of regimental life particularly trying, and he declined invitations to dances whenever he could. 'I think this place will suit Cecil down to the ground,' wrote Louis, 'he need not go out more than he likes and it is very quiet.' In *A History of the Royal Sussex Regiment* G.D. Martineau wrote, 'it was a military tenet of that age that an officer should work hard, ride hard and play hard; and if he also drank hard, it seemed

---

* Sometimes, if circumstances allowed, officers would hire their own transport to carry personal supplies on campaign. In the desert sands of the Sudan in 1884, to maintain the lifestyle to which he was accustomed, Sir Redvers Buller hired 46 camels to keep him supplied with magnums of the best champagne and luxury items from Fortnum & Mason (Asher, p.185). What Cecil and other impecunious officers thought of such excesses we can only imagine.

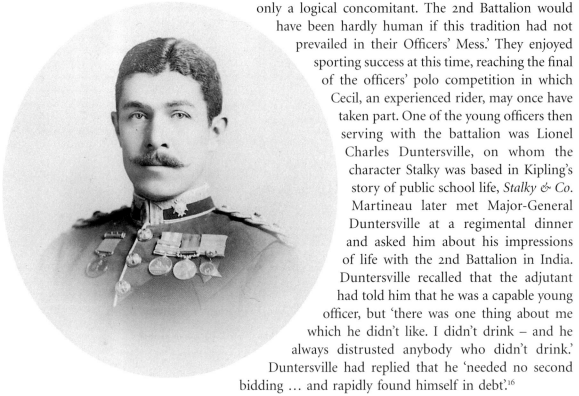

103. Capt. O.C. Le Marchant, Dublin, c.1890.

only a logical concomitant. The 2nd Battalion would have been hardly human if this tradition had not prevailed in their Officers' Mess.' They enjoyed sporting success at this time, reaching the final of the officers' polo competition in which Cecil, an experienced rider, may once have taken part. One of the young officers then serving with the battalion was Lionel Charles Duntersville, on whom the character Stalky was based in Kipling's story of public school life, *Stalky & Co.* Martineau later met Major-General Duntersville at a regimental dinner and asked him about his impressions of life with the 2nd Battalion in India. Duntersville recalled that the adjutant had told him that he was a capable young officer, but 'there was one thing about me which he didn't like. I didn't drink – and he always distrusted anybody who didn't drink.' Duntersville had replied that he 'needed no second bidding … and rapidly found himself in debt'.[16]

In 1890 Cecil returned home on board the troopship *Crocodile* in charge of some men who had exceeded their time. He had been away from England for more than three years, but was soon restless and applied to join the Egyptian Army, which was under British command. Herbert Kitchener was Adjutant-General (and later Sirdar) of the Egyptian Army, and Cecil had almost certainly met him at Abu Klea during the Sudan campaign five years earlier. Robert Le Marchant wrote to General Sir Edmund Whitmore to ask him to use his influence to secure a transfer for Cecil, but later noted in his diary, 'Sir E. Whitmore cannot help Cecil about getting into the Egyptian Army – poor man!' Cecil, now a captain, rejoined the 1st Battalion and spent five years stationed in Dublin, and later Fermoy, before returning with the battalion to Brighton, where he spent much of the next three years. 'I am glad Cecil likes Brighton,' wrote Louis from Burma, 'he seems to be having a very good time there and all the people most kind to the Regt.' Cecil often came home to Little Rissington, and if Basil was there the two brothers loved to go out shooting or spend the day playing golf on the new course at Stow-on-the-Wold. During the early years of the Cotswold Golf Club gentlemen members competed over 21 holes for a monthly medal, which Cecil won in February 1899.

The following month Cecil was promoted to the rank of major, despite suffering from increasing deafness, which his London specialist could not cure. In April he departed for India to rejoin the 2nd Battalion, then stationed at

Sialkot on the border with Kashmir. Within months of his arrival he travelled to Peshawar to visit Edward's grave and speak to officers in The Hampshire Regiment who had known him well. His letter home giving an account of his visit has not survived. Soon after his return to Sialkot plague broke out in the district and no troops were allowed to leave the station. As a result Cecil, now second in command, spent endless hours giving the men military instruction, 'which becomes very monotonous after a couple of days,' he wrote. The tedium was broken in December 1901 when the battalion was given responsibility for some 490 Boer prisoners of war who had been sent to India from South Africa. Because prison camps in South Africa were considered vulnerable to attack from the Boers the military authorities shipped prisoners to various parts of the Empire, and in India a total of 17 such camps were built. The Battalion later received high praise for their handling of the Boer prisoners.

For Cecil, rather a solitary individual who did not relish colonial life, time passed slowly at Sialkot. An excellent shot, he was a member of the team that won the Army Rifle Association revolver shooting competition – the Connaught Cup – four years in succession. Each year he longed for his three months' leave, which he spent in Kashmir. His first leave was ruined when he was struck down with

104. Officers, 1st Battalion Royal Sussex Regiment in full dress uniform with white Foreign Service helmets and spikes, Beggars Bush Barracks, Dublin, July 1892. In the centre, seated, is Maj.-Gen. G.H. Moncrieff, commanding Dublin District, and Capt. Le Marchant is seated second from the right. The three officers in the front row are Lieutenants Hawker, Daunt and Montrésor, their rank denoted by gold lace on the cuffs in a single broad band with a narrow stripe above.

105. Officers from the 2nd Battalion Royal Sussex Regiment, winners of the Connaught Cup – the prize for the Army Rifle Association revolver shooting competition – in 1899. Cecil Le Marchant (far left) is wearing a black armband in memory of his brother Edward, assassinated in Peshawar earlier that year.

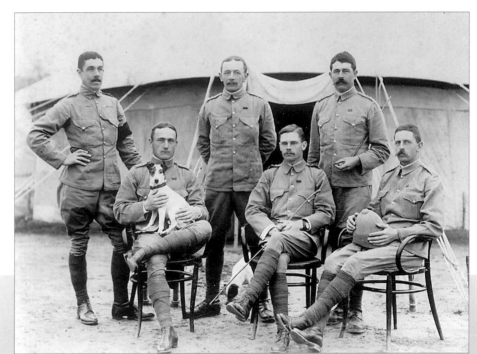

106. Srinagar, Kashmir, 1891.

typhoid; for more than two months he was slowly nursed back to health at the Cottage Hospital in Srinagar, where he made a full recovery. From his sickbed he looked out over a garden full of exotic flowers to the distant hills beyond covered with snow, a scene that lifted his morale and helped overcome the monotony of convalescence. The following year he returned, drawn by the tranquillity and beauty of the place, to relax and make the most of the sporting opportunities available. Duck and snipe shooting were plentiful, and he enjoyed some excellent fishing in the exquisitely lovely lakes and waterways around Srinagar, and in nearby mountain streams.

In December 1902 Major Le Marchant returned to England with his battalion and three months later, at the age of 42, he retired from the Army on a pension of £200 a year. He now turned his hand to poultry farming, at first in Northamptonshire, and later at his farm near Cheltenham, 'where he hopes to prosper by keeping poultry,' commented his father; 'it is the opinion of most people that he will lose stock and block.' Initially Cecil had some success, and his Black Leghorn cockerel won first prize at the Derby Show in September 1905. However, he did not prosper and soon afterwards he gave up and came to live at the Rectory in Little Rissington.

107. Cecil feeding his chickens at the Reddings, Cheltenham, 1906.

108. Annie, Dora, Cecil and Basil Le Marchant amongst bundles of cut osiers in the Rectory garden, Little Rissington, 1904.

Throughout the 1920s and 1930s Cecil travelled to the Continent almost every year, often spending a month or so in Lausanne receiving treatment for his deafness. Sometimes he would travel on to Italy with his sisters, though his interest in the cultural treasures of Florence and elsewhere seems to have been limited. In 1936 he bought Charlton Manor, a substantial house in Cheltenham, where he lived in comfort with several of his sisters. When war broke out, finding it impossible to retain domestic staff, they sold up and moved back once more to the family home in Little Rissington. Now old and frail, it was not long before he was fined for breaching blackout regulations. In 1943, after he had gone to bed one evening, the roller blind in his room fell down. As he tried to put it up and so avoid another fine, he fell backwards off a stepladder and cracked his head. He died in hospital in Cheltenham a few days later, aged 82. Deafness had forced him to relinquish his military career early, and for 40 years he had lived a quiet, socially impaired, life. For a man who loved action and excitement, who had seen active service on two continents, this must have been a cruel disappointment.

109. A bronze statuette presented to the 1st Battalion Royal Sussex Regiment by the surviving members of the 35th Regimental Dinner Club, between 1910 and 1926. The 'under mentioned old officers of the 35th Foot' – several of whom had served during the Nile campaign – were Maj.-Gen. J.C. Young (Colonel of the Regiment, 1914-26), Col. Bowen Buscarlet, Col. C.H.W. Café, Col. H. Browse Scaife, Col. W. Tolson, Maj. Cecil Le Marchant, Capt. A. Harvey Bathurst and Capt. Richard Trimen.

Three Campaigns; Three Continents

LOUIS ST GRATIEN LE MARCHANT
(1866-1914)

Louis, the 13th child and youngest son of Robert and Eliza Le Marchant, was born on a cold winter's day in December 1866 in Little Rissington. Under the guidance of his older sisters the young boy grew up to love and appreciate the countryside. 'Your early life was a sadly disordered one in the Cotswolds, and your speech was of the country,' one of them commented. A generous uncle paid for Louis to attend Somersetshire College in Bath, where he made sufficient progress to pass the preliminary exams for Sandhurst. However, he subsequently failed to meet the entry requirements, and on leaving school he was sent to a Captain Pinney in London for private tuition. In February 1885

110. This photograph of Little Rissington in 1893 was probably taken by Evelyn Le Marchant, a keen photographer, and printed by his youngest sister, Ethel.

Robert Le Marchant used his influence to secure a commission for Louis in the 3rd Battalion The Gloucestershire Regiment (Militia). 'Major Bontein has been very civil in giving him the vacancy,' commented Edward, 'I am sure Louis will like the Regiment, but they are a very expensive lot.' After completing his initial training in Bristol he was sent to a crammer in Broadstairs to study for the Militia competitive examination, and a year later he achieved a high enough pass to obtain a regular commission. It had been a struggle, but in November 1886 Louis was gazetted to the 1st Battalion The East Lancashire Regiment (previously the 30th Foot), and the following January he sailed for India aboard the troopship *Jumna* to join his regiment in Ferozepore.

111. Port Said, *c.*1885, with several troopships in port. SS *Grecian Monarch* (one funnel and four masts, torpedoed and sunk by a German submarine in 1918) is on the left nearest to the camera.

Louis' first impressions of regimental life in India were recorded in the family journal by his sisters in March 1887: 'L. Le Marchant, 30th Regiment, writing from Deolali informs his family of his detention there owing to an outbreak of measles in the draft he is to accompany up country. Deolali [from which the expression 'doolally' is derived] is not a lively station and possesses a very expensive Mess. There are quail and snipe in the neighbourhood, and the holy city of Nasik is well worth visiting.' When at last he reached Ferozepore, about fifty miles

south of Lahore, Louis wrote home to say how much he liked his regiment. Denis Carey, a close family friend from Guernsey who was stationed nearby, came over to welcome Louis. 'He is most good-natured,' commented Louis, 'he drove me over to some sports given by the Artillery the other day. He is going to Umballa next week for the polo tournament.'

Soon, however, Louis realised that he would find it impossible to live on his pay alone. 'There is no doubt our Mess is expensive compared with other regiments,' he wrote. In a letter to his father Louis explained that his pay was just 202 rupees a month, but his expenses during the hot weather

112. 16th Lancers Polo Team in Umballa for the tournament, March 1896. From the left: Capt. H.P. Gough, Capt. H. Dugdale, Col. J. Babington, Mr Leny.

– including his Mess bill (which varied between 120 and 190 rupees a month), drinks, subscriptions, bungalow, house servants, supplies of ice and punkah coolies – came to a minimum of 216 rupees.* Neither did this include his tailor's bills or the upkeep of his pony. A pony was essential because his bungalow was some distance from the barracks, and he had to travel many miles each day in the heat. Furthermore, he had to undertake periods of duty at the fort a mile or so outside the cantonment. By living very frugally he managed to keep his Mess bill well below that of most other officers in the regiment. 'I have given up the Club and the rackets,' he wrote later, 'and drink nothing but water, in fact so do several of us who are no better off than myself.' Initially, he could not even afford a *munshi* to teach him Hindustani. Denis Carey wrote to Louis' uncle James to say that his nephew could not get by without an allowance, but the request for help was declined. 'I suppose he thinks he has done enough for me and perhaps thinks I ought to go to the Staff Corps,' Louis explained to his father. 'Do you think you could let me have £3 a month,' he asked, 'I have been very carefully over my accounts and I don't see how I can possibly do with less.' His father agreed to an allowance of £10 a quarter.

Louis settled in quickly to the routines of regimental life in Ferozepore. 'We are already beginning our hot weather habits,' he wrote, 'we go to Church now at half past six in the morning and parade on other days at 7. The worst of this getting up so early is that it makes such a long day of it, and from eleven till five we cannot do much outside.' Despite the heat, when part of the battalion moved up to the hills Louis asked to remain with those staying behind, for he

---

* There were 16 rupees to the pound in those days.

wished to avoid the additional expense of accommodation in Dalhousie. His request was refused, however, and he proceeded to Dalhousie where he spent the summer months. There he met his brother Cecil, and together they found accommodation at the *Bull's Head Hotel*. For the first couple of months the climate was very pleasant, but it became unusually hot when the rains failed to appear. 'One of our men died last night of sunstroke,' wrote Louis, 'he was on the march up here and died about 20 miles out … we buried him this evening. This is the third funeral I have been to since I came up here.'

At first, Louis found little by way of entertainment in Dalhousie, though later in the season a touring company put on a series of excellent concerts and theatricals. A few dances were organised, but as Louis had not yet learned to dance he did not attend. Notable amongst those staying in Dalhousie for the season was General Sir Charles Gough, who had won a VC during the Indian Mutiny and commanded a brigade throughout the Afghan War of 1878-80, 'but one does not see much of him,' Louis commented. When many people left to spend five days under canvas at Khajiar, about eleven miles away, Louis and Cecil did not go as they did not have ponies at Dalhousie. At Khajiar, a beautiful expanse of open grassland surrounding a small lake, the assembled company relaxed and enjoyed days of horse racing, cricket and polo matches, and dances in the evenings.

113. Lt Louis Le Marchant, 1886.

A small army of servants preceded them, pitching their tents, cooking the meals and attending to their every need.

Before leaving England Louis had agreed to collect and send home to his sisters some exotic butterflies and bird skins, and the months he spent in Dalhousie gave him an opportunity to fulfil his promise. 'I will get you some jungle fowl as soon as I have the chance,' he wrote, 'also some peacocks, I saw some splendid ones when marching up here, but not close enough to get a shot.' The more exotic the species, the greater was the challenge to shoot one to add to the growing collection of stuffed birds at home in the Rectory. 'I have seen some woodpeckers with beautiful plumages,' he added later, 'I should like to try and get some of their skins but I believe they are very difficult to keep.' Louis was greatly impressed by the variety of magnificent butterflies and moths to be seen and he had soon caught and preserved enough to fill an entire case, but getting them home safely was more of a challenge. 'I am afraid they may get smashed to pieces going down country,' he commented. Though he saw several snakes they did not worry him unduly, but the scorpions were a terrible nuisance. 'You find them in your slippers and all over the shop,' he wrote. 'We caught about half a dozen the other night and put them in a plate, one at a time, and lit a fire round them, they went all round trying to get out, but finding they could not they walked into the middle and then stung themselves to death.'

114. Officers of the 1st Battalion East Lancashire Regiment (formerly the 30th Foot) in regimental blazers, Ferozepore 1887. In the front row, centre, is Louis Le Marchant.

When Louis returned to Ferozepore the worst of the hot weather was over, but the following summer he could not escape to the hills and had to endure many discomforts. Terrible dust storms lasting for up to three days darkened the skies and made life very unpleasant. 'We had lamps burning the whole day,' wrote Louis. 'You could not keep the dust out of your bungalow, it lay about an inch thick over everything.' At the fort he was plagued by sandflies and white ants, which got into everything. 'Out here one has to cover all one's things up,' he wrote, 'at dinner they get into your plate and tumblers, and the floor is simply alive with insects.' When the time came for the battalion to move to Benares Louis was very glad to be leaving the extremes of heat and cold and the dust storms of the Punjab.

Benares, however, proved to be rather a disappointment, and Louis did not much care for the place. 'There is very little going on here,' he complained in a letter to his family. Though he played badminton and rackets several times a week, he preferred to ride. But as few people outside his own regiment enjoyed riding he had little opportunity to compete in gymkhanas – so much a part of station life elsewhere in India – and it would be several years before he had the chance to play polo regularly. Hunting jackals with dogs provided an alternative form of amusement, though these wily creatures were difficult to drive out of the jungle into the open and were rarely killed. 'I think the dogs are rather afraid to catch the beasts,' observed Louis after another unsuccessful hunt.

Louis enjoyed many different sports including fishing, but he had not brought his rod out to India. This he now regretted, for there was plenty of good fishing along the Ganges. When the rains came, bringing relief from the intense heat of summer, Louis noticed that fish would appear, as if spontaneously, in the ponds that formed in almost every compound. About two months after the rains had broken he estimated that these fish weighed between two and three pounds. Where they came from he had no idea, as the ground dried out and became rock hard in the hot weather. 'Some people say it rains fish, others that they remain buried in the mud at the bottom till the rain comes again,' commented Louis. Though it may seem implausible, both explanations are possible. Occurrences of fish falling with the rain are rare but not unknown, and instances have been recorded worldwide. Indeed, a rain of fish in Benares was recorded in scientific literature in 1833.[1] The strong winds which accompany the south-west monsoon, when they meet the cold north-easterly winds from the Himalayas, can create whirlwinds and waterspouts with the power to pick up water, fish and all, and carry it some distance. When the updraught subsides, the fish fall to the ground during the heavy rainstorms which ensue. In this case, however, the fish Louis observed were probably catfish or cuchia, which could indeed survive the dry weather, either by moving short distances over land or by burrowing deep down into the mud.

Louis' financial difficulties were eased temporarily when he was appointed acting quartermaster, for which he received an additional 45 rupees a month. Like his brothers before him he was tempted to join the Indian Staff Corps, which would have given him an immediate increase in pay. Louis had sought Basil's advice before his brother returned to England, but after weighing up the options he decided to remain with his regiment. Shortly before going on leave Louis had to prepare a report on the state of some seventy miles of railway line. The work was tedious, but he delayed completing the assignment as he had heard that there was some excellent shooting up the line towards Lucknow. As soon as he finished his report he departed for Ranikhet, a military hill-station more than 6,000 feet up in the Himalyan foothills with spectacular views of the twin peaks of Nandi Devi in the distance. The road up passed through Naini Tal, itself a picturesque hill-station beside a long, narrow lake surrounded by steep hills. Nine years earlier, following several days of torrential monsoon rain, Naini Tal had been the scene of a terrible catastrophe. When a landslip crushed part of the *Victoria Hotel* killing many of those inside, the Commissioner had requested immediate military assistance. As soldiers were digging for survivors an overhanging cliff collapsed, permanently entombing all the soldiers, together with the hotel, library and adjacent assembly rooms.

Ranikhet was the perfect place to combine relaxation with study, and having at last secured the help of a good *munshi* Louis worked hard to gain proficiency in two native languages, subsequently passing the Higher Standard in Urdu and the Lower Standard in Persian. From his bungalow, which he shared with Major

Bannatyne from his regiment, he could look out over some forty acres of what had once been a tea garden. 'There are any amount of leopards, small deer, pheasants and partridges in it,' wrote Louis, 'and a bear comes up at night and eats the fruit off the trees.' The proximity of so much wildlife was not without hazard, however, and one evening a leopard carried off his young spaniel. Two nights later the leopard returned and seized another dog from their verandah, but released it when an officer staying there rushed out and scared it away. 'The dog was bitten in the neck and will, I think, die of the effects,' commented Louis.

After three years in Benares Louis was granted one year's leave. He sailed for England in January 1892 and arrived home four weeks later. Robert observed that Louis 'left us five years ago in snow and now returns in snow from India'. Over the next month the weather remained intensely cold with several more snowfalls, and for Louis the change from the heat and humidity of Bengal could not have been greater. He spent much of his leave shooting and fishing, playing tennis and cricket, and visiting relatives. In December he obtained an indulgence passage on the troopship *Euphrates* and returned to India to rejoin his battalion in Lucknow.

Lucknow – a name associated with the great struggles of the Mutiny 35 years earlier – was a much more lively station than Benares. 'I think I shall like this place very much,' wrote Louis not long after his arrival. He moved into a spacious and very pleasant bungalow which he shared with four other officers, conveniently located close to the officers' mess. At first he was very busy calling on the seven other regiments stationed there, and soon the spring social season at Lucknow was at its height. 'Next week the Polo Tournament begins and after that the races, and Lucknow will be crowded with people coming in from outside,' he wrote. The Assault at Arms, with a variety of contests and displays over several days – including tent pegging and artillery driving – was most

115. An officer's bungalow, Lucknow, c.1895.

entertaining, but for Louis the highlight was a musical ride past by the 16th Lancers. Another year the 16th Lancers amused everyone with a performance of *Ali Baba* featuring a number of new songs written especially for the occasion. 'There was a large civil station as well as a military one,' wrote a young cavalry officer, 'so there were plenty of ladies and we led a gay social life.'[2] And in the autumn the racing season began again. 'Today is the great day, Army Cup day,' wrote Louis, who watched Lieutenant Gough of the 16th Lancers ride Garryowen to victory.

Lucknow possessed two very good clubs around which much of the social life revolved, and Louis was quick to join one. 'Nearly everyone in the Station turns

116. For an assault at arms or a march past, as here in Meerut, ladies watched the proceedings from the comfort of their carriages, 1890s.

up here in the evening,' he wrote. Confronted with such a full and varied social life a young subaltern without substantial private means had to be wary of the attentions of unattached young ladies on the lookout for prospective husbands. Marriage was simply not an option for Louis this early in his career, and as he could not risk incurring debts he had no prospect of repaying he declined invitations when he felt he could do so without causing offence. At gymkhanas he competed in events such as the Polo Ball Race – round a flag and back before hitting a goal – but he steered clear of the Affinity Stakes, in which gentlemen were partnered by ladies. In this event men rode over to their partners, assisted them onto their mounts, and then each couple rode back hand in hand without letting go, the first couple to cross the line being the winners. In the Lucknow Regatta of 1895 Louis rowed for his regiment in the pairs race, narrowly losing to the eventual winners, but he did not enter the mixed events.

In those days Thursday was a holiday for the Army throughout India, and on Thursdays and Sundays in season Louis liked to go shooting in the marshes and lagoons around Lucknow. 'I was out shooting on Sunday and got 24 duck and teal,' he wrote. 'I have seen very few wild geese about so far, they should be in soon now. It is great fun shooting them but they are difficult to get at unless you can find their feeding ground.' Some of his fellow officers went after big game – Lieutenant Lawrence's share of a successful bag from a shooting trip in

the Central Provinces was one tiger and a very fine leopard. Louis' only trophy was a black buck, the horns of which he sent home to England. 'If I am out here next year I will try and get more,' he wrote, 'the worst of it is that they want such a lot of looking after out here or they get eaten by animals at once.'

An officer's life was not all play, however. A month under canvas on manoeuvres and several weeks of musketry practice for the battalion each year kept Louis very busy, and much work had to be done in preparation for birthday parades and inspections by visiting dignitaries. These Louis regarded as 'a great nuisance', and when Prince Albert Victor visited Benares in 1890 Louis was delighted that his stay had been brief. An ambitious officer worked hard and sought opportunities to improve his skills and promotion prospects, and Louis was no exception. He attended advanced courses on musketry and, some years later, military engineering, which he passed with distinction. And the comfortable routine of daily life could be seriously disrupted by illness and disease – 93 men died when a terrible cholera epidemic struck the battalion in 1894. Many letters of condolence had to be written to the families of soldiers back in England.

Louis kept himself usefully occupied in several ways. From time to time he was called upon to act as interpreter at courts martial – a responsibility he found particularly onerous. An awkward case arose during the months he spent on detachment at Chakrata – an awful place with very little to do, according to Louis,

117. Officers of the 1st Battalion East Lancashire Regiment in a variety of regimental uniforms, Lucknow 1895. From the left, fourth row: H. Maclean, R. Cheales, C. Mears, J. Baumgartner, Capt. E.A. Daubeny, G. Stuart, Capt. F.H. Trent; third row: W. Cooper, G. Lawrence, Maj. W. Scott, Capt. Finch, Capt. C. Haynes, Capt. T. Capper, Capt. F. Derham, Capt. H. Twynam, Lt L. St G. Le Marchant; second row: Capt. H.M. Browne, Maj. H. Evans, Lt-Col. W. Little, L. Head; front row: B. De Gex, W. Fletcher.

118. Louis passed his military engineering course with distinction. Here, officers are attending a bridging class at RMC Sandhurst in 1888.

'the ugliest country I have seen at a hill station' – when one of the commanding officer's servants was arrested. The CO there, a major in the Highland Light Infantry who spoke no Urdu, asked Louis to accompany him to the district magistrate's court, where he tried to intercede on behalf of his servant, much to Louis' disgust. The magistrate ignored the CO's intervention and sentenced 'the wretched man' to a month in prison. 'I think our CO is quite mad,' commented Louis, 'I believe he was once in an Asylum for a year, I wonder the Magistrate did not turn him out for contempt of court.' At Chakrata, as elsewhere, the working day began very early for Louis. By 7 a.m. he had breakfasted and ridden three miles to commence rifle practice at the range, but by noon his day's work was usually complete. After lunch he was free to go for a walk, play tennis, or study Persian.

During periods of local leave Louis headed for the hills on shooting and fishing expeditions. Despite such pleasant diversions, however, every officer hoped for the chance to go on active service, and an opportunity arose when trouble broke out once more on the North-West Frontier. The British endeavoured to control this remote region by seeking the cooperation of local rulers in return for subsidies, but such arrangements were always fragile and susceptible to intrigue and treachery. In 1892 the Mehtar (ruler) of Chitral, who had cooperated with the government of India's British representative, died and a family power struggle broke out between rival factions, resulting in the successive murders of two self-proclaimed rulers and the eventual accession of a candidate unacceptable to the British Resident, Surgeon-Major Robertson. Robertson refused to recognise Sher

Afzal and occupied the fort at Chitral with a force of 400 Sikhs and Kashmiris. In early March 1895 Sher Afzal, supported by neighbouring tribes suspicious of British encroachments into the region, laid siege to the fort.

The small mountain state of Chitral lay close to the north-eastern corner of Afghanistan, with the Hindu Kush forming its northern boundary. Robertson and his small force in the fort at Chitral, 190 miles north of Peshawar by the shortest route, were now cut off. Any rescue expedition from Peshawar would have to enter this hostile and mountainous terrain and reach those beseiged before their supplies ran out. A relief force of three brigades under Major-General Low was assembled at Peshawar, and at the same time a small force of 400 Kashmiri troops commanded by Colonel Kelly set out from the garrison at Gilgit, to the east of Chitral. Louis was recalled for active service from the Standing Camp at Ranikhet where he had been adjutant and, eager for glory, was 'quite delighted at the prospect of some fighting'. He arrived at Jalala, about 35 miles north-east of Peshawar, with almost four hundred pounds of kit. 'I had it all packed to send back to Lucknow,' wrote Louis, 'but finding at the last moment there was plenty of transport I brought it on and have still got it.' But at Jalala he had to leave most of it behind. Because of the need for speed the relief force marched without tents and with as little baggage as possible – just 10 pounds per man including a blanket weighing nearly five pounds, and 40 pounds per officer – yet despite this the column was supported by some 10,000 camels, 7,000 bullocks, 5,000 mules, 4,600 donkeys and 3,500 ponies – a total of more than 30,000 transport animals. Huge quantities of food and forage had to be guided over mountain passes, across rivers and through rocky terrain where there was often no discernible path. 'I don't know how they are going to pay for the show,' wrote Louis, 'I believe the transport alone is costing a lakh [100,000 rupees] a month.'

The East Lancs, part of General Low's relief force of 15,000 men, were given responsibility for guarding the lines of communication, an important task in view of the size of the transport column and the nature of the terrain. General Low's force made steady progress but had to overcome stiff resistance at the strategically important Malakand Pass, which had never before been crossed by British troops. The East Lancs reached Malakand Pass a day or two after the fighting. 'The place was covered with dead bodies,' wrote Louis 10 days later, 'most of them have been buried but you still come across one now and then.' The main force pressed on and had to fight again to secure a safe crossing of the

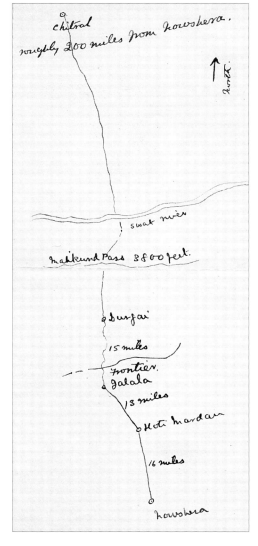

119. Sketch-map of Chitral drawn by Louis Le Marchant, June 1895.

120. Lower camp, Malakand Pass, Chitral Relief Expedition, 1895. The upper camp can be seen just below the top of the pass.

Swat and Panjkora rivers. When hostile tribesmen destroyed a raft bridge built by the engineers, a detachment of guides was despatched to punish and burn local villages. Some of the troops crossed over on inflated animal skins to help secure the river banks, and plans were made to send a small column forward to reach the besieged garrison without delay. Meanwhile, Colonel Kelly's small force overcame tremendous odds and reached the fort at Chitral on 20 April. The siege had lasted for seven weeks, and during that time the garrison survived on inferior half rations and fought an action to prevent the enemy from tunnelling under one of the towers to explode a mine. General Low's column eventually reached Chitral on 16 May, secure in the knowledge that the garrison was safe.

The East Lancs spent almost four months at Malakand Pass guarding the lines of supply and building roads, a tedious and potentially vulnerable duty in an isolated and wild mountain region. Distant views of Nanga Parbat could not adequately compensate for the uncomfortable conditions they had to endure, and during their stay 14 men died from sickness. 'We are all rather disgusted at being kept up here till September as there is nothing whatever to do and it is very slow,' wrote Louis, who was extremely disappointed not to have seen any action. The battalion now split into three separate camps; at the lower camp daytime temperatures inside the tents reached 115°F. Those at the higher camp escaped the dust and heat, but they were buffeted by storms and high winds which blew with such force that some tents were swept away. In the evenings they played hockey on flat ground at the lower camp. 'It is a very good game and gives one lots of exercise,' wrote Louis. He cut several sticks from the wood of olive trees further down the valley. Entertainment had to be improvised, and several light-hearted concerts put on by volunteers proved to be especially popular.

To break the monotony, Louis and Captain Browne of the East Lancs walked to Chitral during a period of local leave to see the fort for themselves. 'It is rather nice marching up here and a great change to remaining on the Malakand,' wrote Louis. 'I am very glad I came. We crossed over the Lowari Pass which has snow on the top and passed through a cutting where it was about 10 feet deep. It was so cold up there but a pleasant change after the heat.' They reached Chitral, a distance of almost 150 miles over rough terrain, in 10 days, 'and some of them good long ones too'. Louis was impressed by the beauty of the Chitral valley, surrounded on either side by steep, barren mountains. A river swollen by melting snow rushed down the valley, and dotted everywhere were orchards and gardens full of fruit, mostly apricots, with grapes growing wild in abundance. In the distance a 23,000-foot snow-capped peak rose above the lesser ridges of the Hindu Kush. Crossing over an old wooden bridge 60 feet above the river the two officers, tired after their long march, entered the fort, where they were cordially entertained by the 4th Gurkhas. The following day Captain Browne and Louis set off on the long march back to Malakand, where they had to endure two further

121. The Fort at Chitral, which was under siege for seven weeks. It took Louis 10 days to walk to Chitral from the Malakand Pass, his base for almost four months. (*Illustrated London News*, 20 April 1895.)

months of inactivity. Their commanding officer, Lieutenant-Colonel Little, could tolerate it no longer and departed for Simla on leave. 'I think he was thoroughly sick of roughing it up here, besides being ill,' wrote Louis, 'the last month he was up here he never moved out of his chair and I could hardly get him to sign his name. Major Wright is commanding now, I am glad to say.'

To make life more comfortable after his return to Malakand Louis extended his living quarters. 'I have been building a small room on to my tent which is a few yards off an old Buddhist wall,' he wrote. 'I have made a large window in the wall and thatched over the space between my tent and the wall, and I get a splendid view from my window right across the Swat valley about twenty miles and then up to the snows beyond.' He was greatly relieved when the battalion was recalled from the pass and returned once more to Lucknow. 'I am afraid we shall have it rather warm going down but as I shall be riding I don't mind much myself,' he commented, 'they are allowing the men a pound of ice every day and are only going to put four men in a carriage in the train.' New forts were built at Malakand and nearby Chakdara to defend the route to Chitral, but any move by the British which could be interpreted as an indication of intended military occupation – including the construction of roads and telegraph lines – aroused the opposition of local mullahs, and two years later there were further uprisings in the frontier region.

After a further six months in Lucknow – during which 180 men were hospitalised with malaria – Louis accompanied the battalion to Thayetmyo in Burma, 200 miles north of Rangoon on the Irrawaddy River. Within the cantonment officers and soldiers alike lived in bungalows built on piles for protection against flooding during the monsoon rains. The area underneath each bungalow was paved and covered with asphalt, and for much of the year it was here that the men dined and played skittles. To keep themselves occupied officers played plenty of tennis, rackets and golf, but at Thayetmyo the twice-weekly games of polo on small Burmese ponies proved particularly popular. Gymkhanas were held fortnightly, and even in this isolated jungle outpost it was possible to generate enough support to stage a successful race meeting over three days. Some officers went on shooting trips into the surrounding jungle, where a typical bag included barking deer, jungle fowl and an occasional panther. During his stay at Thayetmyo Louis was promoted to the rank of captain; for more than two years he had been the senior subaltern in the regiment, and he had grown increasingly frustrated that a vacancy for promotion had not arisen sooner. Now, at last, he would command his own company. But he was impatient to return home after almost five years overseas. 'I am getting so tired of India, and this incessant heat,' he wrote.* In

122. Louis (centre) on board the transport/ troopship *Clive*, a Royal Indian Marine Ship, 1896.

---

* Burma, 5 December 1896. For Louis, 'India' was synonymous with the East Indies, encompassing much of SE Asia.

123. Close to the surrounding jungle, the Officers' Mess at Thayetmyo, 1890s.

June 1897, after spending more than a year in Burma – including a brief spell acting as Deputy Assistant Adjutant-General in Rangoon – Louis was delighted to return to England. For the next two and a half years he was based at Portsmouth, and for Louis this was to be his longest period of service in England. During a military career of 28 years he was to spend 21 years abroad defending the interests of the British Empire.

124. Enjoying a period of home leave, Louis (left) prepares to explore the Cotswolds with his sisters Florence and Ethel and brothers Gaspard and Evelyn, 1897.

At the outbreak of the Boer War Louis had just begun a tour of garrison duty with his regiment in Jersey. The 1st East Lancs had not been included in the initial mobilisation, but after the disasters of Black Week the battalion was recalled to Aldershot, where many regular reservists rejoined their old regiment. On 13 January 1900 Louis boarded the SS *Bavarian* bound for Cape Town. 'We left a lot of men in hospital in Aldershot at the last moment,' he wrote, 'so we are actually only 971 strong.' As adjutant Louis was busy until 2 p.m. each day. The voyage was marred by illness, and eight men – including two from the East Lancs – died following a serious influenza epidemic on board. A prolonged period of stormy weather only served to increase their discomfort. The horses suffered too: 'they don't look at all comfortable,' commented Louis, 'they do not like the rough weather.'

125. Officers, 1st East Lancashire Regiment, at Aldershot shortly before embarkation for South Africa, December 1899. Capt. and Adjt Louis Le Marchant is seated third from right, and to his left is Lt-Col. A.J.A. Wright.

For Robert and Eliza Le Marchant this was a worrying time. Barely nine months earlier they had lost their son Edward to an assassin's bullet, and now two more sons were about to face great danger. 'I am so sorry for you and Father that both Basil and Louis should be off to the war,' wrote Evelyn to his mother

from HMS *Caesar*, 'but the country calls them when she is being hard pressed out there, and so I don't think we can wish them to be out of it. We must hope that fortune will have favoured our arms before they arrive and the heaviest fighting will be over.' Whilst their parents waited anxiously for news the two brothers were eager to see action, little knowing what hardships lay ahead and still confident of early victory.

The *Bavarian* reached Cape Town on 5 February after three weeks at sea, and the following day the battalion departed by train for the front, leaving behind all their heavy baggage. They encamped at Graspan, close to the Orange Free State border, about fifty miles south of the Modder River (see Map 2, page 98). Within days the 1st East Lancs (15th Brigade, 7th Division) were on the move towards their first objective, the small town of Jacobsdaal. During what was later remembered as 'The Great Thirst March' the men, many of whom were reservists, suffered terribly from heat stroke, which was made worse by a desperate shortage of food and water. 'We had two very trying marches in the middle of the day and the heat was awful,' wrote Louis. 'I think quite 200 men fell out during the march to the Riet River.' It was another 24 hours before the supply wagons found a place to cross the river and reached the men, who had not had a substantial meal for more than 36 hours.

A couple of days later the 15th Brigade marched north and occupied Jacobsdaal after a brief fight. 'The South Wales Borderers were on our right and had 15 men killed and wounded,' wrote Louis. 'Most of the bullets passed over our heads and we had no casualties, though a bullet fell between my horse's legs and I heard several pass overhead.' The Brigade remained at Jacobsdaal for nearly three weeks protecting Lord Roberts' lines of communication. Louis could hear the guns at Paardeberg, where his brother Basil was involved in fierce fighting against General Cronje's force of over 4,000 men. For Louis and his fellow officers fighting was infinitely more preferable than waiting around on short rations with little to do. 'We have had a good deal of rain and we get very heavy storms at night,' he wrote, 'we have no tents so we get pretty wet.' During his stay in Jacobsdaal Louis met a number of Boers detained in hospital, whose determination and openness earned his respect. 'They are a very good lot to talk to,' he wrote, 'mostly farmers I think, they say they are sure to win, they hate the war and would do anything to stop it.'

After Cronje had surrendered the 1st East Lancs rejoined the 7th Division and advanced towards Bloemfontein, entering the Orange Free State capital on 16 March. There Louis was delighted to meet up with Basil, who gave him a detailed account of the action at Paardeberg. The two brothers had much in common: both led by example and cared deeply for the welfare of their men. Twelve days later, after less time to rest and recover than they had expected, the 7th Division received orders to attack the Boers at Karee Siding, a small railway station some 30 miles to the north. Forming the rear guard on the first day's march, the East Lancs were responsible for getting the guns and wagons safely across the Modder River. 'The banks are very steep and the road very bad,' wrote Louis, 'and it took us a long time to get our baggage across. We had to put drag ropes on the wheels to pull them up the bank.' Nothing more vividly illustrates the slow and cumbersome advance of British infantry units, so heavily dependent on extended supply convoys. Moving the big guns, hauled by teams of 32 oxen, proved to be a particular challenge.

Next morning the 7th Division advanced towards a line of hills thought to be held by some 4,000 Boers. At around 3 p.m. the East Lancs were ordered to attack a hill forming the eastern spur of a line of heights more than a mile long. As the leading company advanced they were exposed to heavy crossfire from a commanding hill on their right flank. Describing the action Louis wrote: 'We had to cross an open piece of ground about 400 yards across and this is where we had 2 men killed and 13 wounded, three of whom died very soon after. Both

126. This drawing of the 1st East Lancashires attacking at Karee appeared in the regimental Christmas card for 1900.

the mules of our Maxim gun were also shot. We were lucky to escape with so few casualties.' By the early evening the battalion had succeeded in taking the kopje which later became known as East Lancashire Hill. 'We only found one Boer wounded after the fight,' commented Louis, 'I suppose all the others were carried off.' Except for what little each man could carry, they had nothing to eat until the following morning when the supply wagons arrived. Louis, however, was more fortunate. 'I had some lozenges and soup,' he wrote, 'and the Colonel had some chocolate, so we did not do so badly after all.' Congratulating the men next day on their courageous action the brigade commander said, 'You had a damned hard nut to crack and you did it damned pluckily.'[3]

The battalion remained for more than a month at Karee Siding, where conditions were far from comfortable. 'We had to leave all our own things at the Cape except 35 lbs which included our bed, so we could bring up precious little else,' wrote Louis. 'I had two pairs of socks but both are now full of holes. I am rather anxious about my boots as the soles are coming off my present ones and I can't get my other pair up from the Cape. The men are in rags and the railway line is so blocked that nothing can come up at present.' To ease the situation Louis was sent to Bloemfontein to try to get some clothing for the men. There he dined with Basil, and the two brothers discussed the progress of the war. Basil had himself recently been dispatched to Norvals Pont, 130 miles south, to bring back clothing for the 1st West Ridings. Whilst Basil remained optimistic that the war would soon be over, Louis believed that hostilities would last well into the following year. His mission accomplished, Louis returned to Karee. 'I brought back 800 pairs of trousers, 300 pairs of boots, besides a lot of other stuff,' he wrote. 'I also brought up £1,200 in gold and silver which was rather a nuisance as I had to carry this about and travelled by rail in a truck on the top of a lot of boxes.' Parcels from home made life a little easier, and from his family Louis received silk handkerchiefs to wear round his neck for protection against sunburn, a woollen jersey and khaki comforter for the cold nights, socks, soap, a pipe and tobacco, and cocoa and coffee – the latter a welcome treat to add to his restricted diet. 'One gets rather tired of nothing but bread and meat,' wrote Louis. 'I dug up a few potatoes from an old garden which were excellent, but there were very few of them.'

There was little action to break the monotony of their long stay at Karee Siding, though they were often on outpost duty and always on the alert in case of attack. 'The CO [Lieutenant-Colonel Wright] and I live in a Boer house when we come on outpost, so we escaped a ducking,' wrote Louis. 'We have to be up and out before daylight which makes rather a long day of it, but one goes to bed early, generally at 8 p.m. It gets dark now at 6, and as we have only one miserable candle between us there is not much use in sitting up.' When the East Lancashire Mounted Infantry Company were attacked by some six hundred Boers, Louis and Colonel Wright, hearing firing in the distance, rode to the crest of a nearby hill to observe the action unfold. 'I watched a very pretty little fight yesterday morning,' commented Louis, 'I was about 1,500 yards away. The ground over which the Boers were advancing was perfectly open and they were dotted in twos and threes all over it. Our Mounted Infantry advanced out from their hills to meet them, but suddenly we saw them all coming in as hard as they could with the Boers after them.' Louis supposed this to be a feint intended to draw the Boers towards their artillery, for when the enemy were within range the guns opened fire, causing the Boers to turn and gallop away before regrouping to mount a second attack. Although the Mounted Infantry sustained a few casualties during this action, Louis believed that the Boers had come off worse. 'Judging from the number of vultures about over the place,' he wrote, 'I expect the Boers suffered some losses too.'

As they prepared to resume the advance the men were issued with padded khaki overcoats, a necessary protection when sleeping in the open during the cold nights ahead. Reinforcements arrived, including another 5,000 Mounted Infantry and several 5-inch guns, each of which was drawn by 20 oxen. The battalion was soon in action again, initially at Brandfort, and a week later at Zand River. To enable the brigade to cross the Zand River safely, the East Lancs volunteered to attack Boer artillery positions on a hill some two miles away. As they advanced across open ground, with Captain Le Marchant coordinating movements, they came under sustained shell fire but succeeded in reaching the top of a ridge close to Boer positions. 'I heard bullets falling on the stones at our feet on the right and we just had time to lie down when a regular storm of bullets came over our heads,' he wrote in a letter to his sister Annie. About 150 Boers were firing from a trench some 500 yards away, but they fell back when they came under fire from a Maxim gun at the foot of the hill. The East Lancs succeeded in forcing the Boers to withdraw, capturing a key position with losses of one man killed and five wounded. During the battle, Louis noted, 'we fired off 11,000 rounds'.

During the advance northward towards Johannesburg the troops, in the words of Lord Roberts, were 'exposed to extreme heat by day, bivouacking under heavy rains, marching long distances not infrequently with reduced rations'.[4] The nights were bitterly cold and often they slept with their boots on. Frequently there was little or no fire wood. 'I shall be very glad when the marching is over,' wrote Louis, 'one gets very sick of it, starting before sunrise and not getting into camp before dark.' By then it was too late to wash, and in the mornings they could not do so because the water in their canvas buckets was frozen solid. 'Sometimes we have marched over 20 miles a day without a single halt,' Louis continued. 'All the marching was over open roadless veldt covered with long grass and not a single tree of any sort to be seen, except occasionally when we came across a farm, perhaps every five miles or so.' In just seven days they covered 126 miles, a remarkable achievement.

On 30 May Boer forces in Johannesburg surrendered. In return for agreeing to leave all the gold mines of the Rand intact Roberts allowed the Boer army to leave town, taking with them 19 trains of supplies. This 'velvet-glove' strategy – deplored by Evelyn Le Marchant who wished that Roberts would be 'less lenient and not treat the Boers as ladies and gentlemen, for such they are not' – proved to be a costly blunder which considerably lengthened the war. The following day the 7th and 11th divisions, led by Lord Roberts himself, marched triumphantly through the town. 'The procession started at half past eleven and went on until 5 in the evening,' commented Louis, 'the people were astonished to see us, they had been told nothing but lies, that we had been beaten on the Vaal River and had retired.' Now, after four months on the veldt, the hardships of the campaign had reduced the strength of the battalion by more than a quarter. Some had died of typhoid fever during the long march, including the well-liked Major Browne, son of the rector at Bredon, near Tewkesbury, who had trekked to Chitral with Louis five years earlier. Many of those who had succumbed, Louis believed, had probably contracted the disease after drinking water that was 'so dirty one did not like washing in it'. A month later men were still succumbing to typhoid. 'There were 1,500 men in hospital here last week and about nine deaths a day,' wrote Louis on 1 July, 'but I think the death rate has now gone down a good deal. My servant is in hospital with it which is a nuisance, and I am afraid they will invalid him home.'

For the next 11 months 15th Brigade was assigned to garrison the Transvaal capital and surrounding areas of the Rand, from Vereeniging in the south to Pretoria in the north. For the time being the East Lancs remained in Johannesburg. 'They are taking our officers for all sorts of billets,' wrote Louis:

> I was telling the Colonel today that soon only he and I will be left. Station masters, magistrates, escorts for prisoners, all sorts of things. All have to be found from the Battalion in this place. We have a Major trying a murder case. I don't suppose he knows anything about the law and I don't think he can hang the man on his own authority, but I am not sure.

The East Lancs were also required to provide officers and men for the newly formed Johannesburg Military Police. One of Louis' more onerous responsibilities was to locate the units of all those leaving hospital so that they could be returned to their regiments without delay, but the whereabouts of units on the move throughout South Africa often proved very difficult to establish. 'I have had some thousands through my hands since we have been here,' he wrote. 'A lot of the Imperial Yeomanry and City Imperial Volunteers are gentlemen … I fancy they must have a very bad time living with the men, it is of course impossible to treat them any differently to the others.'

Garrison duty had many drawbacks, but initially Louis appreciated having a roof over his head and a camp bed to sleep on within the Agricultural Show grounds. 'I have a very nice room in the ladies' cloakroom building – empty,' he observed drily. After almost six months in South Africa his baggage finally arrived from the Cape, giving him the luxury of several changes of clothes. But military supplies had priority on railway transport, so that everyday goods remained in short supply in Johannesburg. 'One can get nothing in the town now in the way of food or smokes,' he wrote in September, 'only four trains a day come up from the south and they bring rations for the army.' Two months later he complained, 'I don't know when we are going to get any stores. I hear they have all been stopped again on account of people buying them and sending them to the Boers.' The price of eggs rose to seven shillings a dozen, matches – if any could be found – were a shilling a box, and fresh butter could not be obtained. Parcels from home were especially valued, but some were captured by the Boers and never reached their intended destinations. 'I hear De Wet got a fine haul and that the line down by Rhenoster is strewn with letters,' wrote Louis, 'he also got hold of a heap of clothing, provisions, cameras and field glasses, which had come out by parcel post.' Some officers lost entire suits of uniform, and Louis himself lost a much needed pair of boots and a blanket his mother had sent him, items he later ascertained were in the mail of 4 May 1900 captured by De Wet.

After a few months Louis complained that he was tired of being in one place for so long. It was not that he was short of work, but rather that the routine of garrison life had become monotonous. During a short spell in Springs, to the east of Johannesburg, in addition to his duties as adjutant Louis assumed the responsibilities of Station Staff Officer and Railway Staff Officer and was very busy, especially when a column came through. A visit to Pretoria – 'rather a pretty little country town' – was a welcome diversion, and he enjoyed his trip down a gold mine, from which he brought back several pieces of rock to take home as souvenirs. He exercised his horse daily, but he derived no excitement from his work and he could buy nothing in the shops in Johannesburg to ease the boredom. He was a little envious of the wealth of the local population, though they too had little on which to spend their savings. 'This place seems full of money,' he commented, 'every man who is brought to the charge office for being drunk is of course searched and it is not at all unusual to find £100 in gold on them. Natives often have £50 or £60 on them, I don't know where they get it.'

When an opportunity came to go out with a column in search of the Boers, Louis welcomed the change of routine. The column, led by Lieutenant-Colonel Wright, encountered a Boer commando along a ridge of hills about twenty miles south of Johannesburg. As the column advanced they came under fire, but the Boers quickly withdrew when artillery shells burst around them. 'It was quite a nice little fight,' observed Louis, 'no one was killed except one man by accident, and four or five horses.' Next day they cleared out all the farms in the valley and burnt any food and crops they could find. 'We also brought in a lot of Boer

127. Capt. Louis Le Marchant, South Africa, 1901.

families, mostly women and children, 96 of them in all,' wrote Louis. 'They made a great fuss about leaving their farms, and certainly it was a most unpleasant job.' Although he disliked destroying crops and displacing whole families, he later wrote, 'it seems the only way now to end the war is to starve them out'.

Louis was with Colonel Wright when, for a week or two, they had 'rather an exciting time'. 'There were plenty of Boers quite close,' he wrote.

> One day the CO sent out an ambush from one of the Colonial mounted corps. They occupied some Kaffir kraals at midnight. At dawn the usual mounted patrol went out, found the Boers and retired past the kraals, the Boers following as usual. As soon as they got quite close to the kraals the party, previously posted in them, opened fire killing four and wounding another.

When the time came to go out with yet another column Louis, now acting Brigade Major, had grown weary of the protracted conflict. 'I don't see the least chance of the war being over for the next year,' he wrote in January 1901, 'personally I have had quite enough of it.' And some months later he commented, 'I don't like this country a bit … it is nothing like such a good place as India.'

In May, as the war dragged on, four companies of the East Lancs – including Captain Le Marchant and Battalion Headquarters – joined Brigadier-General Hamilton's mobile column. Operating in the Magaliesberg Mountains, which Louis described as 'very nasty country to fight in', the column was constantly on the move, and over the next three and a half months they marched a total of 1,100 miles. 'We had a pretty hard time,' Louis wrote, 'we very seldom got a rest and had plenty of night marches.' Against a highly mobile and elusive enemy, the column failed to capture many Boers. It fell to the infantry to protect the slow-moving baggage convoys and perform outpost duties – unglamorous but exacting and necessary tasks. Louis, however, was frustrated by the tactics adopted. 'As long as we go about with ox convoys I don't see much chance of the end coming,' he wrote. On one occasion it had taken the East Lancs all day to get a convoy of about one hundred wagons over a difficult river crossing. The last wagons reached the far side just before dark, but the convoy was unable to catch up with the rest of the column that night. 'I think the war is practically over for the infantry,' Louis wrote in November, 'the mounted men will have to finish the show now, infantry are much too slow and only hamper the movement of a mobile column.' Louis believed that mobile columns should operate without supply convoys, relying instead on fortified supply depots strategically placed throughout the theatre of operations. Heavy losses of transport animals convinced Louis that he was right: 'oxen are dying in hundreds from rinder pest,' he observed.

After their exhausting trek the battalion spent tedious months extending and garrisoning a line of blockhouses along the railway to the south and east of Johannesburg. 'There is very little to be done,' complained Louis, 'but on the whole I think it is better than trekking, and I am sure the men are glad of a rest.'

At Vereeniging Louis occupied his spare time playing tennis with men from the nearby mine and fishing in the Vaal River. 'I have caught a good many fish,' he later wrote, 'but they are not very good eating, rather coarse I think.' He would have relished the chance to go hunting for big game but the risks of venturing out alone in Boer territory were too great.

Louis was shocked and saddened to hear of the fate of his friend Captain Basil De Gex, with whom he had shared a bungalow for three years in Lucknow. De Gex had obtained promotion into the Lancashire Fusiliers the previous year, but soon afterwards had been seconded to East Africa. There he took part in operations with the Uganda Punitive Force against mutinous British Sudanese troops. During a spell of leave De Gex travelled to Nairobi for some shooting. He engaged several porters and a gun-bearer, and took with him a Mannlicher sporting rifle and a shotgun. Later, whilst searching for game, he caught sight of a lion in the long grass and hurriedly fired his shotgun, wounding it in the foot. The lion lay down out of sight, so De Gex set fire to the grass. Then the lion went for him, and he only just had time to fire the remaining shot in his 8-bore, hitting the animal in the chest. The terrified gun-bearer had, by this time, run off with the Mannlicher. In the ensuing struggle De Gex was badly mauled but he fought fiercely, clubbing the lion over the head with the butt of his gun. 'The beast got him down and worried him,' wrote an officer in the East African Rifles, 'but he stuck his fingers into its eyes, and it seems to have left him alone.'[5] De Gex was carried to the nearest station by porters and put on a special train to Nairobi, where a doctor amputated his right arm. He died the following day.

By November the line of blockhouses for which the East Lancs were responsible had been extended eastward to the town of Frankfort, 'which of course has been completely destroyed', Louis noted, a casualty of Kitchener's ruthless pursuit of the scorched earth policy earlier adopted by Lord Roberts. 'There are a good many Boers around,' wrote Louis, 'and it is not safe to go two miles out of camp.' Though the Boers made sporadic attempts to disrupt the construction of blockhouses and the laying of miles of barbed wire, work proceeded inexorably. 'Barbed wire is awful stuff to handle and cuts the men's hands a good deal but it is a very fine obstacle,' commented Louis. One morning, as he and Colonel Wright rode out to reconnoitre positions for additional blockhouses beyond Dundas Farm, about ten miles east of Frankfort, their safety was seriously compromised by the inexperience of a detachment of Imperial Yeomanry on outpost duty. In a letter home the following day (17 December) Louis gave an account of the incident, which differs from that compiled some years later and published in the regimental journal:

> We had a scrap yesterday. I was riding out to the Yeomanry advanced posts about 7 a.m. when suddenly about 60 mounted men came over a ridge about 500 yards off. Thinking they were Yeomanry I was going on, but I could not make out why there was such a large number. They galloped

128. A blockhouse near Dundas Farm, some ten miles east of Frankfort (see map 2, p.98), constructed by the Royal Engineers and manned by the 1st East Lancashires, 1901.

down to our right Yeomanry post and I saw the Yeomen mount and go along with them, and I then saw they were Boers so I turned round and galloped as fast as I could to a kopje where we had a section of infantry. When I got there I found another party of Boers coming down from the other side and the Boers were firing on us from two other hills. Some of them were not 200 yards off and the Yeomanry and Boers were riding in together. We were in a small kraal but could not fire for some time on account of the Yeomanry. However, as soon as we did start the Boers cleared out, we had a man killed and a lot of Yeomanry were taken prisoner – it was a very smart performance on the part of the Boers who took advantage of the Yeomanry … I am afraid the [33rd Imperial] Yeomanry are not good enough, if they had only fired we should have known what was going on.

Despite the risk of capture the CO and his adjutant continued to visit outposts along the entire length of the East Lancashire line. 'Tomorrow,' wrote Louis from Battalion Headquarters on Tafel Kop in April 1902, 'I am going with the Colonel to the extreme end of our blockhouse line, about 14 miles from here, so we shall have a long ride and change horses half way.' During these final months of the war Louis thought increasingly about his future, and with the support of Colonel Wright he decided to apply to go to the Staff College the following year. To succeed he would not only have to secure a nomination for one of the limited places available but also pass the entrance examination. And as the examination took place in August he urgently needed textbooks from which to revise. Accordingly, he wrote to his brother Gaspard in London asking him to send out the required books as soon as possible. 'The subjects I am taking up,' he wrote, 'are French, Mathematics [three papers], Hindustani, Military Law, Topography, Tactics, Fortification, Organisation and Equipment, Strategy. I hope to be able to qualify but it depends a good deal on when I get the books.' Those he needed most were the Field Manual of Military Engineering, and Chambers Log Tables. Just a week after writing this letter, however, a peace treaty was signed at Vereeniging, and Louis was on his way home.

On 1 June, the day after war ended, Colonel Wright received an urgent request to send an officer and 10 men to London to represent the battalion at the forthcoming coronation of King Edward VII – just 25 days hence. There was no time to lose, and the Colonel asked Louis to make every effort to reach Cape Town, almost 900 miles away, before the SS *Bavarian* sailed for England. 'I started off two hours after receipt of the wire and travelled day and night to reach the railway,' wrote Louis. Leaving at 9 p.m., the contingent covered more than sixty miles to the branch line at Heilbron in 23 hours, though not without incident. As they rode through the night troops in one of the blockhouses, as yet unaware of the ceasefire and mistaking them for the enemy, fired several shots, killing one of their mules. Next day Louis caught a train to Cape Town with his men, arriving on 7 June an hour before *Bavarian* sailed. With extra firemen and engineers on board, who had been promised a bonus of half a month's pay if they reached England in time for the coronation, *Bavarian* made excellent

129. Beatrice Le Marchant hung flags outside the Rectory, Little Rissington, to celebrate the end of the Boer War and, a few months later, the coronation of King Edward VII in August 1902.

progress, arriving in Southampton with less than forty-eight hours to spare. The King's sudden illness, however, meant that the coronation had to be postponed at short notice, and Louis returned home to Little Rissington. He had been on active service for almost two and a half years. Twice mentioned in despatches, he was awarded the Distinguished Service Order 'in recognition of services during the operations in South Africa'.

After six months' leave Louis rejoined his regiment, which was now in Dublin. Two years later he secured a transfer to the 2nd Battalion and embarked once more for India. He spent less than a year with the regiment in Poona, about 120 miles south-east of Bombay, before returning to London for an operation on his varicose veins at King Edward VII Hospital for Officers. In June 1906 he returned to India and was promoted to the rank of major, becoming Brigade Major (chief of brigade staff) a few months later. Louis wrote to Basil, then in Murree, to say that he had 'fallen on his feet' at last and would now be drawing 1,100 rupees a month, enough for him to live very well. For the next four years Louis was stationed at Ahmadnagar, to the east of Bombay, where life followed much the same pattern as that of any other army station in India. It did not take Louis long to re-establish a regular routine – an early morning ride each day with Colonel Sitwell followed by several hours' work. 'There is nothing going on here, it really is not much more lively than Little Rissington,' wrote Louis, 'though of course one does meet most people in the Station at the club in the evening, where one plays tennis and bridge afterwards.' Louis, confident in his ability at the card table, preferred the intellectual stimulation of bridge to the challenge of making a good impression on the dance floor. As a guest at a dance given by the Worcestershire Regiment he spent most of the evening playing bridge, not leaving until the early hours of the morning.

In letters to his sisters Louis, aware of their keen interest in the natural world, described the flowers he cultivated successfully in his garden, and a quail's nest he found with nine eggs inside, 'the same colour as the two in the old egg box at home'. He told them how he had been lucky to escape serious injury when he had been stung by a swarm of bees. But he rarely said much about his social life or any eligible young women he may have met. At the age of 40 Major Le Marchant could now afford to marry, but the prospect of settling down seems not to have tempted him and he remained a bachelor.

In March 1908 Louis was appointed Deputy Assistant Adjutant-General for the Ahmadnagar Brigade, and three years later he spent five months acting as Assistant Adjutant-General at Army Headquarters in Simla, home of the government of India during the hot summer months. Plenty of influential people were there. Young unmarried ladies were attracted to Simla for the season in the hope of finding a husband, and many courtships blossomed in the more relaxed atmosphere of a hill-station with something of a reputation for frivolity and scandal. Though busy, Louis could not avoid altogether the hectic social life of Simla, where he was much in demand. Besides the usual round of tennis parties,

130. The Mall, Simla, looking towards Christ Church (background, centre, and inset) and the Town Hall (right), 1890s. Stretching for a couple of miles in each direction, the Mall was a favourite place for socialites to meet and take a stroll.

lavish dinners and society balls, Louis attended the season's amateur theatrical events put on by officers' wives and daughters, many of whom had little else to do with their time.* These elegant productions were both entertaining and amusing, greatly appreciated by all but the stuffiest members of Raj society.

In December 1911 Louis accompanied the battalion to South Africa, and for the next two years he was based at Wynberg Camp, near Cape Town. Initially detailed to command the garrison at Cape Town Castle, Major Le Marchant and his men were called upon to provide a guard of honour for the Governor General at the reopening of the South African Parliament on 26 January 1912. Apart from occasional ceremonial duties, however, life at Wynberg seems to have had little to commend it, and following the annual inspection of the battalion in 1913 the General Officer Commanding commented, 'The conditions at Wynberg

---

* Amongst the amateur productions staged in Simla in one season (1895) were *Doctor Faust and Miss Marguerite*, *The Cape Mail* (a drama in one act), scenes from *Iolanthe* and *The Gondoliers*, and tableaux from Tennyson's *Dream of Fair Women*.

131 Capt. Fitzclarence, Mrs R. Campbell, Capt. Adam and Lady Elizabeth Bruce dance for the entertainment of guests at the Viceregal Lodge, Simla, 1895.

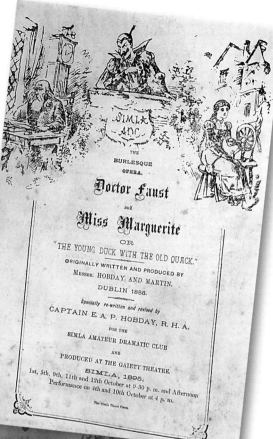

132. For its production at the Gaiety Theatre in 1895 the Simla Amateur Dramatic Club performed a light-hearted opera entitled *Doctor Faust and Miss Marguerite*.

133. Members of the chorus for a performance of *Iolanthe* at 'Snowdon', Simla, 1895. From the left, back row: the Misses Deane, Halliday, Iggulden (Mrs), White, Patterson, Poyser, Boughey; front row: the Misses Johnstone, Craigie, Ogbourne, Lewes, Holdich, Turner.

are unfavourable, but necessary efforts must be made to reduce the drunkenness. If any good results are to be expected, the Commanding Officer and his officers, supported by his NCOs and men who have personal influence, should very seriously take up the temperance movement.'[6] No doubt Louis was glad to return home to England in time for Christmas that year, having spent most of the last nine years overseas. It was to be his last Christmas with his family.

134. The East Lancashire Regiment in Brigade before leaving for France, August 1914.

At the outbreak of the First World War in August 1914 Robert Le Marchant was ninety-four. By now his diary entries were infrequent and very brief, but on 5 August, the day after Britain declared war on Germany, he noted that one of Mr Streatfeild Moore's horses had been requisitioned to support the war effort. Louis, now a lieutenant-colonel in command of the 1st East Lancs, accompanied the battalion to Le Havre on 22 August, from where they boarded trains for the front. They reached Le Câteau on 24 August, the day after the small British Expeditionary Force (BEF) had fought its first battle of the war at Mons. With the French 5th Army in retreat on its right flank, the BEF was ordered to fall back, reaching positions around Le Câteau on 25 August. The East Lancs, part of the 4th Division which had only just arrived at the front, were about to see action for the first time.

At dawn on 26 August Lieutenant-Colonel Le Marchant was summoned to divisional headquarters and he rode off on his charger to Beauvois, west of Le Câteau, only to find that HQ had relocated elsewhere. On his return the battalion marched to take up a new position, but there was little cohesion between units and considerable confusion amongst brigade commanders as to the general situation on the ground. Early that morning General Smith-Dorrien, commanding II Corps, decided that he could not withdraw because of the proximity of units of von Kluck's First Army, and he gave the order to stand and fight. For some eleven hours units of II Corps, including the 4th Division, fought a rearguard action at Le Câteau, and the East Lancs suffered considerable losses. By early afternoon orders were received to pull back about a mile to the village of Ligny across open country devoid of any cover, resulting in further heavy casualties. Louis was with his troops in the front line when he was slightly wounded in the foot. Though lame and in some pain, particularly when the wound later became infected, he retained command of the battalion.

For three hours a detachment of East Lancs and a company of the Rifle Brigade, with artillery support, held up the German advance on Ligny. Late that afternoon, when the order came to evacuate the village, all the wounded who could not walk were left behind as no transport was available. The battalion withdrew in some disorganisation, with elements from all companies now hopelessly mixed up, reaching Ellincourt at 11 p.m., where a little food was obtained from the villagers for the weary troops. In his report on the battle the brigade commander described Lieutenant-Colonel Le Marchant as 'a capable battalion commander and gallant man'.[7] And Major Lambert of the 1st East Lancs, writing of the events of that day, said that Louis was 'constantly going up to the actual firing line himself … he was a man of the greatest personal courage, cool and collected in action'.[8] During the fighting on 26 August one officer from the battalion was killed and four others were wounded or taken prisoner, and more than 250 other ranks were reported killed, wounded or missing. Altogether the British suffered almost 8,000 casualties at Le Câteau – around twenty per cent of the troops involved.

For the next 10 days the BEF retreated almost two hundred miles to the outskirts of Paris. Sir John French, the overly cautious commander of the BEF, feared that the retreat of the French 5th Army on his right would leave his force dangerously exposed. His first priority was the preservation of the BEF from possible annihilation. Accordingly, the retreat proceeded with considerable urgency, and in the intense heat of summer exhausted soldiers marched with equipment weighing around sixty pounds, frequently short of food and sleep. One British officer commented, 'I would never have believed that men could be so tired and so hungry and yet live.'[9] The East Lancs left Ellincourt at 2 a.m. on 27 August and marched more than thirty miles that day. Over the previous 63 hours they had managed to snatch just four hours' sleep. The next day they left at 3 a.m. to cover the retreat of the 19th Brigade and then marched a further 15 miles on half rations. Brigadier-General Hunter-Weston, brigade commander, praised the endurance and fine military spirit of the 1st East Lancs during the early days of the retreat, commenting that the credit for this commendable performance was largely due to Lieutenant-Colonel Le Marchant, 'whose example of cheeriness and self-possession and whose handling of his men was beyond praise'.

135. Members of the Sergeants' Mess, 1st East Lancashire Regiment, after mobilisation, 1914. In the centre of the front row is Lt-Col. Louis Le Marchant.

At Pierrefonds the Battalion had to bivouac in the streets because smallpox was thought to be present in the town. On 1 September at St Sauveur a company of East Lancs were attacked by a detachment of Uhlans, German light cavalry armed with lances. Fourteen men from the battalion were killed, wounded or reported missing during the various actions that day as the East Lancs fought a successful rearguard action which delayed the advancing German 4th Cavalry Division. According to the regimental history, 'Lieut-Col. Le Marchant's withdrawal of the Battalion [from St Sauveur] might well be cited as a model for such an operation.'[10]

By 5 September, after further long marches in intense heat, the battalion had almost reached Brie-Compte-Robert, some twenty miles to the south-east of Paris. In a brief, censored letter scribbled to his father that day Louis commented, 'we have had a hard time of it. We know very little of what is going on … we are not allowed to say anything.' The following day they received orders announcing the end of the retreat. Sir John French had wanted to pull all British units out of the line to rest and 'refit', but he had been overruled by Kitchener. After further hesitation and a personal appeal from General Joffre, French agreed that the BEF would participate in the Allied counter-attack; British forces would advance to the River Marne between the French 5th and 6th Armies. Exhausted, the East Lancs marched north-east with no maps and very little information on the immediate military situation. On the evening of 8 September they reached a farm overlooking the Marne where it flows through the town of La Ferté-sous-Jouarre. The battalion found places to sleep inside some dirty farmyard buildings, but Louis and several other officers preferred to remain in a small paddock nearby. 'The night was fine though it had rained hard during the afternoon,' wrote Major Lambert, 'and the ground (like ourselves) was wet. We got some dry straw to sleep on, and oats and straw for the horses.'

At 3.30 a.m. the Battalion left their billet and advanced towards La Ferté. German troops had withdrawn across the Marne the previous evening to take up positions in houses along the north bank of the river. As the East Lancs entered the town at daybreak they came under machine-gun fire but were able to take cover and suffered no casualties. With orders to relieve the Royal Welsh Fusiliers in the centre of the town, Louis went on ahead to check the route. The battalion then moved forward and set up headquarters in a château near the south bank of the Marne between two bridges which had been destroyed, taking over all positions held by the Fusiliers. 'There were a good many uncollected dead lying about the streets,' observed Major Lambert. Ambulance wagons were later able to take away many of the wounded, and a temporary hospital was set up in the château, part of which also served as the officers' mess. It soon became clear that the Germans had deployed a number of expert marksmen along the north bank of the Marne. 'Every street leading to the river was under a hot and accurate fire,' Major Lambert wrote. 'Every window or shutter that was moved facing the river received one or more bullets through it. There were a good many casualties, it was difficult to get firing places to bear either on the broken bridges or across the river.'

Units of the East Lancs advanced slowly, house by house. At 10.30 a.m. Colonel Le Marchant went forward to visit and encourage a party of men who were in a loft of one of the houses. As he climbed the stairs he was warned that enemy sniper fire was extremely accurate and that it was dangerous to stand near a window. Nevertheless, on reaching the top of the ladder to the loft Louis stopped momentarily to glance out of a small window. He hoped, no doubt, to assess the situation for himself, but in that instant he was struck in the neck by a bullet which killed him outright. A lieutenant in the Rifle Brigade, the Hon. Lionel Tennyson, had visited Louis moments before his death and made the following comments in his diary for that day, 9 September:

> … the General [Hunter-Weston] sent me down on a bicycle with a message for Colonel Le Marchant of the East Lancs who was down in the village. As I was bicycling down this hill the German machine-guns from the opposite side of the river opened fire on me, but I kept close under a wall and so was fairly safe. I delivered my message to him and had some breakfast at the château with him, when I returned to the General. One minute after I left the Colonel of the East Lancs was no more, he was shot through the head by a German sniper … About 5 p.m. the General sent me to the château garden to get hold of the gardener and get some vegetables for his dinner. This I did, but coming back through a small wood, I came right upon 16 dead Englishmen including the Colonel of the East Lancs, Le Marchant by name, all lying side by side ready to be buried.[11]

Louis was buried in the grounds of the château at La Ferté, but some years later his body was reburied several miles away in the small Anglo-French cemetery at La Perouse.

In his diary of the Great War dedicated to Colonel Le Marchant, amongst others, Private E. Roe of the 1st East Lancs wrote these words:

> Our Colonel. Yes! If you want to find him, search where the bullets are falling thickest … He has been engaged all morning seeking out positions where rifle fire can be used to best advantage; he does not say to a section commander, get your section into that isolated house and make loop holes,

you should get a good field of observation and fire from it. No! He goes himself and reconnoitres the enemies position [*sic*] and if he thinks it is too exposed and they could be enfiladed he will not send them. Never send a man where you would not go yourself is his maxim … We had the misfortune to lose our gallant Colonel … He was ever where the danger was most, we will never get another Colonel like him … that familiar figure, beloved by all, will never lead the old 30th into action again, when I write lead I mean lead in the true sense of the word.[12]

By all accounts, Colonel Le Marchant exemplified the very essence of the regimental motto of 'the old 30th', *Spectamur Agendo* – 'Let us be judged by our actions'.

The loss of Lieutenant-Colonel Le Marchant was deeply felt throughout the battalion.

> He had gained the confidence of his officers by being invariably ready to listen to the troubles of even the most junior of them. No officer was afraid to ask his advice, knowing that a firm but kindly helping hand would be given him. His imperturbability under the heaviest fire, his refusal to become rattled when things were going wrong and his complete disregard for his own safety had earned from officers and men a trust which was not only a source of infinite strength to those he commanded, but also to his brigade commander.[13]

136. Lt-Col. Louis St Gratien Le Marchant, DSO, commanding 1st Battalion East Lancashire Regiment.

Following this tribute in the regimental history is a statement, widely believed to be true by officers in the battalion, that shortly before Colonel Le Marchant's death General Hunter-Weston had selected him as the most deserving of the officers of the brigade to receive the French Legion of Honour, which 'was afterwards presented to his sister'. In fact no such posthumous award was made, but it is clear that Louis was very highly regarded by his brigade commander. One of the senior officers of the regiment wrote these words to the family: 'To us, as you know, his loss is irreparable, and we can only ask you to accept our deepest sympathy in the grief you must feel. He was loved and honoured by all ranks, but by none more than those who knew him best.'[14] On 16 September Robert Le

Marchant noted in his diary, 'A telegram was received this evening from the War Secretary to tell me that Louis had been killed. Our first notice.' The next day he received a telegram from the King's Private Secretary 'expressing the King's and Queen's sorrow and regret at our loss of Louis'.*

137.

Less than twenty-four hours after the death of their Commanding Officer the East Lancs crossed the Marne, meeting little resistance as the Germans had withdrawn some hours earlier. By 12 September they had reached the River Aisne, where the Germans were well dug in. Apart from a short advance after the East Lancs transferred to Flanders in October, the battalion would not again be involved in mobile warfare until 1918. Britain's small professional army, which before 1914 had become adept at fighting little colonial wars, had by 1918 been transformed into a vast conscript army capable of fighting a large-scale European war. Private Skin, a Guernseyman from the 2nd East Lancs, reflecting on the need for many more volunteers to replace those that had fallen, wrote a letter to the *Guernsey Evening Press* in December 1914:

> It is pleasing to note that we have already over 1,000 doing their bit at the front, but more are needed, and that very badly. Guernseymen are born fighters and as an example I would like to point out the late Col. L. St G. Le Marchant, DSO … who lost his life whilst leading his troops in the present war. I had the honour of serving under him for three years, during which time he was well respected by every man jack of our Battalion and was referred to as the Father of M Company. He was a gentleman and a born fighter and when he was killed the Army lost a good man.

---

* King George V, who as a young boy had spent two years aboard HMS *Bacchante* with Evelyn Le Marchant, would have felt particular sympathy for the family's loss.

Epilogue

Between 1851 and 1872 the Revd Robert Le Marchant and his wife, Eliza, raised 15 children, yet no descendants are alive today. None of their nine daughters married, a source of great disappointment within the family; the reasons they remained single are explored in *A Victorian Rector and Nine Old Maids*. Only three of the rector's sons married; between them they had just four children, three sons and a daughter. Of the rector's four grandchildren only Evelyn's daughter, Valerie, found a suitable spouse, but she produced no heirs. Neither Gaspard St John nor Valentine showed any inclination to marry, and Edward Herbert was

138. Louis, Cecil and Evelyn in the garden of the Rectory, 1890s. Though they travelled far and wide, the Le Marchant brothers enjoyed coming home to Little Rissington, where they are still remembered today.

killed at the Battle of the Somme in 1916, aged twenty-two. Valentine, the last of Robert and Eliza's surviving grandchildren, died in 1987. But the Le Marchant family is still remembered by many in the village that was their home for more than a century.

On the afternoon of 1 July 2006, as England sank to defeat in the football World Cup, villagers put their cares behind them and celebrated the 150th anniversary of Little Rissington Manor. Many of the ideas for the party that day were taken from a description written by the Le Marchants of a garden party which took place at the Manor over one hundred years ago. The driving force behind much that happened in the village in those days was the rector and his extensive family, and their influence lives on. 'They ran their own social service for the village,' remembered Eddie Butler, and the late Donald Lane commented that 'the Le Marchants were a brilliant family'. Their courage in the face of adversity, and their kindness and generosity, serve as a fine example of community spirit for others to follow. Today many anecdotes are still recounted of their various achievements and eccentricities. Basil and Cecil organised impressive firework displays to mark special occasions, and Beatrice excelled on the sporting field – against teams of both men and women. Miss Dora Le Marchant, who was born and died in the village, lived to be 102 and even when well into her nineties she took a daily walk to Bourton-on-the-Water, a distance of more than four miles including a steep hill back to the village. On her tomb in the village churchyard are the words: 'Five score years and two, thirty-two more than allotted to you'.

Five of the rector's sons distinguished themselves in the service of their country, but until now their stories have not been told. The name of Le Marchant lives on in the Cotswolds, where the family is remembered with considerable affection.

139. On Remembrance Sunday each year, in front of the memorial cross in Little Rissington churchyard, the names of Lieutenant-Colonel Louis St Gratien Le Marchant and others who were killed in the World Wars are read out. Also remembered are the men of RAF Little Rissington who died in the service of their country.

Their name liveth for evermore.

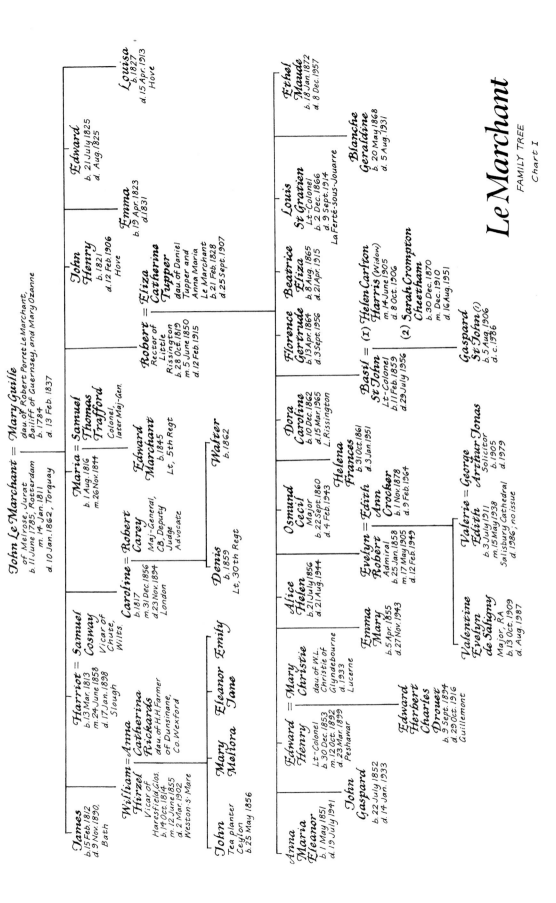

Le Marchant

FAMILY TREE

Chart I

John Le Marchant = **Mary Guille**
of Melrose, Jurat
b. 11 June 1785, Rotterdam
m. 14 Jan. 1811
d. 10 Jan. 1862, Torquay
dau. of Robert Porret Le Marchant,
Bailiff of Guernsey, and Mary Ozanne
b. 1784
d. 13 Feb. 1837

James
b. 15 Feb. 1812
d. 9 Nov. 1890
Bath

Harriot = **Samuel Cosway**
b. 13 Mar. 1813
m. 24 June 1858
d. 17 Jan. 1898
Slough
Vicar of Chute, Wilts.

Maria = **Samuel Thomas Trafford**
b. 1 Aug. 1816
m. 26 Nov. 1844
Colonel, later Maj-Gen.

John Henry
b. 1821
d. 12 Feb. 1906
Hove

Edward
b. 21 July 1825
d. Aug. 1825

Louisa
b. 1827
d. 15 Apr. 1913
Hove

William = **Anna Catherina Rickards**
Vicar of Haresfield, Glos.
b. 14 Oct. 1814
d. 2 Mar. 1902
Weston-S-Mare
dau. of H.H. Farmer of Dunsinane, Co. Wexford
m. 12 June 1855

Caroline = **Robert Carey**
b. 1817
m. 31 Dec. 1856
d. 23 Nov. 1894
London
Maj-General, CB, Deputy Judge Advocate

Edward Marchant
b. 1845
Lt, 5th Regt

Emma
b. 19 Apr. 1823
d. 1831

Robert = **Eliza Catherine Tupper**
Rector of Little Rissington
b. 28 Oct. 1819
m. 5 June 1850
d. 12 Feb 1915
dau. of Daniel Tupper and Anna Maria Le Marchant
b. 21 Feb. 1828
d. 25 Sept. 1907

John
Tea planter
Ceylon
b. 25 May 1856

Mary Meliora

Eleanor Jane

Emily

Denis
b. 1859
Lt, 30th Regt

Walter
b. 1862

Anna Maria Eleanor
b. 1 May 1851
d. 19 July 1941

Edward Henry = **Mary Christie**
Lt-Colonel
b. 30 Dec. 1853
m. 12 Oct. 1892
d. 23 Mar. 1899
Peshawar
dau. of W.L. Christie of Glyndebourne
d. 1933
Lucerne

Alice Helen
b. 21 July 1856
d. 21 Aug. 1944

Osmund Cecil
Major
b. 22 Sept. 1860
d. 4 Feb. 1943

Dora Caroline
b. 10 Dec. 1862
d. 15 Mar. 1965
L. Rissington

Florence Gertrude
b. 13 Apr. 1864
d. 3 Sept. 1956

Beatrice Eliza
b. 8 Aug. 1865
d. 21 Apr. 1915

Louis St Gratien
Lt-Colonel
b. 2 Dec. 1866
d. 9 Sept. 1914
LaFerté-sous-Jouarre

Ethel Maude
b. 18 Jan. 1872
d. 8 Dec. 1957

John Gaspard
b. 22 July 1852
d. 14 Jan. 1933

Edward Herbert Charles Drouet
b. 9 Sept. 1894
d. 29 Oct. 1916
Guillemont

Emma Mary
b. 5 Apr. 1855
d. 27 Nov. 1943

Evelyn Robert = **Edith Ann Crocker**
Admiral
b. 25 Jan. 1858
m. 17 May 1905
d. 12 Feb. 1949
b. 1 Nov. 1878
d. 9 Feb. 1964

Helena Frances
b. 31 Oct. 1861
d. 3 Jan. 1951

Basil = (1) **Helen Carlton Harris** (Widow)
St John
Lt-Colonel
b. 11 Feb. 1859
d. 29 July 1956
m. 14 June 1905
d. 8 Oct. 1906
(2) **Sarah Crompton Cheetham**
b. 30 Dec. 1870
m. Dec. 1910
d. 16 Aug. 1951

Blanche Geraldine
b. 20 May 1868
d. 5 Aug. 1931

Valentine Evelyn de Saligny
Major, RA
b. 13 Oct. 1909
d. Aug. 1987

Valerie = **George Arthur Jonas**
Edith
b. 3 July 1911
m. 15 May 1938
Salisbury Cathedral
Solicitor
b. 1905
d. 1979
d. 1986; no issue

Gaspard St John (1)
b. 5 Aug. 1906
d. c. 1986

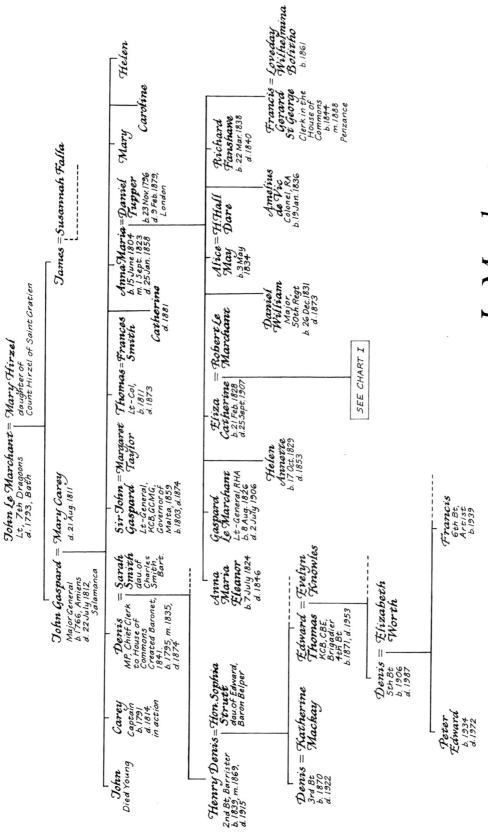

John Le Marchant = **Mary Hirzel**
Lt. 7th Dragoons
d.1793, Bath
daughter of
Count Hirzel of Saint Gratien

James = **Susannah Falla**

John Gaspard = **Mary Carey**
Major-General
b.1766, Amiens
d.22 July 1812,
Salamanca
d.21 Aug.1811

John
Died Young

Carey
Captain
b.1791
d.1814,
in action

Denis = **Sarah Smith**
MP, Chief Clerk
to House of
Commons
Created Baronet,
1841,
b.1795, m.1835,
d.1874
dau. of
Charles
Smith,
Bart.

Sir John = **Margaret Taylor**
Gaspard
Lt.-General,
KCB, GCMG,
Governor of
Malta, 1859
b.1803, d.1874

Thomas = **Frances Smith**
Lt.-Col,
b.1811,
d.1873

Anna Maria = **Daniel Tupper**
b.15 June 1804
m.1 Sept.1823
d.25 Jan.1858
b.23 Nov.1796
d.9 Feb.1879,
London

Mary

Caroline

Helen

Catherine
d.1881

Henry Denis = **Hon. Sophia Strutt**
2nd Bt, Barrister
b.1839, m.1869,
d.1915
dau. of Edward,
Baron Belper

Anna Maria Eleanor
b.7 July 1824
d.1846

Gaspard Le Marchant, RHA
Lt.-General, RHA
b.8 Aug.1826
d.2 July 1906

Helen Annesrie
b.17 Oct.1829
d.1853

Eliza Catherine
b.21 Feb.1828
d.25 Sept.1907
= **Robert Le Marchant**

Alice May = **H. Hall Dare**
b.3 May
1834

Daniel William
Major,
50th Regt.
b.26 Dec.1831
d.1873

Amelius de Vic
Colonel, RA
b.19 Jan.1836

Richard Fanshawe
b.22 Mar.1838
d.1840

Francis Gerard St George = **Loveday Wilhelmina Bolitho**
Clerk in the
House of
Commons
b.1844
m.1888
Penzance
b.1861

SEE CHART I

Denis = **Katherine Mackay**
3rd Bt
b.1870
d.1922

Edward Thomas = **Evelyn Knowles**
KCB, CBE,
Brigadier
4th Bt
b.1871, d.1953

Francis
6th Bt,
Artist
b.1939

Denis = **Elizabeth Worth**
5th Bt
b.1906
d.1987

Peter Edward
b.1934
d.1972

Le Marchant
FAMILY TREE
Chart 2

Notes

Chapter 1: The Burden of Expectation, pp.1-10

1. Charles Oman, *A History of the Peninsular War, Vol.V, Oct. 1811-Aug. 31, 1812* (Oxford, 1914), p.453; R.H. Thoumine, *Scientific Soldier: A Life of General Le Marchant 1766-1812* (Oxford, 1968), p.165.
2. Rory Muir, *Salamanca 1812* (Yale University Press, 2001), p.136.
3. Nicholas Leadbetter, 'Sandhurst to Salamanca' in *Memoirs of the Late Major General Le Marchant 1766-1812* by Denis Le Marchant (Spellmount, 1997), p.xii.
4. Letter dated 25 June 1812, Castello Branco; Priaulx Library.
5. Oman, p.452.
6. Edward M. Spiers, *The Army and Society 1815-1914* (Longman – an imprint of Pearson Education Ltd – 1980), pp.13-25.
7. David Newsome, *The Victorian World Picture* (Fontana, 1998), pp.92 and 140; James Morris, *Pax Britannica* (Penguin, 1979), pp.124-5.
8. Mark Naidis, 'G.A. Henty's Idea of India', *Victorian Studies*, Vol. VIII, Sept. 1964, pp.57-8.
9. James Morris, *Heaven's Command: An Imperial Progress* (Faber and Faber, 1973), p.380 – Ruskin soon lost interest in the Empire but for a brief period he, too, believed in the concept of a civilising empire.

Chapter 2 : Soldier of the Raj – Edward Le Marchant, pp.11-36

1. Andrew Porter (ed.), *The Oxford History of the British Empire, Vol. III* (Oxford, 1999), p.321.
2. C.T. Atkinson, *Regimental History of the Royal Hampshire Regiment, Vol. I, to 1914* (University Press Glasgow, 1950), p.322.
3. Edward M. Spiers, *The Army and Society 1815-1914* (Longman, 1980), p.218.
4. Cited in Vikram Bhatt, *Resorts of the Raj: Hill Stations of India* (Mapin Publishing, Ahmedabad, 1998), p.142.
5. I do not accept – as argued by Mike Davis in his book *Late Victorian Holocausts* – that the British perpetrated 'colonial genocide' by deliberately allowing millions of Indians to starve during the famines of 1876-8 and 1895-7. Colonial administrators were, generally, humane men constrained by the political theories of the day. Though more could have been achieved through better organisation and administration, relief operations distributed food to millions of Indians and undoubtedly alleviated the worst effects of famine and drought.
6. John Lowe Duthie, 'Some Further Insights into the Working of Mid-Victorian Imperialism: Lord Salisbury, the "Forward" Group and Anglo-Afghan Relations, 1874-1878', in *Journal of Imperial and Commonwealth History*, Vol. 8 (1980), p.196.
7. 'An Account of the part taken by the 67th (South Hampshire) Regiment in the Afghan Campaigns of 1878-80', *Our Chronicle* (undated), p.6.
8. Major-General J.G. Elliott, *The Frontier 1839-1947* (Cassell, 1968), pp.109 and 115.
9. *Regimental History of the Royal Hampshire Regiment, Vol. I*, p.334.
10. Ian Knight, *Go to Your God Like a Soldier* (Greenhill Books, 1996), p.23.

11. *Hampshire Chronicle & General Advertiser for South & West of England.*
12. *Pall Mall Gazette,* 17 April 1899.
13. *Wilts and Gloucestershire Standard,* 29 April 1899.
14. Roger Hudson (ed.), *The Raj: An Eye-witness History of the British in India* (London, 1999), p.524.
15. *Regimental History of the Royal Hampshire Regiment, Vol I,* p.389.
16. TNA(PRO) WO339/23209.

Chapter 3: To the Corners of the Globe – Evelyn Le Marchant, pp.37-88

1. John M. MacKenzie (ed.), *Imperialism and Popular Culture* (Manchester, 1994), p.25.
2. Harold Nicolson, *King George V: His Life and Reign* (Constable, 1952), pp.12-13; Denis Judd, *George V* (Weidenfeld, 1993), p.24.
3. *The Cruise of HMS Bacchante 1879-1882,* Vol. I, pp.637 and 672-3.
4. Barry M. Gough, *The Royal Navy and the Northwest Coast of North America, 1810-1914: A Study of British Maritime Ascendancy* (Vancouver, 1971), p.215.
5. TNA(PRO) ADM 196/39.
6. Dr Andrew Lambert, *The Foundations of Naval History: John Knox Laughton, the Royal Navy and the Historical Profession* (Chatham Publishing, 1998), pp.43-5.
7. A. Preston and J. Major, *Send a Gunboat! A study of the Gunboat and its role in British policy 1854-1904* (Longmans, 1967), p.37.
8. Henry W. Cave, *Golden Tips* (Cassell, 1904), p.206.
9. TNA(PRO) ADM 156/20.
10. *Ibid.*
11. Laura M. MacDonald, *Curse of the Narrows* (Walker & Company, New York, 2005), pp.61-2.
12. *Knight Templar* log card Nov-Dec 1917; Admiralty Library.
13. TNA(PRO) ADM 196/39.
14. Arno Spindler, *Der Krieg zur See 1914-1918: Der handelskrieg mit U-Booten Bd. 5* (E.S. Mittler & Sohn, Frankfurt, 1966), pp.11-12; Admiralty Library.
15. Ethel Le Marchant's diary, 13 April 1918.
16. TNA(PRO) ADM 53/45824, 45825 and 137/1493. The ship's log was destroyed when she was torpedoed.
17. TNA(PRO) ADM 137/1493.
18. Other races won by 'The Ghost' were: Royal Artillery Gold Cup, Sandown Park, 1971; Levy Board Handicap Chase, Wincanton, 1971; Fairmile Handicap Chase, Sandown Park, 1972; Fred Withington Handicap Chase, Cheltenham, 1972. Valentine had wanted to call his horse 'The oly Ghost' but was overruled.

Chapter 4: From Paardeberg to the Khyber – Basil Le Marchant, pp.89-120

1. *The Iron Duke,* No 120, 1961, p.65.
2. I am indebted to Scott Flaving at Regimental Headquarters, The Duke of Wellington's Regiment (West Riding), and to staff at the Soldiers of Gloucestershire Museum for their help in throwing light on this obscure action, about which very little has been written. Also to John Broadbent for sending me the unpublished memoirs of his great-grandfather, Colour Sergeant John McGrath.
3. Diary of Capt. (later Brigadier-General Sir John Edmund) Gough, 30 Jan. 1900; Ian F.W. Beckett, *Johnnie Gough, V.C.* (London, 1989), pp.67-8.
4. Andrew Roberts, *Salisbury, Victorian Titan* (Weidenfeld & Nicolson – an imprint of The Orion Publishing Group – 1999), p.716.

5. Spiers, *The Army and Society 1815-1914*, (Longman, 1980), p.230.
6. Letter to Sir Charles Gough, 4 September 1900.
7. Albert Lee, *History of the 33rd Foot (The Duke of Wellington's (West Riding) Regiment)* (Jarrold & Sons, 1922), p.400.
8. Letter from Capt. (later General Sir Hubert) Gough, 24 January 1900.
9. *Illustrated London News*, 6 December 1884, p.551.
10. Lee, p.414.
11. J.M. Brereton and A.C.S. Savory, *The History of the Duke of Wellington's Regiment (West Riding), 1702-1992* (Halifax, 1993), p.225; *Iron Duke*, Vol. XV, No. 43, 1939, p.109.
12. *The Times*, 5 September 1901.
13. Thomas Pakenham, *The Boer War* (Weidenfeld & Nicolson, 1979), pp.572-3.
14. Spiers, p.248.
15. Diary of Capt. J.E. Gough, 21 Jan. 1900; Pakenham, p.265; Beckett, p.64.
16. *The Times*, 25 April 1908.
17. Capt. S. McNance, *History of the Royal Munster Fusiliers, Vol II, 1861-1922* (Aldershot, 1927), pp.38-9.

Chapter 5: Egypt, Abu Klea and the North-West Frontier – Cecil Le Marchant, pp.121-42

1. Lawrence James, *The Rise and Fall of the British Empire* (Abacus, 1997), p.272.
2. Richard Shannon, *Gladstone: Heroic Minister 1865-1898* (Allen Lane/Penguin, 1999), pp.304-5.
3. From the journal of Captain Lionel Trafford, 1st Battalion Royal Sussex Regiment, WSRO RSR MS 1/85, courtesy of the West Sussex Record Office and trustees of the Royal Sussex Regiment Museum.
4. Roy MacGregor-Hastie, *Never to be Taken Alive: A Biography of General Gordon* (Sidgwick & Jackson, 1985), p.170; Charles Chenevix Trench, *Charley Gordon: An Eminent Victorian Reassessed* (Allen Lane, 1978), p.275.
5. Michael Barthorp, *War on the Nile: Britain, Egypt and the Sudan 1882-1898* (Blandford Press, 1984), p.98.
6. Michael Asher, *Khartoum: The Ultimate Imperial Adventure* (Viking, 2005), pp.189-90; Philip Warner, *Dervish: The Rise and Fall of an African Empire* (Macdonald, 1973), p.116.
7. Lord Elton (ed.), *General Gordon's Khartoum Journal* (London, 1961), p.219.
8. Adrian Preston (ed.), *In Relief of Gordon – Lord Wolseley's Campaign Journal of The Khartoum Relief Expedition 1884-1885* (Hutchinson, 1967), p.79. By permission of The Random House Group Ltd.
9. Ian Knight, *Marching to the Drums* (Greenhill Books, 1999), p.222.
10. Trafford.
11. *Illustrated London News*, 7 February 1885, p.137.
12. J.M. MacKenzie (ed), *Imperialism and Popular Culture* (Manchester University Press, 1986), p.56.
13. By kind permission of Peter Newbolt.
14. Alan Harfield (ed.), *The Life and Times of a Victorian Officer* (Wincanton Press, 1986), p.153.
15. Lawrence James, *Raj: The Making and Unmaking of British India* (Abacus, 1998), p.400.
16. G.D. Martineau, *A History of the Royal Sussex Regiment* (Chichester, 1969), p.125.

Chapter 6: Three Campaigns; Three Continents – Louis Le Marchant, pp.143-78

1. *Journal and Proceedings of the Asiatic Society of Bengal,* New Series, Vol. XXIX (1933), p.100.
2. General Sir Hubert Gough, *Soldiering On* (Arthur Baker, 1954), p.44.
3. *The XXX*, Journal of the 1st Battalion The East Lancashire Regiment, June 1912, p.6.
4. R. de M. Rudolf (ed.), *Short Histories of the Territorial Regiments of the British Army, Vol. I* (Naval & Military Press, undated), p.303.
5. *The Lancashire Fusiliers' Annual*, 1901, p.204.
6. A.S. Lewis, *The Lilywhite 59th, The 2nd Nottinghamshire & 2nd Battalion The East Lancashire Regiment* (Blackburn, 1985), pp.65-6.
7. Capt. E.C. Hopkinson, *Spectamur Agendo: 1st Battalion The East Lancashire Regiment, August and September 1914* (privately printed), p.23.
8. Letter (of 24 October 1914) to Miss Annie Le Marchant from Mrs Geraldine Lambert enclosing extracts from her husband's diary.
9. Barbara W. Tuchman, *The Guns of August* (London, 1995), p.387.
10. Hopkinson, *Spectamur Agendo*, p.40.
11. Field Marshal Lord Carver, *Britain's Army in the 20th Century* (Pan Books, 1999), pp.33-4.
12. The Diary of Private E. Roe, courtesy of the archives of The Queen's Lancashire Regiment Museum.
13. Hopkinson, *Spectamur Agendo*, p.53.
14. Sir O'Moore Creagh VC and E.M. Humphris, *The Distinguished Service Order 1868-1923* (Hayward, 1978), p.195.

Bibliography

Unpublished

Admiralty Library, Portsmouth: HMS *Knight Templar* log cards

The Duke of Wellington's Regiment (West Riding): diary of Major E.N. Townsend (Paardeberg); Digest of Service, 1st Battalion; notes on the life of W.A. Wynter

Lambert, Major T.S.: diary extracts, Aug. 1914; description of the action at La Ferté-sous-Jouarre on 9 Sept. 1914 (author)

Le Marchant albums (Corinium Museum, Cirencester, 1999/84)

Le Marchant letters, diaries, journals, sermons, and albums (author)

McGrath, Colour Sergeant John, 33rd Regiment: memoirs

The National Archives – TNA(PRO): Admiralty records; Army and Navy service records; war diaries

Priaulx Library, Guernsey: albums; Le Marchant correspondence; family trees

The Queen's Lancashire Regiment Museum: Digest of Service, 1st Battalion The East Lancashire Regiment; diary of Private E. Roe

West Sussex Record Office: journal of Captain Lionel Trafford; Records of Service, Royal Sussex Regiment

Published

Contemporary sources, autobiographies and diaries

Albert Victor, Prince, and George of Wales, Prince, *The Cruise of HMS Bacchante 1879-1882* (London, 1886)

Anon, *An Account of the part taken by the 67th (South Hampshire) Regiment in the Afghan Campaigns of 1878-79-80* (Regimental Press, n.d.)

Elton, Lord (ed.), *General Gordon's Campaign Journal* (William Kimber, 1961)

Forbes, A., Henty, G.A. and others, *Battles of the Nineteenth Century*, Vols I and II (London, 1896)

Gough, General Sir Hubert, *Soldiering On* (Arthur Baker, 1954)

Jane, Fred T., *The British Battle-Fleet: Its Inception and Growth throughout the Centuries* (1912; republished Conway Maritime Press, 1997)

The Lancashire Fusiliers' Annual (1901)

Le Marchant, Sir Denis, Bt, *Memoirs of the Late Major General Le Marchant 1766-1812* (1841; republished Spellmount, 1997)

Preston, Adrian (ed.), *In Relief of Gordon: Lord Wolseley's Campaign Journal of The Khartoum Relief Expedition 1884-1885* (Hutchinson, 1967)

Robertson, Sir George, *Chitral: The Story of a Minor Siege* (1898; republished R.J. Leach, 1991)

Younghusband, G.J. and Younghusband, F.E., *The Relief of Chitral* (London, 1895)

Newspapers, journals and magazines

Daily Telegraph, Guernsey Evening Press, Hampshire Chronicle & General Advertiser for South & West of England, Illustrated London News, Iron Duke (Journal of The Duke of Wellington's Rgt), *Lady's Pictorial, Le Bailliage, London Gazette, Morning Post, Our Chronicle* (Journal of the 67th Rgt), *Pall Mall Gazette, Salisbury and Winchester Journal,*

Pioneer Mail, *Tenby and County News*, *The Times*, *The XXX* (Journal of the 1st Battalion East Lancashire Rgt).

Articles

'A.Z.', 'The Heavy Cavalry at Salamanca', *United Service Journal*, No. 60 (November 1833), pp. 351-4

Boyle, T., 'The Liberal Imperialists 1892-1906', *Historical Research*, Vol. LII (1979)

Durand, Ralph, 'Major-General John Gaspard Le Marchant', *La Société Guernesiaise, Report and Transactions*, Vol. XXIII, Part I (1991)

— 'Lord Lytton and the Second Afghan War: A Psychohistorical Study', *Victorian Studies*, Vol. 27, No. 4 (1984)

Duthie, John Lowe, 'Some Further Insights into the Working of Mid-Victorian Imperialism: Lord Salisbury, the "Forward" Group and Anglo-Afghan Relations, 1874-1878', *Journal of Imperial and Commonwealth History*, Vol. 8, 1980

Gallagher, J. and Robinson, R., 'The Imperialism of Free Trade', *Economic History Review*, Second Series Vol. VI, No. 1 (1953)

Gudger, Dr E.W., 'Do Fishes Fall from the Sky with Rain?' *Scientific Monthly*, Vol. XXIX (December 1929)

Hopkins, A.G., 'The Victorians and Africa: A Reconsideration of the Occupation of Egypt 1882', *Journal of African History*, 27 (1986)

Hora, Sunder Lal, 'Rains of Fishes in India', *Journal and Proceedings of the Asiatic Society of Bengal*, New Series Vol. XXIX (1933)

Mowat, R.C., 'From Liberalism to Imperialism: The Case of Egypt 1875-1887', *Historical Journal*, XVI, 1 (1973)

Naidis, Mark, 'G.A. Henty's Idea of India', *Victorian Studies* Vol. VIII (September 1964)

Payne, R.W.J., 'Soldier and Artist', *Quarterly Review of the Guernsey Society*, Vol. 23, No. 2 (1967)

Other secondary sources

Asher, Michael, *Khartoum: The Ultimate Imperial Adventure* (Viking, 2005)

Atkinson, C.T., *Regimental History: The Royal Hampshire Regiment, Vol. I, to 1914* (University Press Glasgow, 1950)

Barthorp, Michael, *War on the Nile: Britain, Egypt and the Sudan 1882-1898* (Blandford Press, 1984)

Beckett, Ian F.W., *Johnnie Gough, VC: A Biography of Brigadier-General Sir John Edmond Gough, VC, KCB, CMG* (Tom Donovan, 1989)

— *The Victorians at War* (Hambledon & London, 2003)

Bhatt, Vikram, *Resorts of the Raj: Hill Stations of India* (Mapin Publishing, Ahmedabad, 1998)

Boyes, Michael, *A Victorian Rector and Nine Old Maids: 100 Years of Cotswold Village Life* (Phillimore, 2005)

Brereton, J.M. and Savory, A.C.S., *The History of The Duke of Wellington's Regiment (West Riding), 1702-1992* (Halifax, 1993)

Carver, Field Marshal Lord, *Britain's Army in the 20th Century* (Pan Books, 1999)

— *The National Army Museum Book of The Boer War* (Pan Books, 2000)

Clark, Victoria, *Holy Fire: The Battle for Christ's Tomb* (Macmillan, 2005)

Cook, Andrew, *Prince Eddy: The King Britain Never Had* (Tempus, 2006)

Court, W.H.B., *British Economic History 1870-1914* (Cambridge University Press, 1965)

Creagh, Sir O'Moore, VC, and Humphris, E.M., *The Distinguished Service Order 1868-1923* (Hayward, 1978)

Davis, Mike, *Late Victorian Holocausts: El Niño Famines and the Making of the Third*

World (Verso, 2001)

Dixon, Conrad, *Ships of the Victorian Navy* (Ashford Press, 1987)

Downham, John, *Red Roses on the Veldt: Lancashire Regiments in the Boer War, 1899-1902* (Carnegie, 2000)

Fletcher, Ian, *Salamanca 1812* (Osprey, 1997)

George, James L., *History of Warships: From Ancient Times to the Twenty-first Century* (Constable, 1999)

Gough, Barry M., *The Royal Navy and the Northwest Coast of North America, 1810-1914: A Study of British Maritime Ascendancy* (Vancouver, 1971)

Harfield, Alan (ed.), *The Life and Times of a Victorian Officer* (Wincanton Press, 1986)

Harlow, Barbara and Carter, Mia, *Imperialism & Orientalism: A Documentary Sourcebook* (Blackwell, 1999)

Heathcote, T.A., *The Afghan Wars 1839-1919* (Spellmount, 2003)

Holt, P.M., *The Mahdist State in the Sudan 1881-1898* (Clarendon Press, 1970)

Hopkinson, Capt. E.C., *Spectamur Agendo: 1st Battalion The East Lancashire Regiment, August and September 1914* (privately printed, 1926)

Hopkirk, Peter, *The Great Game: On Secret Service in High Asia* (Oxford University Press, 2001)

Hore, Captain Peter, *The Habit of Victory: The Story of the Royal Navy 1545 to 1945* (Sidgwick & Jackson, 2005)

Hudson, Roger (ed.), *The Raj: An Eye-witness History of the British in India* (London, 1999)

James, Lawrence, *The Rise and Fall of the British Empire* (Abacus, 1995)

— *Raj: The Making and Unmaking of British India* (Abacus, 1998)

Judd, Denis, *George V* (Weidenfeld, 1993)

Judd, Denis and Surridge, Keith, *The Boer War* (John Murray, 2002)

Keegan, John, *The First World War* (Pimlico, 1999)

Kennedy, Paul, *The Rise and Fall of British Naval Mastery* (Fontana Press, 1991)

Keown-Boyd, Henry, *A Good Dusting: A Centenary Review of the Sudan campaigns 1883-1899* (Leo Cooper, 1986)

Knight, Ian, *Go to Your God Like a Soldier: The British Soldier Fighting for Empire, 1837-1902* (Greenhill Books, 1996)

— *Marching to the Drums* (Greenhill Books, 1999)

Kochanski, Halik, *Sir Garnet Wolseley: Victorian Hero* (Hambledon Press, 1999)

Lambert, Dr Andrew, *The Foundations of Naval History: John Knox Laughton, the Royal Navy and the Historical Profession* (Chatham Publishing, 1998)

— (ed.), *Steam, Steel & Shellfire: the Steam Warship 1815-1905* (Conway Maritime Press, 1992)

Lee, Albert, *History of the 33rd Foot (The Duke of Wellington's [West Riding] Regiment)* (Jarrold & Sons, 1922)

Lewis, A.S., *The Lilywhite 59th, The 2nd Nottinghamshire & 2nd Battalion The East Lancashire Regiment* (Blackburn, 1985)

Lunt, James, *The Duke of Wellington's Regiment (West Riding)* (Leo Cooper, 1971)

Lyon, David, *The Ship: Steam, Steel and Torpedoes; the Warship in the 19th Century* (HMSO, 1980)

MacDonald, Laura M., *Curse of the Narrows* (Walker & Company, New York, 2005)

MacGregor-Hastie, Roy, *Never to be Taken Alive: A Biography of General Gordon* (Sidgwick & Jackson, 1985)

MacKenzie, J.M. (ed.), *Imperialism and Popular Culture* (Manchester University Press, 1986)

McNance, Capt. S., *History of the Royal Munster Fusiliers* Vol. II (Gale & Polden, 1927)

Marr, L. James, *A History of the Bailiwick of Guernsey* (Phillimore, 1982)

— *Guernsey People* (Phillimore, 1984)

Martineau, G.D., *A History of the Royal Sussex Regiment* (Chichester, 1969)

May, W.E., Carman, W.Y. and Tanner, J., *Badges and Insignia of the British Armed Services* (Adam & Charles Black, 1974)

Morris, James, *Pax Britannica* (Penguin, 1979)

— *Heaven's Command: An Imperial Progress* (Faber and Faber, 1973)

Muir, Rory, *Salamanca 1812* (Yale University Press, 2001)

Newsome, David, *The Victorian World Picture* (Fontana Press, 1998)

Nicoll, Fergus, *The Mahdi of Sudan and the Death of General Gordon* (Sutton Publishing, 2005)

Nicolson, Harold, *King George V: His Life and Reign* (Constable, 1952)

Nowell-Smith, Simon (ed.), *Edwardian England 1901-1914* (Oxford University Press, 1964)

Oman, Charles, *A History of the Peninsular War, Vol. V, Oct. 1811-Aug. 31, 1812* (Oxford, 1914)

Padfield, Peter, *Rule Britannia: The Victorian and Edwardian Navy* (Pimlico, 2002)

Pakenham, Thomas, *The Boer War* (Weidenfeld & Nicolson, 1979)

Perrett, Bryan, *At All Costs! Stories of Impossible Victories* (Cassell, 1998)

Porter, Andrew (ed.), *The Oxford History of the British Empire, Vol. III, The Nineteenth Century* (Oxford, 1999)

Preston, A. and Major, J., *Send a Gunboat! A study of the Gunboat and its role in British policy 1854-1904* (Longman, 1967)

Pretorius, F., *The Anglo-Boer War 1899-1902* (Struik Publishers, Cape Town, 1998)

Roberts, Andrew, *Salisbury: Victorian Titan* (Weidenfeld & Nicolson, 1999)

Robson, Brian, *The Road to Kabul: The Second Afghan War 1878-1881* (Arms and Armour Press, 1986)

— *Fuzzy Wuzzy: The Campaigns in the Eastern Sudan 1884-85* (Spellmount, 1993)

Rudolf, R. de M. (ed.), *Short Histories of the Territorial Regiments of the British Army*, Vol. I (Naval & Military Press, n.d.)

Sanger, Ernest, *Englishmen At War: A Social History In Letters 1450-1900* (Alan Sutton, 1993)

Shannon, Richard, *Gladstone: Heroic Minister 1865-1898* (Penguin Press, 1999)

Spiers, Edward M., *The Army and Society 1815-1914* (Longman, 1980)

— *The Late Victorian Army 1868-1902* (Manchester University Press, 1992)

Spindler, Arno, *Der Krieg zur See 1914-1918: Der handelskrieg mit U-Booten Bd. 5* (E.S. Mittler & Sohn, Frankfurt, 1966)

Strawson, John, *Gentlemen in Khaki: The British Army 1890-1990* (Secker & Warburg, 1989)

Swinson, Arthur, *North-West Frontier* (Hutchinson, 1967)

Thompson, Julian, *The Imperial War Museum Book of the War at Sea 1914-1918* (Pan Books, 2006)

Thoumine, R.H., *Scientific Soldier: A Life of General Le Marchant 1766-1812* (Oxford, 1968)

Trench, Charles Chenevix, *Charley Gordon: An Eminent Victorian Reassessed* (Allen Lane, 1978)

Tuchman, Barbara W., *The Guns of August* (Constable, 1962)

Warner, Philip, *Dervish: The Rise and Fall of an African Empire* (Macdonald, 1973)

Watts, Anthony J., *The Royal Navy: An Illustrated History* (Arms and Armour Press, 1994)

Webb, J.V., *The Abu Klea Medal Rolls* (published by the author, London, 1981)

Wykes, Alan, *The Royal Hampshire Regiment* (Hamish Hamilton, 1968)

Index

Page numbers in **bold** refer to illustrations; the letter *n* refers to a footnote, and endnote references include the letter *n* followed by the number of the chapter and note concerned.

Abbreviations: BEF   British Expeditionary Force
Bn   Battalion
BW   Boer War (1899-1902)
Rgt   Regiment
SA   South Africa
WW1   First World War

Abbreviations for naval and military ranks are usually self-evident, and are too numerous to list here.